THE
CLAM-PLATE
ORGY

THE CLAM-PLATE ORGY:

*And Other Subliminals
the Media Use to
Manipulate Your
Behavior*

◆

Wilson Bryan Key

**PRENTICE HALL INC.,
ENGLEWOOD CLIFFS, N.J.**

Grateful acknowledgment is made for permission to reprint the following material:

From *The Brothers Karamazov*, Fyodor Dostoyevsky, translated by Constance Garnett. New York: Random House, Inc., 1955.
From *The Hidden Order of Art*, Anton Ehrenzweig. London: Weidenfeld Limited.
From *Propaganda: The Formation of Men's Attitudes*, Jacques Ellul. Copyright © 1965 by Alfred A. Knopf, Inc. New York: Alfred A. Knopf, Inc.
From *Civilized Man's Eight Deadly Sins*, Konrad Lorenz. London: Methuen & Co., Ltd., 1974.
From *The Time of the Assassins*, Henry Miller. Copyright 1946, 1949, 1956 by New Directions Publishing Corporation. Reprinted by permission of New Directions.
From *The Mountain People*, Colin M. Turnbull. Copyright © 1972 by Colin M. Turnbull. New York: Simon & Schuster, Inc., 1972.
From *The Pornography of Power*, Lionel Rubinoff. Reprinted by permission of Times Books, a division of Quadrangle/The New York Times Book Co., Inc. Copyright © Lionel Rubinoff. New York: Times Books, 1968.
Figure 20, courtesy Museo del Prado, Madrid.
Figure 21, courtesy Cabinet des Dessins, Musée du Louvre, Paris.
Figure 26, by courtesy of the Vatican Museums.
Figure 30, courtesy Museo e Galleria Borghese, Rome.
Figure 34, © S.P.A.D.E.M., 1978.
Figure 35, Karsh of Ottawa.
Figure 45, courtesy of the Trustees of the National Gallery, London.

The Clam-Plate Orgy: And Other Subliminals the Media Use to Manipulate Your Behavior, by Wilson Bryan Key

Copyright © 1980 by Wilson Bryan Key

Printed in the United States of America

Prentice-Hall International, Inc., London
Prentice-Hall of Australia, Pty. Ltd., Sydney
Prentice-Hall of Canada, Ltd., Toronto
Prentice-Hall of India Private Ltd., New Delhi
Prentice-Hall of Japan, Inc., Tokyo
Prentice-Hall of Southeast Asia Pte. Ltd., Singapore
Whitehall Books Limited, Wellington, New Zealand

10   9   8   7   6   5   4   3   2   1

Library of Congress Cataloging in Publication Data

Key, Wilson Bryan
The clam-plate orgy and other subliminals the media
use to manipulate your behavior.
Bibliography: p.
Includes index.
1. Mass media—Psychological aspects. I. Title.
P96.P75K4   301.16′1   79-24638
ISBN 0-13-135038-2

CONTENTS

Otra vez, para mi Irisita,
Who discovered the priest
In the face
On the rock
At the mountain of Arco
y muchas otras.

1 • MORE REAL THAN REALITY

De-individualizing effects are desired by all those whose intention is to manipulate large bodies of people. Opinion polls, advertising, cleverly directed fads and fashions help the mass producers on this side of the Iron Curtain, and the functionaries on the other side, to attain what amounts to a similar power over the masses.

Konrad Lorenz,
Civilized Man's Eight Deadly Sins

THE IGNORED MEDIA CONNECTION

Across the United States during 1978, dozens of school boards approved for their lunch programs hamburgers, tacos, pizzas, and other junk food products of the type merchandised by fast-food restaurants. Some parents made muted protests.

Across the nation, a very small number of school administrators successfully resisted the conversion, but the majority argued that students refused to eat dietetically balanced lunch menus, which are often prepared at much less expense from USDA surplus foods. CBS News filmed school lunchrooms where students threw hundreds of pounds of food into garbage cans. In a world where two-thirds of the population go to bed hungry every night, this was profoundly upsetting to watch.

Within months, in numerous schools that had switched to junk lunch menus, public health officials recorded startling increases in cholesterol levels among teenagers. Many students had also unknowingly depended upon the former lunch programs for nutrition not available in their homes. The converted schools bragged about how successful their lunches had become, with students gulping down hamburgers doused in ketchup, mustard, and relish. For several months the issue was nationally discussed, until it was milked of popular interest.

At no point during the controversy did anyone point a finger at media involvement—let alone their responsibility—for the popularization of junk food. Fast-food corporations spend several hundred million dollars in advertising annually, yet the young people's preference for gastronomical garbage was considered merely a whim of adolescence, just another of the countless teenage fads. Saturation advertising in behalf of extremely expensive, nutritionally deficient food—aimed principally at young people—was never even brought up.

During a famine in the Philippines after World War II, shiploads of rice were imported from Egypt. In spite of exorbitant black market prices for local rice and a large population bordering upon starvation, the Egyptian rice rotted in warehouses. Filipinos refused to eat rice they considered inferior to their own.

Food preferences, which anthropologists consider one of the fundamental characteristics of every culture, are most resistant to modification or change. And yet the U.S. commercial media have initiated significant cultural change by drastically modifying the food preferences and eating behavior of millions of consumers, a fact virtually unnoticed by any of the people affected. Perhaps the media's most pernicious potential is its ability to modify behavior without the subject's awareness. Very few Americans are aware of the significant role advertising plays in both their lives and health.

CLAMS AT HOWARD JOHNSON'S

One of the world's great art treasures was discovered, not in the *Louvre*, the *Prado*, nor in Rome's *Galleria Borghese*, but lying inconspicuously on a table at Howard Johnson's. After a University of California lecture in San Diego, several students and I dined at a nearby HJ restaurant. Our heated talk, which had begun at the university, continued as we squeezed ourselves into the booth. As we chatted, several students casually glanced through menus. When the waitress finally materialized, four out of the six of us, including myself, ordered clam plates.

Shortly after the waitress had taken the order and disappeared, I incredulously recalled that since childhood I have loathed clams in any form. Only were I near starvation would I seriously consider eating fried clams, and I was extremely annoyed with myself for ordering something I really didn't want to eat.

No one else at the table appeared to share my strong aversion to fried clams, however. "It's entirely possible," I remarked, "that someone has put something into our heads since we entered the restaurant."

"What about the music?" one student volunteered. Indeed, the crowded restaurant noises were dampened by ceiling loudspeakers playing innocuous, not unpleasant background music. For a few moments we concentrated upon the recording, but as far as anyone could tell, there were no faint subliminal voice tracks audible under the music.

Finally someone noticed the placemats that had been on the table, before each of us, since we first sat down. The students and I began to "psych out" or analyze the mat, which was really an ad for the featured clam plates, a high-profit item on HJ menus throughout the world. At first glance, no one could find anything startling on the placemat which could have been so persuasive. Each mat was titled, "Dig Into Our Clam Plate." None of us could recall having consciously perceived the mats before we placed our orders (see Figure 1).

FUNCTIONAL MEDIA

Most of us tend to think of such casual media as placemats as either *functional* (they provide a clean area for our eating utensils and designate our territory on the tabletop); or as *decorative* (the nice Howard Johnson people are simply showing us how good their special clam plates appear). But neither of these assumptions about placemats—or other casual media—is correct. Placemats, and everything else featuring a product or service found in merchandising situations, serve to sell something—a most specific and single-minded objective.

I have no idea what percentage of the total U.S. clam dig is merchandised, at a high-profit margin, through HJ restaurants, but it must be substantial: there are many thousands of HJ food outlets from coast to coast.

Over several years I found these clam-plate placemats in such cities as Miami, Montreal, New York, Toronto, Chicago, Kansas City, Denver, El Paso, Los Angeles, and San Francisco. The simple, rarely noticed, taken-for-granted placemat is a primary sales medium, extremely effective in that it is rarely paid attention to, is considered of little consequence, and is never perceived critically or consciously.

Most reasonable individuals would ask, "So what?" Why make a big deal out of a piece of printed paper no one ever pays any attention to? Conventional logic, however, simply does not prepare us to live in a media-dominated environment.

Carefully examine the seemingly innocuous placemat, much as the students and I did that night in San Diego.

Before proceeding, look carefully at the copy and picture. How does it make you feel? While concentrating on the placemat, try a few free associations. Consumers rarely read ad copy. With an ad such as the placemat, as few as one person in fifteen might read through the text—and then only if the service is very slow. Such texts serve mainly to provide ads with an informative image even though this copy, like most, contains no real information about clams, or anything else for that matter.

The clam-plate copy is modestly suggestive, describing "a batch of succulent tender clams. . . ." The poetics would hardly compare with the imagery of an Elizabethan sonnet, but they are erotically vivid. A line at the bottom of the left column remarks casually that, "They always *come* . . . out crispy and crunchy [italics and interruptive punctuation added]."

One copy line at the top of the right column also might be interpreted as sexually suggestive: "Piled high and crowded with creamy cole slaw and french fries." If you read this line aloud slowly, your tongue as it curls about the vowel sounds does produce a certain feeling of sensuosity.

Still, were anyone seriously to elaborate a case for morally objectionable verbiage out of these lines—even in a Bible-school classroom—they would likely be ridiculed.

Were you to intimate that these well-turned phrases had a salacious, unwholesome intent, a barrage of indignant corporation attorneys would descend to denounce—maybe even sue—anyone corrupt enough to read dirty thoughts into their clean, wholesome placemat. The clam copy seems clear of salacious content, at least in any definable legal sense. There appears to be nothing here that would provoke the FTC into a charge of deceptive advertising. But then, the copy is only part of an overall image.

AD COPY RARELY READ

Copy usually serves only as reinforcement for pictorial art, providing an aura of validity for the picture.

The consumer block-reads the paragraphs, at a glance, consciously accepting them as something meaningful. Nevertheless, should a consumer carefully read the copy, it is like money in the bank for the advertiser. It keeps individual attention on the layout for an extended period, during which the brain can assimilate the illustration. If the copy were deleted, individuals might be more inclined to concentrate critically upon the picture. Of course, the actual stimulus that motivates the purchase—the psychological trigger that justifies the expense for art, reproduction, paper, and distribution—resides in the picture.

Let's move on to the picture (see Figure 2). Few individuals are likely to become enthusiastic over a photograph of a plate of clams. But wait! Think carefully and critically. There is dissonance in this picture—a very important element in both visual and auditory subliminal stimuli.

At first glance, we appear to be viewing the clam plate from the outside of a ship's porthole, looking in.

When I asked the students whether we were inside looking out through the porthole or outside looking in at the clam plate, they all quickly answered, "Outside, looking in." But we were *not* outside looking in.

The viewer is inside the boat. The porthole opens inward—the screw located on the right and the hinge on the left. The lush clam plate is presumably on the dock next to the boat. Further, there is, if we can recall the real thing, a heavy plate of glass between us and the clam plate. There is no way we could possibly reach out and touch, pick up, or gain access to the "succulent tender clams."

In the world of commercial media, where every artistic detail is carefully calculated for its sales effectiveness, this would seem a careless oversight on the artist's part. Logically, the clam plate is out of reach unless the consumer opens the porthole. One might think an open porthole would have been a more desirable frame in which to feature HJ's clam plate.

Now concentrate upon the clam-plate picture itself—the object of a large financial investment. Things are simply not correct, not quite as they should be in reality, or in what we perceive as the real world.

LOVE A CLAM

A simple, reliable, and very effective technique of media analysis, one rarely taught in universities, is to compare the media representation with the real thing and to note discrepancies. Reality usually pales into insignificance when compared with the polished, manipulative craftsmanship of the modern media creator.

When the four clam plates arrived at our table, we compared the fried clams on our plates with those in the picture.

We were astonished. The real clams and those in the picture were dramatically different. In fact, the clams in the picture appeared far more desirable than those on our plates. As a civilization, we may be well on the way to a complete rejection of reality in favor of the much more desirable perceptual illusions supplied by commercial media. (See Figure 2.)

Looking critically at the clam plate, on the vertical centerline—within the porthole scene, just below the parsley—one can see a heavy dark dot, the only dot of its kind in the picture. At first we thought it a flyspeck, but that seemed illogical: the HJ corporate image projects *cleanliness* so strongly. We checked our clam plates. No one had a comparable dot on any of their clams. The large dot is in precisely the center of the elliptical plate.

Around the dot appears another elliptical shape, presumably representing a piece of fried clam—outlined by the dark and light shading that divides one clam from another. On the top of the ellipse appears a small triangular shape. This ellipse, or egg shape, with its central dot and triangular appendage at the top could—if you can relax your perceptual restraints for a moment—be interpreted as the head of an animal, perhaps a dog or a donkey. The students and I checked our plates for a real clam that looked like an animal's head. None of us found a shape even remotely close.

THE HEAD BONE CONNECTS TO THE NECK BONE

Extending to the right of the head-shaped clam is a short, narrow nape which could be a neck. Further to the right, the back arches down to rear legs extended into the pile of clams. The animal's forelegs extend vertically down from just below the neck. Give yourself a moment to discover the donkey-shaped clam before you turn to Figure 3 for an outline of the figures crowded into the clam plate.

The placemat illustration is not a photographic representation of actual clams, of course, but an airbrush painting. It includes nine caricatured human figures as well as a donkey astride a human figure. The donkey seems to be licking the stomach of the figure upon whose lightly shaded face is a long moustache.

To the left of the prostrate face-up male figure appears a female figure with a highly piled coiffure. A head can be seen between her legs.

Who would believe a sexual orgy, oral sex, and bestiality could be so deftly incorporated into an innocent restaurant placemat? But, then, shellfish—clams and oysters—are themselves archetypal symbols of virility. Had this painting been commissioned during the Renaissance, it might have ended up in one of the world's great museums instead of being ignominiously mass-produced for tables in Howard Johnson restaurants.

This obscene information will be unconsciously perceived by every man, woman, and child who regards this placemat for even an instant.

From what little we know about how information is processed through our brains, perception appears to be both total and instantaneous. Our senses pick up every minute, seemingly insignificant detail, but since it is transmitted into the brain virtually at the speed of light, what we consciously recognize is only a small portion of the total. Perhaps, as some theorists have speculated, as little as $1/1000$th of a total percept is consciously available. The remaining $999/1000$th remains in the brain for varying periods before being stored permanently or dumped as irrelevant.

Over the years, my students and I collected a dozen HJ menus and placemats with subliminally embedded material. There is very little recommendable about the food at HJ, except perhaps the coffee. We have spent many happy hours over coffee cups at HJ restaurants while we psyched out their merchandising media.

AN UNSPECIALIZED SPECIALTY

One of the most frequent questions I am asked is, "How did you stumble into subliminal dimensions of art? They had been around a very long time without being discovered." There is no simple answer; at least I don't have one. But I suspect my blundering into the subliminal area was a product of a rather fluid cultural background, since subliminals appear to be culture-bound.

A culture is a way of perceiving the world, a way that excludes other perspectives, an aggregate of unconsciously perceived, unverbalized, tacit agreements. We constantly confirm our perceived realities by asking others (sometimes so-called experts) if our perceptions are valid. Do they see what we see? If our individual perceptions are confirmed, we usually accept them. If they are denied, we most often concede to "experts," "authorities," or group consensus.

My specialty, if it can be called that, was intercultural research as it related to corporate investments, marketing potentials, and media effectiveness.

Earlier, I had spent many years in the Philippines and in Spanish-speaking America. Working out of Puerto Rico as director of an international research group for ten years, I completed over 300 research projects for governments and such corporations as General Foods, Nabisco, Schlitz, Volkswagen, Eastern Airlines, Seagrams, Sea-Land, Simmons, IBEC, Del Monte, NABISCO, Gillette, General Motors, Texise, and a sizable collection of large international ad agencies, including J. Walter Thompson; Irwin Wasey; Lennen & Newell; Norman, Craig & Kummel; Compton; and McCann-Erickson.

This research covered a wide range of investigations into language and behavior phenomena such as public opinion and attitude change, economic feasibility, consumer market analysis, government policy development, political party dynamics, new product development, mathematical modeling and systems evaluation, and media utilization studies.

My view of the world was that of a perceptual outsider—always looking into someone's cultural window. But in many ways the outsider has an advantage in making cultural studies. The alien's vested interests are limited (at least temporarily). Aliens often perceive things that are invisible to group members, perceptions consciously repressed by those within the group or culture. I often exploited this perceptual advantage for my business research clients.

Abetting my lack of cultural inhibitions was more than 25 years of familiarity with the theoretical literature of behavior and language. I had always been intrigued by subtle ways of thinking—and thinking about thinking—that prevail from place to place. The most resourceful and flexible of the several hundred technicians and field workers I employed each year always seemed to be those few with an interest in theoretics. Most technicians are unfortunately limited to doing what they have been taught instead of constantly reevaluating changing situations. And, of course, my experience in business and marketing research helped make sense out of media strategies.

Upon returning to North America I accepted a professorship in Canada's Western Ontario University (UWO), and suddenly found myself involved with media insights that seemed unavailable to those around me, especially to "trained experts" on mass media, society, human perception, and psychology.

ARE ACCIDENTS ACCIDENTAL?

The discovery appeared accidental—as most discoveries do. During a class lecture, I happened to glance at an open copy of *Esquire* upside down. In an illustration I noticed phallic designs that, by conventional reasoning, should not have been there.

When I showed the embed to my students, at least half of them thought I was out of my mind. The other half appeared curious, however—even pleased.

I continued to find these unusual pictures-within-pictures. At first they seemed to be jokes perpetrated by ad artists on their employers. But as our collection grew from a few dozen the first year to several hundred the second, and to over a thousand the third, it became apparent that perceptual tricks in commercial art were the rule, not the exception.

The collected ads began to fall into categories. As I developed hypnosis and relaxation techniques as a form of perceptual training for media research, new types of subliminals appeared. It was at least a year before we attached to our findings the label "subliminal art." I tried to explain our continuing discoveries through medical, psychological, sociological, and philosophical insights into human perception. My students and I waded through a Niagara of literature on perception. Once in a while we found bits and pieces of insight which seemed to make sense, but mainstream cognitive psychology, sociology, anthropology, and the other so-called social sciences are so tightly organized around quantitative data, so narrow in their specializations, that they told us little of any value. Our problem was not data collection (there was an abundance of data) but *meaning* and *significance.*

There is no such thing as an inert (motiveless) communication. The entire question of conscious and unconscious motivation is an integral aspect of any human communication system. Media cannot be meaningfully discussed unless the question of *who is doing what to whom for which reasons* is first carefully considered. For this reason, commercially motivated media are a delight to study. The motive is simple and always known—to sell, to sell, to sell, to sell . . .

HOW "AN OLD SOFTIE" TAKES ADVANTAGE

For many decades, the gigantic Kraft Corporation has supplied, at substantial profit, processed foods for the American home.

The Kraft Soft Parkay Margarine ad shown in Figure 4 was published in *Family Circle Magazine*'s November 1973 issue, as well as in virtually all the other women's home magazines and in many newspapers. Over several years, several million dollars were invested in purchasing media space for this single piece of advertising. *Family Circle*—usually sold in supermarkets, a multimillion-circulation magazine with tens of millions of readers—is a bastion of middle-class morality. Nothing more controversial than how many egg whites should be used in an angel food cake ever intrudes upon the ads. Housewives are portrayed as clever, attractive, independent, morally righteous members of an affluent, food-oriented society (in which, the National Institute of Health tells us, 60 percent of adults are overweight). On the surface *FC* is pretty dull stuff—unless you are turned on by endless articles and pictures of food, which is apparently the case for many women (and men) across the nation.

The Soft Parkay ad is banality itself. When we observed people aimlessly thumbing through the pages of *FC*, no one appeared to pay much attention to Kraft's sizable investment in art. Average exposure, or reading time, for this particular page was 1 to 2 seconds. About one in fifteen readers used 3 to 4 additional seconds to read the brief paragraph of copy. A Kraft stockholder watching these *FC* readers might have angrily protested the waste of money on an ad that readers appeared to ignore.

Indeed, in the Parkay ad, there is really nothing to see. A glob of greasy Parkay, on the end of a knife blade, is about to be spread on a muffin—pretty unexciting, at either the emotional or intellectual level! But, unexciting only if you take the world of media at face value.

IN THE EYES OF THE BEHOLDER?

Before reading further, please study carefully every detail of the Kraft ad. Ask yourself: how does the carefully lit photograph of the Parkay patty make you feel? As your eye takes in the words and pictures, try to relax. Let your vision wander aimlessly across the picture, taking in every line and shadow. Most readers agree that the ad presents a "wholesome," "nourishing," "desirable" "food product."

Now become critical. Check every detail. In any serious study of media, it is vital to accept nothing at face value. Whenever reason tells you something is unimportant, look or listen even more critically. In human perception, the content of the unimportant (or background) often becomes of greatest significance. The *apparently* important is often mere decoration, like icing on a cake.

The lead line of the ad firmly advises the housewife to "Take Advantage of a Softie . . ." and to guess "what happens when you're an old softie."

The Soft Parkay copy is generally undistinguished as literary metaphor. That, of course, is precisely how it is intended to be perceived—as pure banality. The word "Softie," however, through free association, could describe the flaccid male genital. Male genitals are often referrenced in ad copy as "hard" or "soft," adjectives attached to an incredible range of products.

Illusions presented in the commercial mass media are far removed from reality. In a media-dominated society, it becomes increasingly difficult to find or identify reality. Americans have been carefully media trained not to be able to tell the difference between fantasy and reality. Clearly separating the two is often quite difficult, and sometimes nearly impossible in the world of commercial huckstering, where fantasies are designed to seem more real, more desirable, more rewarding, and more stimulating than reality could ever become. And, indeed, the Parkay patty, knife, and muffin are *not* photographic representations, but cleverly airbrushed paintings executed by a skilled, highly paid artist.

FANTASY-REALITY ARE DIFFICULT DISTINCTIONS

Even though it may appear realistic, a painting is pure fantasy, an artist's creative imagination. A simple unretouched photograph represents one limited dimension of reality—time has been stopped at a particular instant. Of course, a skilled photographic artist can manipulate perception by choice of perspective, background, and lighting as readily as could an artist with his brush. Several technical devices can help determine whether a picture is a photographic representation of reality or a photographer's fantasy—for example, a linen tester (microscope for studying dot structures in engraving), computer enhancement spectographic analysis techniques, and ultraviolet photography. It is quite simple to make these distinctions.

One simple test for determining fantasy characteristics is to check with the real thing. For example, does the ad Parkay look like actual Parkay in a similar situation? A group of students and I tried to scrape off on knife blades a Parkay glob that resembled the one in the ad. In several hundred attempts, we never even came close.

At this point many readers will accuse me of exaggeration or projection—having a dirty mind or a wild imagination. Such accusations are difficult to defend oneself against—at least until you find the "Softie" in the Parkay painting. A quite identifiable glans (head of the penis) is gently peeping out from the patty on the right side.

Were only *one* penis represented in the Parkay patty, one might rationalize that anyone can see anything he wishes in any picture. But another quite identifiable glans also has been worked into the Parkay design. Notice the coronal ridge that extends down the left side of the Parkay patty. As any medical text on genital anatomy will demonstrate, the coronal ridge at the base of the glans is fairly standard male physiological equipment.

Media present symbolic *illusions* via words, pictures, and sounds that are perceived on at least two levels, conscious (or cognitive) and unconscious (or subliminal). At the unconscious level, the male genitalia concealed in Soft Parkay being spread with a phallic knife blade inside a muffin would most certainly be unconsciously perceived instantaneously.

A CUTTING SYMBOL

Portraying the heads of two penises on a knife blade could also suggest male castration—a quite possible unconscious motive for the highly insecure American housewife. If she can fatten up her husband, he may, at least theoretically, become less vulnerable to the attractions of a younger woman—a fear dutifully exploited by the ad agencies. Presumably *"old* softies"—men whose age has rendered them impotent—get castrated as punishment. The last sentence in the copy explains, ". . . guess that's what happens when you're an old softie."

Moreover, the rich, golden, nourishing goodness portrayed in the Parkay patty is ultimately intended to be put in the mouth. Some very respectable psychoanalytic theory would explain the ad's effectiveness in terms of unconscious oral regression. It is not at all difficult to envision millions of housewives across the nation salivating over their *Family Circles* —without the slightest suspicion about what was really turning them on.

If only one such piece of subliminal pornography were introduced daily into our brain systems, perhaps it could be argued as being harmless. But literally dozens of such embedded obscenities, involving human reproductive behavior or death, enter our brain systems each day—for some individuals, hundreds daily. Most junk food advertising utilizes subliminal techniques, of course; if such media were only a simple information source, it could not so dramatically affect basic cultural value systems. Even worse, some unconscious memory systems may retain the obscene information for a lifetime. Pioneering Montreal neurosurgeon Wilder Penfield believes the brain retains everything perceived throughout life (Penfield and Roberts, 1959).

The average individual in our culture perceives well over a hundred ads daily, from a variety of media. Some or all of this information is retained in the individual's perceptual system, though few people have any conscious idea about their unwitting involvement. Merchandising battles are fought almost entirely at the unconscious level.

A NEW WORLD OPENED

For a very long time, at the University of Western Ontario, my students and I were uncertain just what we had blundered into as we began to collect examples of subliminal art. But, because of the cries of outrage and indignation from people around us in the university, from the beginning it seemed significant. Every few weeks something new appeared that no one had consciously been aware of before. For dealing with repressed media content, we developed techniques not dissimilar to those used by psychoanalysts.

I am grateful to those students who continued to probe their own perceptual limitations and those of the world around them. Often it took courage to question conventional wisdoms. Several times students came to class with faces bruised after a fight with roommates over something they had discovered in such media as *Playboy*. In fact, the *reactions* to what we had turned up were often almost as curious as the discoveries themselves: I have watched young men become furious or actually shed tears over the shattering of a *Playboy* illusion.

Our examinations of the so-called "men magazines" provoked the strongest, angriest responses. For many young men, these publications serve as puberty manuals, offering an assortment of commercially profitable though cruel, narcissistic, masturbatory fantasies about both women and themselves.

AT THE PLAYBOY TOWER

A recent tour of the Playboy Building in Chicago produced confirmation that the real world is rarely what the U.S. commercial media would have us believe.

At the invitation of *Oui's* managing editor, I spent a full day interviewing several dozen of the magazine's senior editors and production staff. I was intrigued at how many were familiar with my research. In virtually every interview, the discussion quickly turned to masturbation—at their initiative, not mine. One rather learned editor described their primary day-to-day dilemma as constantly developing "new dimensions of American masturbatory fantasies" in order to sustain and increase circulation and, of course, advertising.

Having always believed these crotch magazines dealt with real, live women, I was stunned. I had always thought of men's magazine readers as red-blooded American he-men, constantly surrounded by hordes of sexually demanding women. From the *Oui* staffers' admissions, the so-called men's magazines were in fact *masturbation manuals*. The exhaustive detailed information available to these executives on masturbation frequencies, manual techniques, fantasy variations by demographic group, and useful (salable) duration of fantasy projections was fascinating. They knew precisely and in great detail what their magazines were used for by their readers. Obviously, their readers do not know they know.

These manufactured masturbatory fantasies, of course, are simply merchandising *modus operandi* that serve to sell the magazines, which sell the ads, which sell the products, which offer an ever-unfulfilled promise the fantasies will become reality if only you buy and buy and buy.

I spent an entire day in the Playboy Tower talking about *jacking off*. I left Heffner's citadel with the unsettling conviction that these experts knew more about the masturbation fantasies of both young and not so young American males than anyone in the nation.

Since my visit to the Playboy Tower, however, I have met numerous media executives who have made or financed scientific research on both male and female masturbation. One president of a California porno publication empire, specializing in bondage and discipline books, discovered via sophisticated research that when a very small proportion of his readers stopped masturbating with his magazines and began acting out the fantasies (actually participating in B & D), they stopped reading the publications. Apparently, the acting out of sexual fantasies is commercially undesirable. This publisher regularly uses subliminal art in his B & D books to intensify fantasy projection.

America's so-called sexual revolution—largely a product of media hype—primarily involves refinements in narcissistic masturbation. Apparently it has little to do with heterosexual relationships. The sexual revolution turns out to be only another media rip-off.

IN DEFENSE OF FANTASY

The hostile, ridiculing, even violent reactions to our research are powerful demonstrations of the U.S. media's power over individual lives. I was proposing only that individuals critically examine something many did not wish to deal with—for good reason, as you can see. But little by little, we learned to deal with subliminals without provoking anger and confrontation, though I did underestimate the threat seemingly new ideas always pose to those deeply attached to conventional wisdoms of the status quo. Socrates was forced to drink hemlock for probing his environment in much the same way we were probing ours. And, professors are still hemlocked for asking unsettling questions. From the beginning, we knew it was only a matter of time until our media studies ended in conflict with the university.

During our first two years of research on subliminals, no one outside my classes paid much attention. I completed a long study of Attitudinal Resistance to Change, commissioned by the Commonwealth of Puerto Rico. When published, it weighed several pounds and like so much research of its kind, it was purposely dull reading. Boring academic prose is rarely criticised. Yet it did look very impressive in its heavy academic binding. Along with a dozen other studies done for large corporations, it resulted in my being granted tenure during my third year at UWO—theoretically, at least, a lifetime assurance of job security and academic freedom.

With the Puerto Rican project completed, I began to assemble the subliminal data for publication. I submitted the resulting 45-page academic paper, heavily footnoted and illustrated, to several academic journals. All the editors rejected the piece with such comments as: "Nonsense!" "This simply couldn't be going on." "Too wild an idea, better suited to science fiction." "We would have known about subliminals if they were really being used," and so forth.

I then carried my article around to half a dozen scholars whose specialty was perception. Four of them literally ordered me out of their offices. Two laughed hilariously, commenting that this was the craziest thing they had ever heard. One kindly advised me to drop the project, warning that this could finish my academic career. After thirteen years as a professor, I was vividly aware of the political tightropes that must be walked in terms of promotion, tenure, and survival in academia.

HOW TO LOSE FRIENDS AND ALIENATE EMPLOYERS

I never expected everyone to accept my discoveries uncritically, but I did want a hearing. The only way to get the material into print, it turned out, was as a popular book. So during 1972 I expanded the paper to book length, chopped out most of the footnotes, and tried to convert my pedantic jargon into more or less readable English.

Thinking I had better prepare the people around me at the university for what was to come, I took the Gilbey's Gin ad (*Subliminal Seduction*, Figure 1)* from *Time* magazine into the office of my department chairman, who had headed the small four-man journalism department for over 25 years. He had once been the London, Ontario, stringer for *Time*'s Canadian edition and spent much time in his classes lecturing on the glories of advertising.

"Morning," I greeted him with enthusiasm. "This Gilbey's Gin ad is strange. Take a look."

I dropped the magazine on the desk in front of him. Immediately he became distraught. He would not, perhaps could not, look at the ad. His eyes darted nervously from me to the door to the window, almost as though he was looking for a way to escape. "That's nonsense!" he finally muttered, almost trembling. "You can see anything you want to see in any picture. I'm not interested in such trash. I never pay attention to ads anyway." He was angry now, apparently having already heard from students about my new research project. "Ads have no effect upon anyone, especially anyone who controls his mind and emotions. I make up my own mind about gin and everything else."

At first I had thought he would find the gin ad amusing. I tried to explain, but his face became livid, his jaw rigid, his eyes defensively narrowed. "Just look at the damned thing," I almost pleaded. "It won't hurt you!" I pointed out the airbrush details. He avoided looking at the ad, acting as though I

*Key, Wilson Bryan. *Subliminal Seduction,* New York: Signet, 1974.

were attempting to force him into some highly repugnant and fearsome experience.

Finally he shouted me out of his office. As I closed the door, he yelled something about my "dirty mind."

"You're making up all this filth," he shouted. "You are destroying young people's confidence in the press. You should be locked up as a public menace."

That interview was typical of many that would occur over the next couple of years. Somehow, my research into advertising triggered bizarre, defensive reactions—especially from individuals whose professional experience and education should have made them at least skeptically curious. After all, what could be so harmless as a gin ad in a national magazine? I would have been much more warmly received had I been showing around hard-core pornography.

THE REWARDS OF IRRELEVANCE

In research, one test for significance has always been the degree of opposition the findings stimulate. If research findings are generally applauded and considered sound, the work is likely of little significance. Pleasantly received research merely tells people what they wanted to hear, reinforcing conventional prejudices and convictions. This innocuous research includes the preponderance of work that qualifies university faculty for tenure and promotion, professional status, and, of course, financial reward. But when individuals—especially the so-called "experts"—respond to new ideas with outrage, frequently a breakthrough is near. Innovative discovery invariably threatens traditional concepts. Individuals with vested interests will of course attempt to ridicule or suppress any threat to the conventional wisdoms upon which they have based their careers.

Thus this, my third book on subliminal phenomena is—at least partly—the story of what happens to somebody who discovers something that someone else has already discovered and kept secret from a society that really did not want to know about the discovery.

My discovery appeared about as enthusiastically accepted as a typhoid epidemic.

This made the subject unavoidably personal, indeed—and sometimes even fun.

2 · WHAT WE HIDE FROM OURSELVES WITH MEDIA'S HELP

To be effective, propaganda must constantly short circuit all thought and decision. It must operate on the individual at the level of the unconscious. Critical judgement disappears altogether. The responses of the neurotic are identical with those of the propagandee [i.e.: consumer].

Jacques Ellul,
Propaganda

HUMAN PERCEPTUAL DEFENSES

Among Sigmund Freud's major contributions were his early studies on the limits of man's conscious behavior; these have been developed and expanded by scores of modern writers on psychological phenomena. In order to avoid anxiety, we construct perceptual defense mechanisms that either limit or distort our perception of reality. Perceptual defenses include repression, isolation, regression, fantasy formation, sublimation, denial, projection, and introjection—possibly all describe different aspects of the same mechanism. These defenses erase memories of upsetting experiences, prevent disturbing conscious memory associations, inhibit certain emotions from relating to experiences, or modify the perception of a drive, wish, or fantasy, transforming a drive stimulus which produces guilt into a more acceptable form (Lidz, 1968, p. 256).

Repression is often termed the central mechanism of perceptual defense. R. D. Laing's simple definition is often useful: "We forget something, then forget we have forgotten." Though unavailable at the conscious level, repressed information does affect behavior, usually in ways impossible to consciously recognize. These defenses, unconscious ways in which conscious awareness excludes information that might provoke anxiety, are compulsive acts. Indeed, there is no control over a perceptual defense, nor even any conscious awareness such a defense is in operation. They operate automatically and invisibly, and appear related to individual adjustment within cultures or subcultures. Each culture uniquely confronts its members with an effort to control or manage basic drives. These defensive perceptual strategies actually make it possible for an individual to adapt to a society's imposed restrictions.

One of the most unsettling discoveries anyone researching substimuli must eventually confront is that once the subliminal information is pointed out, it is easy to perceive consciously. From the point of discovery, in fact—even years after the discovery—it is the primary feature that will be dealt with consciously. Substimuli have a powerful effect upon memory.

The artists do not really hide anything! It is always available to anyone who could consciously deal with the information. *Viewers* actually hide the taboo images from their own conscious awareness, lest they arouse culturally forbidden memories, feelings, or perceptions.

This view of human perception is profoundly disturbing to many, especially to those with highly repressed views of themselves and their social and sexual behavior. The United States may well be one of the most repressed societies on earth—purposefully educated in vast areas of reality avoidance. This is an extremely dangerous condition that could threaten both individual and national, if not world, survival.

REPRESSION OF THE FORBIDDEN

The Kanon Man's Cologne ad (Figure 5) appeared in many of the so-called "men's" magazines. An estimated half million dollars was invested in the rather innocuous photograph of a hand holding a bottle of Kanon. There is certainly little here that could be considered threatening, but again, please study the ad before you read further. Write down anything unusual you perceive, any feelings of which you are aware which might have come from the ad. How, for example, might men and women perceive you if you were to use Kanon Cologne?

Through a one-way mirror, we videotaped readers thumbing through a magazine in which the ad appeared, and observed that virtually no one spent more than a second or two with the Kanon ad. Remember, however, that perception is both total and instantaneous. Most print advertising is *designed* for a perceptual exposure time of less than one second. If the ad is to justify its investment, any information capable of motivating a purchase must enter the reader's brain in this instant, even if the actual purchase situation may not arise until days, weeks, or even months later.

So how does the Kanon ad do its job? When the ad agency sent the Kanon ad to its client for approval, some corporation executive must have asked this same question.

Let's carefully examine the hand. One of the best techniques for psyching out any sensory stimulus is to compare what you *perceive* as the real thing with the *actual* real thing. Compare your own left hand with the hand in the Kanon ad. Are they similar?

Vaguely similar, perhaps, but several things are distinctly different. Did you notice the thumbnail—and its relation to the thumb knuckle? Though the entire knuckle does not appear in the picture, there's no way you can get your thumb and thumbnail into the position shown in the picture. The thumb, bottle, thumbnail, hand, and knife were first photographed separately, then all pasted together in the layout. Note that no fingers show through the supposedly transparent bottle. Several artists I consulted estimated that the complex composite picture involved an art fee of between five and ten thousand dollars. There is no way such a perspective between the two hands and bottle could be achieved in a straight photograph, even with a special camera lens. The wrist, hair, and thumb details have been thoroughly retouched with an airbrush.

Now look at the palm where the thumb joins the hand. Compare the picture with your own left hand. Are they similar? The vertical line dividing the wrist and palm bisects two rather bulbous areas that strangely also resemble testicles—or could this be merely your imagination? The rigid thumb, of course, becomes the semi-erect penis. It may take you a few seconds before the repressed genital registers in your consciousnss.

The hand-genital illusion is *syncretistic*, that is, two-sided, much like the old "Rubin's profiles" first described around

1910 by Danish perceptual psychologist Dr. E. Rubin. Several of these old illusions—vases and faces, old woman and young woman, duck and rabbit—appear frequently in a wide range of elementary psychology texts, presented as perceptual curiosities. I have never met a psychologist who even suspected syncretistic illusions could have a practical use.

But if one side of a syncretistic illusion is loaded with taboo or strong emotional content, as in the Kanon ad, it will be repressed, perceived only at the subliminal level. And as the technique is applied in the Kanon ad, the total perception may be retained for a lifetime in some people's memory systems.

Tests on the Kanon ad were done with subjects who, as far as could be determined, were unfamiliar with the subliminal issue. Roughly 20 percent of women instantly recognized the erect penis, though some were reluctant to admit it for fear of being accused of having "dirty minds." Only about 2 percent of male subjects consciously spotted the erect genital in its published context. The ad could not have been safely published in a women's magazine.

An erect penis is certainly taboo when published in a "man's magazine," advertising a man's product to be sold to men. The symbolism is predictably repressable, in view of readers' macho self-fantasies. The overt macho image is often considered a camouflage for a more ambiguous, covert sexuality, and a large amount of psychoanalytic theory suggests the illusion's appeal is directed at latent homosexual tendencies—which all men presumably share in some measure.

The ad is clearly not directed at *overt* male homosexuals—few homosexuals read the men's magazines; many find them highly offensive. As yet, there are not enough homosexuals to justify sizable magazine marketing investments. This may be changing in America, however, in response to such manipulations of the human unconscious.

Another theory of the ad's subliminal significance might be that Kanon will help readers achieve a large, erect penis. There is, of course, always the possibility that hand-genital symbolism unconsciously alludes to masturbation.

There is much more to come in the Kanon ad, however.

A CUTTING BLOW

Did you notice the knife about to slip on the bottle cork? When it slips—castration! The artist has deftly injected another of the psychological common denominators that, in one degree or another, have united all men who have ever lived.

As if an appeal to latent homosexuality and fear of castration were not enough, did you notice the beagle or Labrador's head just below the bottom of the bottle? One floppy ear hangs just to the right of the wood awl. This is a rather pathetic dog, however, as it is dead. The awl has been driven through its head.

I am frankly uncertain as to why a dead hunting dog would help sell Kanon Cologne. Subliminal animals embedded in waterfalls, rivers, lakes, and hillsides are usually found in advertising for women's hygiene products; it is rare to find them in ads aimed at men. Theoretically, the subliminal dog might be explained as an appeal to some anthropomorphic unconscious projection, but this is only theory. Dogs are highly emotionalized symbols in America—symbolic surrogates for children and many other things. (This is not the case with dogs in most other countries.)

Go back now and check your response notes from the beginning of the analysis. What feelings or ideas did you consciously experience when you first viewed the ad? At first glance, the ad appears to show merely a hand holding the product. But a *mere* hand and a bottle would not communicate anywhere near the feeling of strength, desirability, and imperative use that the picture transmits. Without the taboo subliminal information surfacing, conscious perception is strengthened, reenforced, and emotionalized. It is entirely possible, however, that these nonverbal effects upon conscious perception are also presently unverbalizable. We simply do not know *how* and *why* the brain functions. Art, like music, is a nonverbal medium. It is often difficult for North Americans to accept that much, or most, of human perceptual phenomena cannot be meaningfully represented with words except in theories far removed from actual brain functions.

THE ADMEN SPEAK

Terrence Healey, while a graduate student at Bowling Green University in Ohio, was curious about how ad executives would comment on the subliminal issue. As part of his thesis research, he wrote numerous large international agencies whose ads appeared in my books and asked two simple questions: "To what extent is subliminal stimulation used by your agency in ad preparation?" and "If not, why not?" Most simply did not answer, but he did receive a handful of almost uniform replies.

The Senior Vice President and Executive Creative Director of Foote, Cone, & Belding (the world's fifth largest ad agency) said, "I have read Key's book . . . and consider it to be a total crock. Subliminal seduction is not used by FC&B because it is dirty, devious, and shows a total lack of respect for the people we ultimately work for—those being the consumers of the products we represent. I despise the whole idea of subliminal stimulation."

FC&B was, of course, responsible for the Miss Clairol "Does She or Doesn't She" ad discussed on page 57 of my second book, *Media Sexploitation.** I once discussed this ad with their creative director on television. She ended the program in hysteria. They must still remember.

The Director of Public Affairs and the Senior Vice President and Research Director of Batten, Barton, Durstine & Osborn, Inc., both responded with: "Subliminal techniques including subliminal stimulation are not used by this agency—or any other competent agency. To waste time considering trying to create a subliminal message that will overcome the intended message would be counter-productive in time and effectiveness." "The technique is not used because (a) it has not been proven to be effective; (b) there is some question as to the validity of the technique; (c) we do not see any reason to use advertising techniques such as these."

The Vice President Account Supervisor of Doyle, Dane, Bernbach, Inc., replied: "Mr. Key's dissection of the 1971 Calvert Extra ad [*Subliminal Seduction*, Figure 16, pp. 102–7] may epitomize the delusions of a disturbed personality. Anyone who has looked at Rohrschalk [*sic*] tests or cloud formations knows that perception varies from person-to-person and generally the more neurotic the individual, the more devious the interpretation. Key's book evoked nothing but laughter among those of us at the agency who were involved in that particular Calvert ad . . . it would amaze me if any other agencies or advertisers employed this device. We would never jeopardize our reputation or integrity by utilizing dishonest and devious advertising methods."

*Key, Wilson Bryan. *Media Sexploitation*, New York: Signet, 1976.

YOU CAN TRUST CLOUDS

There is no meaningful way to discuss human perception without dealing, in some way, with projective phenomena.

One of the most frequent charges ad executives have made against my work is that I am making up these images, much as children do when they fantasize faces in clouds. In his diary, Leonardo da Vinci described field excursions with his students: they sat before stone walls or stared into the sky, projecting images. Da Vinci believed such projective exercises to be excellent training for artists. In my classes, after the first lecture I often take students out on the lawn where we study clouds for an hour. You would be astonished at the filth and obscenity floating about in cloud formations!

The projection mechanism was extensively studied by Dr. Hermann Rorschach during the early years of this century. His essays are rarely used today, even in undergraduate psychology courses, and that is a pity as they are brilliant explorations of the human psyche. The famous Rorschach inkblot is an automatic design in which content has been deliberately excluded. As with cloud formations, anything projected into a Rorschach inkblot comes out of a subject's mentation system and is frequently an expression of underlying conflict or neurosis. Thus the Rorschach inkblot is a useful tool in psychotherapy.

A simple, though not infallible, test of whether you are projecting (making up) is to ask other individuals if they see what you see. It is usually difficult to persuade others to see your individual projections; they tend to come up with their own projective version. But if it is *really* there, most other people will perceive the stimulus in much the same way you do.

Someone should explain, then, how the lizard, fish, birds, skulls, and other death and self-destruction symbols found their way into that Calvert ad. These images are clearly not projections, as the Vice President Account Supervisor claims. They were painted skillfully and expensively into the ice cubes of an ad in which they invested many millions of dollars.

The Publicity Director of McCann-Erickson, Inc., said: "We do not subscribe to hidden or devious methods of manipulating consumer behavior, nor do we feel that anyone in the advertising business could do it, even if they wanted to. To believe that it can be done, regularly, on a commercial basis, is to underestimate and disrespect the consumer."

An account executive at Ross Roy of New York, Inc., wrote: "It's virtually impossible to implement through photography. And very few people would recognize it even if one could implement it, which would make it quite cost-inefficient and therefore useless."

The Vice President in Charge of Media Research at Leo Burnett said: ". . . there has been only one 'test' of the subliminal mode of presentation . . . upon the sale of Coke and popcorn to movie-goers. This report [by James Vicary] is now considered as much a hoax as the doctored remains of pre-historic man routinely discovered during the latter half of the 19th Century. Vicary was discredited by the market research community and has dropped completely out of sight." He quoted the TV Code of the National Association of Broadcasters (IV, 14): "Any technique whereby an attempt is made to convey information to the viewer by transmitting messages below the threshold of normal awareness is not permitted."

"As far as I know," this executive continued, "subliminal presentation and perception remains confined to college laboratory classes. After careful analysis of the various psychological models of human beings' response to advertising and the available data, I've come to the conclusion that the most frequently occurring mode of response to advertising is rejection after scanning."

The account executive for Virginia Slims at Leo Burnett also wrote: "Subliminal stimulation is not purposely used by the Leo Burnett Co. in the development of Virginia Slims advertising. The reason is that we are advertisers, not psychologists. Our expertise is in the communication of ideas and images, not in the probing of stimulation of the subconscious."

One of the more honest answers to Terrence Healey's inquiry came from the Business Manager of the Art Department at William Esty Company, Inc., who said simply, in regard to Camel Filters ads, "Due to the nature of cigarette advertising and the various controversies that often surround it, it has become our and our client's policy not to divulge any information as to our marketing, advertising, or media plans."

WHOSE IMAGINATION IS REAL?

There appear several possible conclusions. First, the ad industry is correct. Subliminal techniques are a figment of this writer's imagination; no such thing exists.

Second, it is entirely possible the individuals who answered Mr. Healey's letter really did *not* know anything about subliminal techniques. Several appeared to be low-ranking research, publicity, account, or administrative executives who would have no real *need to know*. Were I a senior executive in an ad agency who received such an inquiry, I would probably have the letter answered by someone who knew nothing about the subject.

Third, there is a possibility that subliminals *do not* really affect human behavior.

As a writer, scholar, and researcher, I believe subliminal advertising is indeed effective. This conclusion is based upon ten years of research, years of prior work in the advertising industry, and the personal testimony of colleagues and associates in both academia and the business world. But then, I may have sold myself a bill of goods. Having written three books and invested ten years of my life in the subject, I certainly have a vested interest in believing that subliminals are effective; I am in the same biased position as my colleagues who spend their lives arguing against the idea.

PROOF: A COMPLEX QUESTION

Perhaps the most frequent question lecture audiences ask is, "Do these embedded taboo obscenities in ads *really* sell the product?"

I believe subliminal stimulus techniques, indeed, have a most significant potential to change human behavior in measurable ways. A great many scholars, scientists, philosophers, artists, and technicians, working over many years, have reached similar conclusions. A prodigious amount of published evidence appears to answer the question directly—that of Dixon, Becker, and Dichter, for example. The more indirect evidence from such as Freud, Jung, Ehrenzweig, Thass-Thienemann, Fromm, Menninger, and others is also reinforcing.

But one other question often brought up during my university lectures is whether I have clear, specific *proof* that subliminals affect behavior. My answer (often unsettling to those who read my books) is that *I do not*. Nor do I know anyone else who has clear, specific, simplistic, demonstrable data to settle the question once and for all.

Available evidence, however believable it appears, is nevertheless theoretical, conjectural, deductive, and inductive—even though now backed up by a prodigious quantity of published experimental research.

The question focuses upon how the brain works. We simply do not know. There are hundreds of theories as to how it might function, but they are only theories. Some of this theorization, produced over the past century or two, is often useful. Theories do not have to be true to be useful. A theory is only a conjecture, sometimes a *learned* conjecture, but at best only a guess.

Ad researchers are in an enviable position. They need not prove *how* or *why* subliminals work—only that they *do* work, that is, sell. The multibillion dollar annual media investment in research can usually determine clearly whether any specific media technique works—that is, sells—or not. Purchasing behavior, of course, certainly classifies as significant human activity.

This problem regarding indisputable proof also applies to such questions as the smoking-lung cancer polemic. Few physicians (except those on the tobacco industry's payrolls) doubt that tobacco is a direct cause of cancer, emphysema, and other pathologies. But even though statistics persuasively point to shorter life spans for smokers, the cause-and-effect relationship is so difficult to prove that no one has yet been able to establish unequivocally that cigarettes cause cancer in humans. It simply cannot yet be proven in court, so to speak—for which the tobacco industry is probably most grateful. For practical purposes, of course, it would be extremely unwise to smoke if you wish to enjoy maximum longevity, whether or not the cancer link has been legally and scientifically "proven."

The most persuasive evidence for the effectiveness of subliminals is the billions of dollars annually invested by advertisers and media industries on the assumption that subs *are* effective merchandising stimuli. I find it difficult to argue with an industry that year after year spends billions annually on advertising, a very large portion of which is allocated to subliminal selling. Businessmen are not omniscient, of course:

their assumptions and conclusions are wrong as often as anyone else's. But U.S. capitalistic enterprises use a ruthless, basic, decision-making premise: if it does not make money, investment cannot be justified. And, it is widely known that U.S. corporations have invested many billions of dollars in the study of human behavior over many years—far more money and research effort than has ever been available to the universities. Unfortunately, no one has access to this research, upon which U.S. corporations justify mammoth (and continually expanding) media expenditures. But certainly these business organizations have demonstrated the strength of their convictions.

If subliminals do *not* work, the indictment against the ad agencies is even more shocking: they have invested tens of billions of dollars of their clients' merchandising funds in worthless subliminals, misappropriating enormous quantities of client money, and endangering their clients with public censure and eventual government intervention—on a communication scheme that most Americans would consider grossly immoral.

A ROCKY SELL

The Johnny Walker Black Label Scotch ad (Figure 6) appeared in virtually every major U.S. national magazine, including *Playboy, Time, Newsweek,* and *New Yorker.* Over a three-year period, an estimated $2 million was invested in magazine space in which to display this single ad, which must have been extremely successful in selling Scotch to have justified the prodigious investment. According to the U.S. Bureau of Commerce, distillers reinvested 6 percent of their gross receipts into advertising in 1977. Therefore, each one million dollars invested in the ad would have had to produce $15 million in sales. At the $2 million investment level, this ad would have had to sell some $33 million in JW Scotch to break even. Nobody who merely breaks even is going to remain in business—there must be profit. The $2 million investment in this single display would have to gross upwards of $50 million in order to pay for itself.

Admittedly, it is difficult to believe—because we have been educated to believe just the opposite—that six ice cubes in an empty glass on a black background could be responsible for a $50 million Scotch whiskey transaction. Yet, the economics of advertising—like those of most business transactions—are relatively simple, in spite of ad executives' frequent public statements that "advertising really doesn't work." Were they to repeat such nonsense in front of their clients, they would be instantly unemployed. Advertising does indeed work, and it works well. It works *best,* of course, when the consumer believes it doesn't.

Considering the literary talent available in the English-speaking world, it is curious to consider the JW ad's two lines of copy: "The road to success is paved with rocks. Let us smooth them for you." Could this assemblage of words have anything to do with over $50 million in Scotch sales? The glass and ice cubes are even more banal. Logically, a half inch or so of golden Scotch might have been poured into the glass, at least to demonstrate the product. But, nothing—only an empty glass with six ice cubes.

Considering that the ad appeared in *Playboy,* a lipstick stain could have been placed on the edge of the glass to add a touch of romance. But no, only an empty glass with six ice cubes—waiting to be filled with Scotch.

Were you an executive at Somerset Importers, Ltd., the company that imports Johnny Walker Scotch into the United States, how might you react to this ad? Your ad agency has seriously proposed you invest $2 million of your hard-earned capital to purchase display space within every major magazine in the United States for this clumsily executed photograph.

By the inexorable, simplistic logic taught in business management university courses, you might justifiably fire the account executive who had proposed this apparently irresponsible investment. As anyone can clearly see, the photographer was careless. He allowed one ice cube to fall out on the table. For all that money, you might think they could find a photographer who could get all six ice cubes in the glass where they belonged. Audience reading time on this ad was designed to be no more than a second or two—a fact that makes it even more difficult to explain. You would even be justified in saying there is really not much to see in this ad.

THE HAPPY SCOTCH DRINKERS

The copy mentions "rocks," presumably the ice cubes that appear to be the ad's primary subject. JW Scotch is mentioned only in the trademark at the bottom of the page. So, let's carefully examine the "rocks" (see Figure 7).

Observe the right one-third of the ice cube that has fallen from the glass. On the cube's surface was painted an inexplicable screaming, agonized, terrified face (Figure 8). The face is surrealistic, certainly not representational, hardly the sort of thing you'd expect to find in a whiskey ad.

Turn the cube upside down. Next to the screaming face appear a man's feet and legs, dangling or floating in midair (Figure 9). On the cube's left (when still viewed upside down) appears another face in agony, this one melting away in a white heat, the tongue hanging limply from the open mouth (Figure 10).

The JW ice cubes and glass are not photographs of the real thing. Twenty years ago commercial artists painted on actual photographs. Even plastic ice cubes were sometimes used as models. Today, however, the technique is so well developed—and readers so well trained *not* to deal consciously with visual subtlety—that photographs are rarely used. Because of their heavy advertising budgets, the alcoholic beverage industry can hire the best creative talent available. The entire JW ad is an artist's fantasy, a sophisticated airbrush painting executed by a master craftsman. One slip of his brush, and some of his imagery might have surfaced in the reader's conscious awareness. This would mean big trouble for the advertiser. Painted into the JW ice cubes are twelve clearly recognizable images.

On the far right surface of the cube at the bottom right within the glass appears a skull (Figure 11). Turn the ad on its right side, and a monster with encircling arms appears on the left surface of the bottom right cube (Figure 12). Turn this same cube upside down, and you see a snake charmer with skull face, wearing a turban and sitting in a lotus position with a cobra (Figure 13). The left bottom ice cube includes a teddy-bear monster with smiling mouth and flipper, a rather cute animal but not one of this world (Figure 14). Another twisted, agonizing face appears in the topmost ice cube. The shallow forehead, long nose, and twisted mouth portray a tortured face (Figure 15).

On the right surface of the cube at top right appears the pained face of an old man, his tongue protruding from his lips (Figure 16), perhaps another satisfied JW drinker. On the right surface of the center cube, turned on its right side, is a standing figure wearing a grotesque mask reminiscent of the Japanese ceremonial *devil's mask*. The figure's torso is in a posture of torment, pubic hair is apparent, and the left arm seems to end in a stump. Objects, perhaps spirits, swirl about the masked head (Figure 17).

On the left surface of the center cube, turned on its right side, appears a bird—the body, eye, and beak easily recognizable (Figure 18). My first thought was of a raven, an archetypal symbol of death, hardly the kind of bird one might logically select to sell Scotch whiskey.

The object below the raven's beak, however, is even more curious. When you turn the ad on its left edge (Figure 19), the object under the beak appears to have two orifices at the bottom and a headlike appendage at the top. A physiology text confirmed that the object is a quite accurate representation of a castrated penis. In cross-section, the penis displays two symmetrical chambers such as those illustrated in the ice cube. There are actually three chambers in the penis, two filled with spongy tissue that expands when blood pumps in under pressure; the third, much smaller, surrounds the urethra. As readers can perceive for themselves, this is a very special castrated penis, as a most somber human skull appears behind it.

How can the brain perceive images presented upside down and in various conflicting perspectives? During hypnotic trance, many subjects read quite fluently textual material presented upside down and even in mirror image—an impossible task for most people while awake. The brain appears to be able to perceive certain kinds of distorted information at the unconscious level. This discovery opened up vast new areas of manipulation potential for Madison Avenue, as we shall see in Chapter 11.

Adding together the JW ice cube symbology, we seem to be dealing with imagery that involves nightmare hallucinations, self-destruction, even self-immolation. You are unlikely to find an explanation for such unusual imagery in any textbook of which I am aware in the field of advertising, communication studies, or in any conventional system of logic. For the advertiser, of course, the only question is whether such bizarre imagery *can sell* Scotch whiskey.

It is impossible to spend much time around heavy alcohol consumers, especially those who have not yet formally been classified as alcoholics, without becoming aware they are involved in some monstrous kind of self-destructive syndrome. Many are quite intelligent individuals, some even appear consciously aware of the devastated future toward which they are pushing themselves. But, alcoholic consumption easily (and invisibly to the drinker) becomes addictive, leading the compulsive drinker into indescribable agonies undreamed of even by Dante.

THE ALCOHOLIC'S NIGHTMARE

I demonstrated the JW ice cube imagery at several Alcoholics Anonymous meetings. Numerous recovered alcoholics related the ice cube imagery to their withdrawal hallucinations. The body, legs, and feet floating in midair is apparently a common hallucination among alcoholics and other drug users. So is the melting face: during withdrawal hallucinations, various portions of the body often appear to be melting or burning, also a common LSD hallucination. The snake charmer conforms to various reptilian images common to withdrawal hallucinations; and the castrated genitalia are a very common hallucination among virtually all male users of perception-distorting drugs.

One AA member commented that the JW ice cube imagery could have been researched at an AA meeting, simply by listening to testimonials of hallucination experiences.

I also used the JW ice cube imagery in a lecture at a Palm Springs Information Film Producers Conference. The following morning at breakfast an attractive middle-aged woman joined our table. A noted film producer, she identified herself as a recovered alcoholic. She explained that after viewing the subliminal ice cube images, she had been unable to sleep and found herself craving a drink—for the first time in twelve years. Finally in desperation, she called the local Alcoholics Anonymous chapter for help. Yet she could not recall ever having seen the ad when it had appeared a year or so earlier.

Some research suggests that subliminal stimuli appear to operate much like post-hypnotic suggestions. A substimulus is induced at the unconscious level and surfaces consciously at a later date, say, at the moment of a purchasing decision. The actual reason for the decision, however, is never known to the subject, who may verbalize a complex, even bizarre rationale for his behavior—as do most addicts trapped in compulsive behavior.

Apparently, when I demonstrated the ice cube images, the woman's earlier memory of the ad was unconsciously activated, setting off the cravings which ended in a sleepless night. At least this is as good an explanation as I can offer. The same thing could conceivably happen to readers of this book, but they at least will know what's going on.

Ninety-nine percent of alcohol beverage advertising contains one or more techniques of subliminal excitation stimuli. And the JW ice cubes ad is only one of several hundred alcohol ads collected that utilize subliminal death and self-destruction imagery.

On March 8, 1976, I demonstrated the JW ice cubes in testimony before the Senate Committee on Labor and Public Welfare in subcommittee hearings on alcoholism and narcotics. Senator Harrison A. Williams of New Jersey, Committee Chairman, mentioned he was considering the introduction of a bill that would require a warning label on every alcoholic beverage container, similar to that used on cigarette packages. We briefly discussed the distinct possibility that self-destruction could be an important factor in sustaining alcoholic consumption.

One theory, of course, is the old notion—going back at least to British philosopher Thomas Hobbes (1588–1679)—that self-destruction is an inherent human motivation or instinct. Freud discussed the suicidal urge (Thanatos) as a powerful human compulsion present in all individuals in one degree or another. Modern psychoanalysts such as Karl Menninger also utilized the notion of life and death instincts.

What *appears* as self-destructive behavior, in young people especially, may be a very normal part of the maturation or puberty process. Young people today risk their lives with motorcycles, hang gliders, and parachuting. But while often frightening to parents, this behavior is nothing new. Plato wrote of such potentially lethal antics among the young in Athens around 400 B.C. Such behavior may serve positive maturation goals, establishing sexual identities or autonomy from parental domination.

Advertisers may have simply appropriated a normal biological growth phase in behalf of marketing alcoholic beverages. Thus the senator should certainly entertain some second thoughts about a warning label that might turn out to actually *induce* consumption, as it apparently has in cigarette marketing (see the Benson & Hedges Hockey Players ad in

Media Sexploitation, pages 170–72). But one thing is apparent at this point: the alcoholic beverage industry knows a good deal more than do its consumers, and even the medical profession, about why individuals continue to drink.

According to the National Institute for Alcohol and Alcoholism, there are already well over 12 million alcoholics in the United States, and the rate of increase, especially among women and the very young, is accelerating rapidly. The taxpayer picks up the tab for the damage heavy alcohol consumers do to both themselves and society. The bill grows larger each year, as do the number of alcoholics, the quantities they consume, and alcoholic beverage corporation profits.

Considering the growing millions of pathetic, dying alcoholics in the United States (less than 5 percent are believed to ever recover), the research that justified the corporate investment in this JW advertisement should be made public.

If self-destruction is a viable technique of merchandising alcoholic beverages, then this fact should be made common knowledge—and very quickly.

NOTHING NEW UNDER THE SUN

In university classes I often advise ambitious students not to waste their time looking for something new. Very little of that which surrounds us is new. Incessant sales propaganda only makes it appear new by changing labels, interpretations, or pretensions. It would be flattering to say I discovered something new in the widespread use of subliminal manipulation techniques—flattering, perhaps, but untrue. What I did accidentally stumble into was that over a period of several decades, America's advertising agencies and some of their client corporations had engineered subliminal techniques into a fascinating new technique of behavior modification through a direct communication with the brain's unconscious systems.

In fact, however, ad agencies and their behaviorist psychologists had not discovered the techniques either. Subliminal embedding and illusion techniques date far back into our history.

What I appear to have stumbled into is a discovery *of* a discovery made at least five hundred years ago, perhaps even as far back as 400 B.C., possibly even earlier. Plato, Aristotle, and later even the Bible alluded to nonconscious phenomena.

It can be argued that ancient Greek sculpture included elements that suggest their creators possessed a knowledge of unconscious perception.

We have always studied art from the point of view of how it represents reality, but *studying* art is quite distinct from *creating* it. Many of the great masters apparently studied art in terms of how it affected and controlled human perception. The master artists were far more advanced in their comprehension of human perception than the so-called "scientific" psychologists of this century.

3 ⋅ PERCEPTUAL ENGINEERING IN FINE ART

Superficially insignificant or accidental looking detail [in art] may well carry the most important unconscious symbolism.
Anton Ehrenzweig,
The Hidden Order of Art

ENRICHMENT AND UNDERSTANDING

Several years' study of the subliminal dimensions of commercial media often made me wonder: were these embedding and illusion techniques—aimed at the viewers' unconscious—products of our highly competitive, modern, consumer economy? Or had they somehow evolved from the work of earlier artists? Several essays on embedded images in Renaissance art demonstrated that these techniques were utilized long before Madison Avenue adapted them to mass merchandising.

Patrik Reuterswärd, curator of the National Museum in Stockholm, found over a dozen examples of embedded skulls, death heads, and sexual symbols in fourteenth-, fifteenth-, and sixteenth-century paintings (Reuterswärd, 1970). He called them "chance images and visual puns," explaining the techniques as merely "artistic curiosities" or "a scholarly game indulged in by Renaissance artists and their wealthy sponsors." The scholar apparently saw no behavioral significance in their imagery.

Several years earlier, I had drawn almost the same conclusions about advertising embeds. After the first few dozen had been collected, I was convinced they were artistic caprice, pranks, even accidents. No other plausible explanation appeared. Not until hundreds of examples were accumulated, organized, and analyzed, and not until a theoretical background in language and psychology was acquired, did the embeds start to make sense as instruments of behavior modification. It took over a year of perceptual training for myself and a group of students to discover the hidden embeds and evolve ways to establish that they were not merely our individual projections.

These essays on embedded Renaissance art were exciting, even though their scholarly authors appeared inexplicably uninformed about perceptual processes. The articles opened up a whole new area for studies in perception. However, when these art treasures were considered in the context of advertising, it was stunning to find subliminal embedding—*perceptual engineering*, in effect—going on in the fine arts as far back as the fourteenth century.

The following examples illustrate that a new, exciting analytic technique is available to reexamine these treasures from the past. My most important objective here is not to debunk these superb creations. They are undisputably the work of genius, as may be many of the pieces of art which go consciously unnoticed and unacclaimed under the label of advertising. Studies in art and perception could enhance our conscious awareness of how we perceive both art and the world which surrounds us. Or, perhaps to phrase it better, to enhance our conscious awareness of what we exclude from consciousness as we perceive our environment. It appears obvious that most of us have missed a good deal of the action.

ST. ANTHONY'S MEDITATIONS

Among the "artistic curiosities" Reuterswärd cites are the paintings of Hieronymus Bosch—*The Peddler, The Prodigal Son, Garden of Earthly Delights,* and *St. Anthony in the Wilderness* (Figure 20), presently in Madrid's Prado Museum, which has been the subject of hundreds of studies. Wilhelm Fraenger (Fraenger, 1958), who has been called one of the greatest interpreters of Bosch, noticed that the old oak in the center resembles a stag's skull, the branches forming the antlers. Fraenger said the oak held a secret (though he did not explain it), concluding the stag's head was a sexual or virility symbol.

Many other Renaissance renditions of St. Anthony included a tempting woman at his side. In this painting, Bosch replaced her with the tree-skull of a stag. Reuterswärd explained that the artist thereby avoided losing the picture's meditative mood. He wrote, "The conflict of the story told here is, in fact, mainly a conflict on the level of contemplation. St. Anthony is represented as an old, hardened hermit who would hardly succumb to those mischievous agents of evil which approach him from all directions."

But a stag's head as a sexual symbol—as many of the painting's interpreters claim it to be—appears a remote interpretation. One of the general conclusions developed in studies of advertising was that, once discovered, meaning is usually very simple and direct. Even Bosch's magnificently complex *Garden of Earthly Delights* is the essence of simplicity once it is understood.

In both the commercial and the fine arts (the distinction is not nearly as clearly defined as we wish to believe) objects placed over people's heads often depict what they are thinking (see *Subliminal Seduction*, Figure 9). It is reasonable to assume the upper portion of the decayed oak trunk, in which the tormented St. Anthony sits, has something to do with his meditations. If the reader will invert the *St. Anthony* and mask out the branches, the upper portion of the oak stump becomes, almost magically, the torso, legs, and exposed genital area of a woman. Bosch deftly shaded in curled lines around the genital area which appear to be pubic hair.

It is not astonishing that superb perceptual craftsmen would insert such imagery in their work to enhance its effects upon viewers at the unconscious level. It *is* surprising, however, what such artists accomplished intuitively centuries before perception was studied as a "science." It is even more surprising that it remained a secret. Paintings such as the St. Anthony portrait have been studied and interpreted endlessly without, it appears, anyone even getting close to the artist's secrets. This apparent repression within art scholarship says much more about how societies have used art than it does about art and artists.

DÜRER'S LITTLE JOKE

On his way back to Germany from Venice in 1495, just three years after America's discovery by Columbus, Albrecht Dürer stopped on the slopes of the Italian Alps to capture what has been described as "one of the first and most beautiful watercolor landscapes in history." The lovely picture depicts the great rock at Arco, north of Lake Garda, with its stronghold, houses, and olive trees below.

Reviewing Dürer's *Fenedier Fortified Rock at Arco* (Figure 21), Reuterswärd wrote that the artist "cannot have taken it seriously" when he painted a face into the famous rock. According to Reuterswärd, the painting "lost a great deal of its charm because of the chance image." Once the face in the rock becomes apparent, the viewer cannot get rid of it. The face dominates perception of the painting. According to Reuterswärd, Dürer had rendered his watercolor "pictorially unsatisfactory," destroying much of the painting's artistic value by including the obvious and crudely drawn profile as a joke. Another critic who actually journeyed to Arco to view the fortified rock from Dürer's perspective commented that the mountain does not have a face on its slope as portrayed by the artist and that the artist muddied up the otherwise excellent composition with the ridiculous profile.

Perhaps Dürer made a joke of sorts, but the painting (presently in Paris's Louvre Museum) has survived nearly five centuries, a quite remarkable accomplishment for any painting, even Dürer's "disfigured" watercolor. A more careful examination of the painting reveals several reasons why it is still considered a great and significant work of art. Tens of thousands of far "prettier" or more "satisfying" paintings, in the words of the critics, have ended up in garbage cans with their author's dying anonymously.

The face indeed dominates the viewer's perception: apparently Dürer accomplished precisely what he intended by capturing—or *distracting*—the viewer's perception with the crude profile. As long as viewers consciously concentrated on the face, they would never (at least they have not over the past 485 years) consciously perceive the kaleidescope of cartoon faces, animals, and grotesque figures that virtually infest the landscape.

The supposed face in the rock (see Figure 22) is also a standing figure, with a wide-brimmed hat, looking forward. In the standing figure's right hand appears a heavy club, in his left, a book. The figure wears a robe—likely the attire of a priest. Italian priests still wear distinctively broad-brimmed hats, as they did in the fifteenth century. The book in his left hand could be the Bible.

Dürer positioned his priest to dominate a seemingly harmless pastoral Italian landscape. He painted the scene during the Holy Inquisition—a fearful time in Italy and Spain. Dürer's priest, a threatening grimace on his face, dominates Italy. This Dürer watercolor is well known among artists, students, and critics. Considering that the priest has remained hidden for 485 years, at least at the conscious level, this was a rather exciting discovery.

Reuterswärd and his scholarly colleagues totally missed Dürer's perceptual game that must have provided the artist with endless amusement. He ruthlessly and quite humorously caricatured the Italian landscape and its inhabitants.

SUBLIMINAL REINFORCEMENT

There are at least 33 faces in the watercolor (Figures 23, 24, 25). Some can be found when the painting is viewed from the top or sides. Just below the face in the rock, viewed from the right side, is the large face of a woman. The thick lips, narrow cheeks, and long eyelashes suggest the stereotyped notion of a prostitute's face (Figure 23) which has not changed much in five centuries. Below the woman's face, viewed from the bottom, is a sleeping face with a very long beard—possibly someone who has been asleep a long time. A devilish face is embedded in the lower right corner. A skull appears, when viewed from the top, where the horizon disappears behind Arco.

Below and to the right of the face in the rock appears a large, fat, fish-like profile (Figure 24). The large Roman nose could certainly caricature the Italian profile. Another face, shaped similarly to the face in the rock, appears just above the sleeping, bearded face. A sleeping moustached face is embedded just below the face in the rock.

Another large, sleeping face—large nose and eyes—appears in the painting's foreground (Figure 25). When the watercolor is looked at from the left side, a large head and right shoulder extends up the left edge, a figure which also appears to be sleeping. Next to this large face's right ear, Dürer embedded a boot. Italy is still often referred to by Europeans as "the boot." Numerous other caricatured faces are scattered throughout the painting.

Dürer's portrayal of Italy as full of fat, indolent, indulgent people dominated by priests would not likely be considered flattering by either Italians or the Catholic Church. It was likely a parting shot Dürer took just before leaving the country.

Dürer included such embedded material in many of his paintings and engravings, most of which have never been discovered by the art scholars, critics, and experts who wrote about his work over the centuries since his death. What such subliminal dimensions add to the conscious perception of the *Rock at Arco* can really only be conjectured. Clearly, they do affect conscious perception, but in nonverbal terms; the effects are similar to those of embedded contemporary commercial media. However, subliminal effects would serve to enrich the painting's consciously perceived significance. As the experimental data and theories suggest, the exhaustively embedded *Rock at Arco* could, at least, reinforce the negative attitudes of individuals antagonistic to Italy and the Church.

FROM CREATION TO DELUGE

For over four years (1508–12) Michelangelo lay on his back on scaffolding 80 feet in the air to complete the Sistine Chapel ceiling. The series of frescos include 300 biblical personalities, all of whom, except for God, are naked—physically as well as in their questionable motives and sensual indulgences. The characters have been described as superhuman—"godly beings devoured by worldly passions."

Millions of words have been written about the Sistine vault and about Michelangelo's portrayal of mankind from the first days of creation to the deluge.

In the over forty critiques of the Sistine vault reviewed, however, nowhere does there appear a detailed analysis of individual frescos. Perhaps the total effect of the ceiling has overpowered critics for over four centuries. Certainly, the ceiling's effect upon a viewer is like an artistic hammer-blow—a *perceptual overload*. The eyes and brain are so overpowered by the spectacle that the nervous system defends itself from an onslaught of meaning that could become threatening or anxiety-provoking were it consciously available. And so, detailed information is repressed.

GREAT ART IS NOT ACCIDENTAL

One thing appears clear, nevertheless: the artist was not merely decorating a ceiling in the private chapel of Pope

Julius II, who commissioned the work. Michelangelo was involved with probing far more of human experience than could be included in mere decorative embellishments. Pope Julius was so concerned with heretical ideas filtering into the work, even inadvertently, that he assigned several advisors to "supervise" or "counsel" the artist on each scene's content.

Artists have rarely been trusted throughout the world's history, but in this period in particular virtually all artwork was carefully censored and controlled. The Holy Inquisition attempted to control both minds and bodies in the Christian world.

It is known that Pope Julius II and the Holy Inquisition trusted neither Michelangelo nor most other artists of the time. While his work was in progress, numerous disputes over content and biblical interpretation were recorded between Michelangelo and Vatican officials. Considering this censorship, it is surprising that the Sistine vault managed to become one of history's most significant artistic creations. Most of the art produced by the period's thousands of lesser artists has disappeared into the dung heaps of art history—trite junk executed merely to achieve status or wealth.

The techniques of transmitting subliminal information were apparently known in some way to Michelangelo and other great Renaissance artists. Because of his work's complexity, Michelangelo had to know what meaning (even though at the unconscious level) he would communicate to his viewers. He must have been acutely aware of how he would either offend or please Vatican officials, who, of course, perceived the painting as propaganda for the faith.

It would take several years to study all of the panels in the chapel, not to mention the interrelationships among the biblical narratives. But most art critics' and historians' attempts to deal with the Sistine vault focus on Michelangelo's prodigious technical abilities, his knowledge of anatomy, and his skill in scene design—perspective, color, symmetry and asymmetry, biblical interpretations, and the like. The question of meaning has been virtually ignored. Certainly there is much more dramatic *meaning* inherent in those frescos than has ever been publicly discussed over the past four and a half centuries.

One fresco, *The Original Sin and Expulsion from the Garden of Eden* (Figure 26), is divided into two sections. On the left appears Adam and Eve with the crafty serpent. Eve is reaching for the forbidden apple, handed her by the snake depicted with a human head and shoulders. The right section portrays the hapless, humiliated couple, terrified and agonized, being driven out of Paradise at swordpoint by an angel. At an obvious, cognitive level this is all that appears to be going on.

AVOIDANCE OF MEANING

Typical of traditional criticism of the scene was an analysis written in 1896 by famed art historian Bernhard Berenson, who apparently thought the work a poor example of Michelangelo's ability: "Compare [Michelangelo's] 'Expulsion from Paradise' with the one by Masaccio [a Florentine artist of a century earlier, 1401–28]. Michelangelo's figures are more correct, but far less tangible and less powerful; and while he represents nothing but a man warding off a blow dealt from a sword, and a woman cringing with ignoble fear, Masaccio's Adam and Eve stride away from Eden heart-broken with shame and grief, hearing perhaps, but not seeing the angel hovering high overhead." (Berenson, 1896).

Berenson simply compared one artist with another in terms of technical strength and weakness of their executions, "good or bad art." Like so many of his followers including highly publicized authorities such as Kenneth Clarke, he studiously avoided any examination of meaning.

In contradiction to the "art experts," why not assume that Michelangelo portrayed Adam and Eve in precisely the way he wished? That his choice purposefully evoked a specific meaning from his viewers? Any artist with the extraordinary knowledge of human anatomy Michelangelo displayed in his statue of *David* would certainly be in control of his subject and his interpretation.

A careful examination of the central figures in the fresco reveals content that has apparently never been consciously perceived. Any art critic and historian discovering these details would certainly have written about them, and the artist's secrets would quickly have become public. As far as a review of the literature could determine, however, the fresco's subliminal content has remained repressed for nearly five centuries.

THE TIME DIMENSION

Time is a basic, though unconsciously perceived, element in representational art. In a painting or sculpture, just as in a simple photograph, the artist has stopped time at a special instant. The viewer evaluates action in seconds, minutes, hours, days, weeks, or even months both *before* and *after* the stopped motion—in other words, what *has been* or *will be* going on in the painting. On the right, in his *Original Sin* portrayal, Michelangelo illustrated *time after* or *the future*. The two cringing, trembling, humiliated, pathetic humans are driven from Paradise at swordpoint. We know, therefore, what happened to the couple *after* Eve received the apple from the snake.

Now consider the *present*, the instant time was stopped by the artist, as depicted in the scene on the left. The snake is represented with a human head. Just below the snake's left shoulder protrudes a female breast. The snake, or the source of temptation, is female—one woman is tempting another toward destruction through sensuous indulgence. The snake is an ancient symbol of the forces of destruction, temptation, corruption, and evil. In mythologies, the snake often relates to female symbolism. In the language of symbols, therefore, the source of the forbidden fruit—the snake or the temptress of Eve—was a woman.

Eve sits comfortably relaxed on the ground, supporting her body on her right elbow as she turns to accept the apple. She appears to have been in this position for quite a while, perhaps five minutes or longer. Her legs are drawn comfortably up beneath her (Figure 27).

Adam is hardly relaxed, however. Standing with his feet wide apart, he appears braced, his hands gripping the tree branch for support. His shoulder muscles appear tense. Adam's right forefinger is bent as though gesturing or beckoning to the snake. All this, of course, is an obvious description of what appears to be going on at the moment Michelangelo stopped time.

Now, what was going on before? What was Eve doing one minute before she turned to receive the apple from the snake? Please do not read further until you have studied the scene for yourself.

Even today, when movies such as *Deep Throat* are casually shown at neighborhood theaters across the nation, the discovery of a fellatio scene on a Vatican ceiling is somewhat unsettling.

One distinct possibility that might contradict this interpretation is that the interpreter has a *dirty mind*. If this is merely an individual projection, however, there would be alternate interpretations. For example, perhaps Adam and Eve were merely looking at the view. This hypothesis would be most unlikely, as the two figures were facing each other before the artist stopped time. A careful examination of details demonstrates that Michelangelo went to considerable trouble in posing his figures. He had virtually an infinite number of postures and positions available. Numerous alternative sketches of the figures survive in Vatican archives. Yet, the artist selected these specific postures, presumably with conscious intent. Try to list alternative meanings for Adam and Eve's postures and positions in the painting. In several years of discussion and argument over the work, no other supportable meaning for the scene ever developed.

Keep in mind that in all media, *meaning,* not technique, is the name of the game—even if, or particularly if, the meaning is not consciously apparent on the surface. The question arises whether Michelangelo inserted the salacious meaning consciously or unconsciously. Could the artist have had (as individuals who think they do not have one put it) a "dirty mind"? Though it is entirely possible for artists to include unconsciously perceived material in their work, it is doubtful this artist did not consciously know what he was doing. Consider the precise, complex craftsmanship involved in designing and executing this scene from the Bible on such a massive scale before the ever watchful Holy Inquisition. One slip of the brush and Michelangelo would have shared the painful fate of any other sixteenth-century heretic.

It is, of course, conjectural what any artist consciously knows at any specific stage of a work in progress. Nevertheless, a strong argument can be built that Michelangelo must have clearly and consciously known precisely what he communicated. He must also have known the salacious content would be repressed by both critics and general viewers. His life depended upon knowing this.

It seems reasonable to view the painting's sensuous implica-

SANOREX®Ⅲ
(mazindol)

consistent weight loss for up to 12 weeks of thera

tions as part of some commentary or insight the artist wished to conceptualize for posterity. To me, at least, it is inconceivable that Michelangelo was merely painting obscene pictures on the ceiling of the Pope's private chapel or indulging himself with a crude joke at the Vatican's expense. Even with today's modern technology, to complete the Sistine ceiling would be a prodigious task, involving far too many years of effort to throw away on nonsense or superficial pornography. The word "repressed," with its psychological meaning, would have been unknown in the sixteenth century, but the repression *process* has operated in humans for thousands, if not millions of years. It just took a long time for so-called scientists to find a label for it, probably because they did not really want to deal with it.

SEXUAL GUILT SINCE GENESIS

Eve's attempt to excite Adam orally appears to have been unsuccessful: his penis remains flaccid, contracted. On the other hand, Eve's nipples are tumescent—suggesting sexual arousal. Adam's right forefinger appears to be signaling or beckoning the snake to approach, perhaps to distract Eve with an alternative indulgence. His mouth is open, suggesting he was speaking—perhaps with the snake.

Eve sits at the foot of a dead tree stump whose thin forked branch points toward the snake. The heavier branch, however, points toward the two hands exchanging the apple. Turned on its right side, this tree branch has two bulbous appendages at its base, forming a rather obvious erect penis and testicles (Figure 28).

Extending from the penis-shaped branch, the forked branch resembles a snake's tongue—an ancient symbol of duplicity, double meaning, betrayal, even treachery. Recall the phrase, "spoken with a forked tongue." The statement is better written as a question for the reader rather than a declaration of fact: Could the phallic tree stump symbolize human sexuality as two-sided, treacherous, devious? Eve has turned away from her lover to accept a sensuous indulgence from another woman.

There is one final symbolic mystery in the scene. Next to the tree stump, Michelangelo placed a rock of a different color, shape, and texture than the surrounding ones. On the rock's surface he painted a laughing face with a big nose and large mouth (Figure 29). One of the most learned men of his day on the appearance of both people and things, Michelangelo would not have shaped a rock to look like a human face by either accident or oversight.

There were, of course, only two people in the original Garden of Eden. Michelangelo added a semihuman snake, but the biblical narrative includes a third personality—God himself. If Michelangelo meant the laughing face on the rock to represent God, he designed an ironic twist into the biblical narrative.

God was, of course, perceived as being everywhere and knowing everything. God designed woman from Adam's rib, giving them each the pleasures of sensory and sexual indulgence. Recall from Genesis that the Lord God warned Adam not to eat from the Tree of Knowledge. The forbidden fruit would open his eyes and make him aware of right and wrong, good and evil. Sexual guilt was certainly one of the consequences of eating the fateful apple; presumably before Eve ate the apple, there was no sexual guilt. The original sin was portrayed as a sensory indulgence, committed first by woman; it was an act that condemned all women to an eternity of guilt and atonement. Later, as punishment, He cursed Eve with the necessity of bearing children in intense pain and suffering.

In summary, God gave humans a capacity for exquisite joy, pleasure, and endless sensual indulgences. He then imposed the ultimate irony, making it impossible for them to enjoy his gift because of guilt. In Michelangelo's painting, at least, He is still laughing at the human comedy he created.

SACRED AND PROFANE OR VICE VERSA?

The sixteenth-century Italian artist Titian painted *Sacred and Profane Love*. Unquestionably one of the great art masterworks of all time (Figure 30) the work today hangs in Rome's *Gallerìa Borghese*. Titian is believed to have painted the scene around 1515 while in his late thirties.

His two models are seated on a bench at a well in the country. The conventional designations are obvious: "Sacred" would likely be represented by the clothed model; "Profane" would likely be nude. As far as we can determine, the rather dull conventions of upper-class Renaissance morality were not dissimilar from those of our own contemporary middle class. Reality, of course, is always complex and contradictory. Only fantasy images are consistent.

Sacred's body is completely covered by her gown—sleeves down to the wrist, gloves covering the hands, body and legs invisible beneath the billowing skirt. The breasts are also covered, though an area of the chest and neck is exposed. Her protective right arm rests across her lap and genital area, covering all. Her red silk sleeve sternly cautions any human who might approach her. Her water bowl, a symbol of fertility, is tightly encircled and protected by her left arm and hand. Nobody is about to get into her bowl. A very proper lady, without question! Sacred is a righteous, respectable woman whom the Italian Renaissance world would approve of and respect. Such women are still with us.

One detail about Sacred borders upon the ominous, however. She has clumsily, perhaps even cruelly, crushed the flowers she has been picking. Her hand is curiously heavy and tense. A rose blossom and several leaves appear to have been plucked and casually thrown on the bench. The flower, of course, is the plant's reproductive organ and richly symbolic. Sacred's background is dominated by a dark field: two almost apprehensive rabbits sit widely apart in the shadows, doing not at all what rabbits are supposed to do. Above the field is a castle, a formidable military bastion of power and destruction that commands the peaceful and fertile valley.

Profane, on the other hand, hides nothing. Her left arm and hand holding her symbolic water bowl gestures toward heaven. Her right arm easily supports her weight. Her palm is open; she is not apprehensively prepared to defend herself. Her voluptuous body is at ease, not tensed into sexual provocation, but natural and beautiful. Behind her head are lovely white clouds against a clear, blue sky. Her background is rolling plains where sheep peacefully graze. On the horizon appears a small, quiet village with a church steeple.

And, quite curiously, Profane is looking with an enigmatic smile at Sacred's arm-protected genital area. Something, perhaps best described as a vague feeling, is communicated that there may be something profane about Sacred and something sacred about Profane. The innocent, chubby cupid or child reaching into the well with his right arm favors Profane; he is turned away from Sacred.

Another curious inconsistency appears in the carved bas relief beneath the well bench. Under the austere Sacred appears a strutting white horse, its mane and tail flowing in the wind. The horse symbolizes physical and emotional freedom, and the release of sexual inhibition and restraint. The horse, one might logically conclude, should have been positioned under Profane, who appears to fit the symbolic description more consistently.

Beneath Profane, carved into the bas relief, is a flagellation scene. Someone in the scene's background is chained to a post. In the foreground, one figure lies face down and is being whipped by another kneeling figure. Bondage and punishment are represented beneath the nude Profane, again inconsistent with Profane's overt character. Or is it?

Titian's statement does not become clear, however, until the viewer carefully studies the faces of the two women in the painting. *These faces are identical* (see Figure 31).

The smallest facial details have been precisely reproduced in each model: *eyelids, eye shape, complexion, jaw structure, lips, coloring, forehead, ear positioning,* and *nose structure.* Even the hair is identical in *texture, color, curling,* and *length.* The two women, Sacred and Profane are, in fact, the same woman.

Technically, it is quite easy for any artist to differentiate facial structures or expressions—a line, a shadow, a bone structure under the skin highlighted or darkened. It is quite difficult for an artist to paint two recognizably identical faces. One slip of the brush and the faces become two women instead of one. But Titian's brush did not slip on even one of these many details.

Titian's profound subliminal statement is that all these conflicting, contradictory influences—the simultaneous desire for both freedom and bondage, for propriety and voluptuousness, for conformity and rebellion—the desire to be both sacred and profane—are inherent in all women. For 460 years Titian's *Sacred and Profane Love* has been admired, studied, and copied by countless art lovers who sensed or felt its genius, but apparently the specific subliminal structure remained invisible.

WORDS REINFORCE PICTURES

Though modern commercial artists regularly use verbal embeds in their work—words such as SEX and a small vocabulary of four-letter words not intended to be consciously perceived—the technique appears in painting at least as far back as the fourteenth century.

Famed art historian Erwin Panofsky (Panofsky, 1953, pp. 138–47) discovered in the Jan Van Eyck (1390–1440) painting *Virgin of the Annunciation* inconspicuous upside-down lettering—ECCE ANCILLA DEI (Here is the servant of God). The statement, thought to have been made by angels describing Mary, would have been very familiar to fifteenth-century Catholics. These words usually do not appear when viewers are initially exposed to the painting. Only after a viewer begins to feel there is something "wrong" with the painting does the lettering sometimes become apparent. Panofsky explained the reason for the hidden phrase briefly: ". . . so that God in His Heaven can read it."

Similarly, the grotesque eagle at the gates of Hell, painted by Orcagna (1344–68) on the walls of Santa Croce Cathedral in Florence, has the letters LASCIATE OGNI SPERANZA (Leave outside all hope) printed backward—a famous quotation from the First Canto of Dante's *Inferno*, widely quoted in fourteenth-century Italy. These letters are also not consciously apparent to most viewers of the painting (Offner, 1962).

Readers of my earlier books will recall the Bacardi rum ad (*Subliminal Seduction*, Figure 8, 8a) with the words "U BUY" ingeniously printed upside down and backward in the bottom of a brandy glass. In *Media Sexploitation*, there were also numerous examples of the word SEX lightly embedded in commercial art, even on Ritz crackers.

Only a few examples of famous paintings with subliminal embedding are reproduced in this book's illustrated section. Small reproductions are inadequate for the careful study of complex compositions. Subtle details may not reproduce. Readers are strongly advised to seek out larger, more precise reproductions.

For example, try to find a large reproduction of Rembrandt's *Syndics of the Drapers Guild*. Painted in 1640, *Syndics* today hangs in Amsterdam's *Rijksmuseum*, one of the world's most important national galleries (Figure 32).

SELF-FLATTERING ANAESTHESIA

Syndics is a portrait of six leading citizens of Rembrandt's time, each of whom is known to have paid the artist handsomely to be included. They are dressed modestly, piously, and expensively—as befitted successful textile merchants of the time. They are well fed and cared for; their long hair or, more likely, wigs have been carefully curled. Rembrandt's business executives were sleek, rich, pompous, and very self-satisfied.

The six rich men were likely most pleased at the mirror image the artist provided them, and were charmed and narcotized by the not at all subtle flattery. These stalwart men of commerce controlled the world of Rembrandt—and, incidentally, mercilessly exploited the artist during his lifetime as he endured problems with propriety, women, and bankruptcy.

At one level, the work was a seventeenth-century public-relations portrait by one of the world's most gifted artists. Any twentieth-century Board of Directors would pay a king's ransom to indulge themselves in such a flirtation with immortality. If you take a more careful look at possible implications in the painting, however, some subtle—even troubling—suggestions intrude.

Was the artist trying to tell his audience something quite different from the obvious message? These more subtle implications of feeling, which art critics have never quite been able to put their fingers on, may well be the unknown reason for the timeless quality or significance of Rembrandt's work.

The painting, considering a time dimension stopped at a particular instant by the artist, depicts a group of textile merchants in an exclusive private meeting. Someone has just intruded, not merely entered the room. The intruder—presumably the artist—is an inferior who threatens the group, perhaps an outsider capable of seeing them as they really are rather than as they would desire the world to view them. All eyes are turned down with defensive expressions toward the intruder. People in pictures look upward at superiors, straight across at equals, but down at social inferiors. Look carefully at the facial and bodily expressions: they are neither friendly nor welcoming.

The second figure from the left appears startled and threatened. The unannounced entry has caused him to rise anxiously and self-protectively from his chair.

The senior member, third from left, appears to pretend involvement in a serious discussion of some sort. Placed in front of this senior member is the book that the group was studying and presumably discussing. The Chairman of the

Board's right hand, palm up as though asking for alms, covers or hides a portion of a page in the book. His facial expression is simply too sincere to be authentic. As Rembrandt portrayed him, the man is a transparent actor.

The second dominant member of the group, fifth from left, is prepared to turn the page, as though to hide from the intruder what the group has been discussing. His facial expression and tense body position suggest his apprehension over anyone's discovering what might be drawn or printed on the page, or possibly what the group has been up to.

The one bareheaded figure in the picture, the fourth from the left, has a trace of smirk, humor, or cynicism in his expression. The youngest of the six, he apparently removed his hat to peer at the book between the heads of his two seniors.

The figure on the right, surprised and anxious, responds to the intruder's threat by protectively grabbing the money bag.

THE PRIMARY FOCAL POINT

The book is a primary focal point around which the entire scene was constructed; it is the key to the painting's meaning. Only seconds before the artist stopped time for the painting, it was the subject of the group's attention. What was the book about? As far as can be determined, very few among the millions who have viewed, studied, analyzed, and copied this painting over the past 325 years have consciously concerned themselves with this question.

Rembrandt, like most artists and magicians, went to his grave without divulging the secret of the drapers' book. However, he did leave several clues to what the very proper business leaders were discussing and reading.

In the upper left green wall of the room, above the wood paneling, appears a subliminally embedded SEX. The "S" can be found directly above and to the left of a line drawn vertically from the shirt cuff above the hand of the draper on the extreme left (Figure 33).

Another embedded SEX appears in the green wall to the right, the "S" starting directly above the bareheaded draper's head. Still another SEX appears in the red table carpet directly below the cuff of the fifth-from-left figure; the "S" would be just to the right of a line drawn from the cuff to the bottom of the painting.

If these staunch Dutch defenders of the business ethic

were, indeed, discussing sex—and if the book, perhaps a seventeenth-century version of *Playboy*, was about sex—the meaning of the famous painting becomes quite interesting.

Rembrandt could have been making *covert* fun of these good citizens: while he *overtly* flattered them. The rich, old men react as though someone had just walked in on their verbal masturbatory session.

A VERY OLD WORD

In checking the possible meanings of SEX in seventeenth-century Holland, several possibilities occurred. The devious Rembrandt (and geniuses are most often devious) read Latin. The word SEX in Latin is a numerical term and apparently did not involve erotic implications. Indeed, there are six men in the painting. But then why should the artist go to the trouble of embedding numerics in his painting? Difficult, deft brushwork is required to keep the lettering invisible to the conscious casual eye. In a photographic enlargement of the area, Rembrandt's precise brush strokes which formed the SEX were clearly apparent. It is not necessary to hide anything unless the idea cannot be handled openly, or unless the artist, for some perceptual strategy, does not wish the information consciously exposed to his audience. And a numerical "6" could just as well have been visibly included if it added anything at all to the painting's meaning.

A seventeenth-century Dutch dictionary presented an almost too simple solution to the mystery. In the seventeenth century Dutch idiom, sex—as we presently use the term—was spelled *seks, seksual, sekse,* and *sexe.* Apparently the word meant roughly the same thing then as it does now throughout the world.

After being shown Rembrandt's SEX, however, Herman Pleij, a Dutch linguistic scientist, insisted that the seventeenth-century Dutch word SEXE had nothing to do with sex, only with *gender* (*Holland Herald*, April 1974). It is curious how verbal labels completely block the intellectual process. A quick look in any dictionary, or a brief discussion with any high school student, will verify that gender is a basic consideration in sexuality. In the popular language of the streets of 1640 Holland, SEX would have meant pretty much what it means today.

No one, as Rembrandt may have quietly known, would

remember even the names of the drapers, but the painting helped ensure Rembrandt's immortality.

FARFETCHED SEX

It is fascinating how defensive so-called art experts become when their clichés are challenged. Pieter van Thiel of the Amsterdam *Rijksmuseum* said about my discovery of Rembrandt's hidden SEX: "Complete nonsense and scientifically based on nothing. Finding letters and words on seventeenth-century paintings is totally farfetched." Had van Thiel not been so nearfetched, he might have checked out the fourteenth-century painting by Orcagna and the fifteenth-century painting by Jan Van Eyck, only two of many examples where artists used verbal embedding in their works.

"In those days, there were pornographic books," van Thiel admitted, "but people then weren't easily shocked," he explained (as though people have *ever* been easily shocked). "Many paintings," he continued, "did have double meanings, but these were immediately recognizable to the intellectuals of the day and weren't hidden in walls or table carpets."

Van Thiel persisted, "I have done my own research into the book the *Staalmeesters* [Syndics] have before them. Some art historians feel it is a financial report the Syndics are reading to the Guild members, but my studies show that the Guild never used a book of that size for financial reports. I feel that it must be a book of samples of white linen. The man with his hand on the book, palm up, is expressing the thought that this sample has possibilities."

Another Dutch "art expert" explained Rembrandt's *Syndics* as, "A sharp-witted evaluation of men busy fulfilling an honest task. Some art historians believe the Syndics are shown bringing out a financial report to the Guild members, but this is wrong. Rembrandt had the men looking down to get a dramatic element into the portrait. X-ray photos show he had difficulty in getting a balanced composition and changed the figures' position three times."

A "dramatic element," indeed, but what does the drama *mean*? Whatever Rembrandt was doing, he went to considerable trouble and did it quite purposely. But once again, the "expert" avoids dealing with the fundamental question in all art—*meaning*.

Had Rembrandt been as witless, unimaginative, and pedantic as these contemporary art experts, his works would have been forgotten long ago—adding nothing but further banality to the heritage of Western civilization. The world can be thankful Rembrandt was an expert artist instead of an art expert.

4·MODERN ART—NOT SO NEW

Specialists don't welcome discovery . . . only
new proofs of what they already know. All
specialists understand that discoveries are
fatal to the stockpile of their unclassified data.
Discovery makes the field of the specialist
and expert obsolete.
         Edmund Carpenter and Ken Heyman,
         They Became What They Beheld

PICASSO'S DREAM

Wondering how modern advertising media had discovered subliminal techniques, I once hypothesized that artists could have handed them down over the centuries as craft secrets, from master to apprentice. For a while this was an attractive and romantic possibility. One can almost visualize a deathbed scene in which Leonardo da Vinci tells a favored disciple his secret discoveries about human perception.

But, this is most unlikely. Sadly, very few of the men who apprenticed to the great masters ever distinguished themselves. They usually copied rather than pursue the always speculative and often dangerous innovation. Moreover, subtechniques appeared widely during the Renaissance (perhaps even earlier) in ways and places where direct communication between artists was virtually impossible.

If such techniques were discussed in the various academies and universities, substimuli would not have been a secret. Eventually someone would have written a book or article on the subject. No such publications have been discovered.

The most likely answer appears that individual artists stumbled onto these techniques on their own, century after century, without ever attempting to verbalize them. These individual discoveries could have been made repeatedly in much the same way—simply through a sensitivity to perceptual response.

One of the most hilarious modern examples of perceptual repression in art is Pablo Picasso's masterpiece *Woman Asleep: The Dream* (see Figure 34). First exhibited in Paris during 1932, the painting is presently in the W. Ganz collection in New York and valued at something approaching half a million dollars. It is truly a masterpiece by the North American criterion of "great art."

It is difficult to understand, however, how this abstract representation of a woman asleep could ever have made it into the big time. The woman's figure is grotesque, the colors annoying, the theme inspecific. Yet *The Dream* somehow communicates a subtle feeling of significance. In the clumsy figure there is an almost exciting quality that defies verbal explanation.

The earliest critique of *The Dream* was published in *Life* magazine during April 1932, as part of a six-page photo essay on Picasso, one of his first publicity exploitations in the United States. *Life* reproduced the painting full-page in four colors. The crisp text spoke eloquently of the great Spanish artist's unique contribution to modern art, how he had portrayed the woman asleep in flowing, voluptuous, abstract curves. The review described only the obvious, avoiding the question of how such a clumsily drawn figure could be called an artistic innovation and completely avoiding the question of meaning.

Over the next half century, 18 other reviews published in art journals, popular magazines, art anthologies, and books about Picasso similarly avoided telling their readers what about the painting made it so expensively important. Gaston Diehl, art critic and professor who knew Picasso intimately (so his book jacket proclaimed), wrote, "Sometimes the scintillation is toned down [in Picasso's paintings of women] and develops like a symphony the powerful network of its interlaced design giving way [in *The Dream*] to the melody of sensuosity interwoven in sweet cadence" (Diehl, 1960).

Diehl continued with even more incomprehensible verbal gymnastics: "Is it not only from observation that [Picasso] gets his idea of displaced and interpenetrating planes which will lead him to abandon geometrical perspective? Is it not from pacing around his model, as any sculptor would, and registering successive impressions that he deduces the principle of simultaneous points of view of the same object or of fragmentation of various objects glanced at?"

Such verbal obfuscation awes the unsophisticated reader and enhances the confusion over what constitutes "art." The question of meaning rarely, if ever, is mentioned. Mystification, of course, is also a business asset for the art hustler. Were the works clearly and simply described in easily understood metaphor, the mystique might disappear and the work's financial value quite possibly diminish.

Diehl's essay is sadly typical of the 18 reviews and critiques on *The Dream*. They all say little of consequence that might help explain the painting. Several discussed the use of noncomplementary colors, others the sensuousness of the female figure, others the total relaxation of the female anatomy. One even cautiously mentioned the woman's left nipple peeking provocatively above her low-cut bodice. Nothing in any of the reviews would not have been obvious to a ten-year-old child after he had viewed the painting for several minutes. They merely described the obvious, often in the artistic doubletalk of Diehl's essay.

Typical is Lael Wertenbaker's text for Time–Life's expensive book on Picasso: "In 1932, Picasso's vengeful attack on the female figure abated. He became interested in a new woman and the lift of his spirits is evident in *The Dream*. The torment of earlier works is gone, although an unsettling quality remains. The face and the body of the girl asleep are curiously halved, perhaps to suggest the dual reality of dream and waking." (Wertenbaker, 1967)

"The lift of his spirits," indeed. Picasso's title for the painting was *Woman Asleep: The Dream*. Considering the thousands of high-priced words published about the painting, it appears curious that no one has asked simply, *what was she dreaming about?* This logical, reasonable question was not even suggested in any of the 18 reviews.

OFF THE TOP OF HER HEAD

This kind of omission is not unusual in art history and criticism. It is extremely rare to find any writer who probes questions of *meaning—what's going on?* You might conclude that critics either don't know or merely consider such questions irrelevant.

In any respect, as you view the painting, ask yourself the simple question: *What* is she dreaming about? What does she have on her mind?

Don't read further until you have studied the painting and thought about these two questions.

It is easy to perceive what she has on her mind—on top of her horizontally drafted face. The top plane appears to be growing out of her left jaw. If you mask off the lower portion of her face, the left plane appears as a long, cylindrical object. The left eye forms the coronal ridge at the head of an erect penis.

From studies I made of the painting, about 3 percent of viewers consciously perceive the genital before having it pointed out. Consistently, however, some 97 percent unfamiliar with subliminal embedding will not consciously detect the erect genital without being told.

If anyone had discovered the embedded genital after the picture's publication in *Life* in 1932, it would have been a scandal of major proportions. Such discoveries are usually quite exciting. The finder knows something no one else appears to know, and the compulsion to talk about it is almost uncontrollable. Yet in nearly half a century, no one has apparently discussed Picasso's ingenious dream in public.

Such perceptual discoveries are also quite unsettling to many individuals. One art historian acquaintance wrote his doctoral dissertation on Picasso, devoting an entire chapter to *The Dream*. He has not spoken to me since I explained to him what he had missed. Culturally supportive repression is the problem of nearly all modern media studies. As long as the focus is upon what media *appear* to be, the secrets of how and what media are doing and why will remain hidden.

Might Picasso have unconsciously designed the woman's face in this manner? This appears most unlikely. The design is too complex. Picasso would have had to consciously know what he was doing. He also had to predict that no one would discover his secret. Had the erect genital been consciously discovered, the painting might well have been worthless, its author denounced as a cheap pornographer. It certainly would not have been published in a full-page color reproduction had *Life*'s puritanical Henry Luce even suspected the salacious content.

MASSAGING THE PROBLEM

By now, some readers will have discovered another discrepancy in Picasso's masterpiece—a dissonant element which, by conventional logic, should not be in the painting. Did you notice the sleeping woman has six fingers on each hand? This might be considered an error that would have wiped out the painting's value—had it ever been discovered. After all, any artist so careless with basic anatomy could hardly be called a genius. But, for the moment, let's give Picasso the benefit of artistic license. He might have accidentally painted six fingers on one hand, but he would have hardly made the error on *both* of her hands unless he really wanted them that way. Six fingers on each hand must *mean* something.

Let me suggest a hypothesis. There are numerous precedents where artists have portrayed *movement* through multiple hands, feet, or limbs. A hand whose fingers are not moving clearly has only five fingers, but when the fingers are moved rapidly, the illusion of more than five fingers appears.

The sleeping woman, therefore, appears to be dreaming about an erect male genital while she moves her fingers over her genital area, masturbating. Strangely, several reviews emphasized how *relaxed* the woman's hands appeared as they lay in her lap. Several other reviews alluded to a strange "sexual quality" about the painting, without specific explanation.

You can almost visualize Pablo Picasso, back in those Depression years, laughing his way to the bank—amused not over what critics thought they saw in his work, but over what they did *not* consciously perceive.

Exceptional artists often appear anti-intellectual; very few feel comfortable making explanations of their work. Most, however, appear to possess extraordinary sensitivity to perceptual nuances. After all, artists were studying audience reactions long before market research was invented.

UNMASKING HIDDEN DIMENSIONS

Anyone whose photograph has been published experiences an endless series of comments about how "you don't look like your pictures," most often repeated in a disappointed tone of voice. Sometimes people feel they should tear themselves up and let friends just keep their pictures. The artist or photographer has portrayed them as they want to be perceived, not necessarily as they are perceived by others.

Distrust of the artist appears universal, except in media-dominated North America, where large consumer audiences are trained to prefer illusions over realities.

Artists are feared for their ability to, in effect, manufacture perceptual reality, impose their own individual perspectives—or those of their employers—upon the viewer's perception. Photographers accomplish the same thing essentially, but, in the interest of economic survival, often humbly pretend that all they do is simply take a picture. As long as they play their role, society may be prone to trust them.

In North America, photography is a vast business enterprise based upon reality manipulation. In their expensive media promotion and advertising, film and camera manufacturers and distributors emphasize that what is recorded on film is "pure reality," or "the natural image," which can be preserved indefinitely. The illusion becomes fixed when the photographer stops time for an eternity by merely clicking the shutter.

What happened an instant before or after the shutter clicks is communicated in the picture, but this is usually repressed. Think of the standardized pose assumed by American families for their portraits. Some effort has usually been expended to make the portrait appear as though nothing happened before or after. Faces look into the camera, expressions frozen, carefully posed smiles, awkward hand positions, forced postures of relaxation, and carefully chosen costumes. But just think of the hectic, nervous minutes, hours, even days of preparation and the final period of relief when the session is over. But then, complicating simplistic perceptions of reality will not likely result in obedient consumers and profitable sales.

Ottowa-based Yousuf Karsh is one of the twentieth century's most astute, sensitive photographic portrait artists. Over the past quarter century, Karsh's photographic subjects have included John Kennedy, Robert Frost, Albert Einstein, Winston Churchill, Pablo Casals, George Bernard Shaw, Albert Schweitzer, and many others, both famous and infamous.

PROBING THE MASK

Karsh once said about his work: "Within every man and woman a secret is hidden. As a photographer, it is my task to reveal it if I can. The revelation [of greatness], if it comes at all, will come in a small fraction of a second with an unconscious gesture, a gleam of the eye, a brief lifting of the mask that all humans wear to conceal their innermost selves from the world. In that fleeting interval of opportunity, the photographer must act or lose his prize."

Karsh does not merely click a shutter. He intellectually probes beneath the skin with film imagery and makes symbolic use of lighting, backgrounds, posture, expression, costume, textures, props, and sets. A Karsh portrait sometimes reveals far more about the subject than would several pages of description. His intellectually penetrating compositions could well be a product of the photographer's integrated conscious and unconscious probing of his celebrities. But, beneath his creative, intuitive insights, Karsh is also the superb craftsman, consciously exploiting every conceivable dimension of photographic and perceptual technology. He uses reflections, shadows, highlighting, cross lighting, and filtering much as a painter might apply pigments.

In a Karsh portrait every detail appears to have been planned. Small, consciously unnoticed details often appear retouched, possibly with an airbrush. Prints are retouched, then rephotographed (often several times) to soften and obscure the retouch marks. Though successful photographers rarely admit it, virtually all published photographs of any consequence have been reworked, including so-called news photos. And yet North Americans appear to have an innate desire to disregard this fact of life. People or things as symbolized in photographs are looked upon as the "real thing."

McLUHAN'S MASSAGE

Karsh first photographed Marshall McLuhan in 1965 for an exhibit at the Montreal Exposition the following year. By McLuhan's recollection, he and Karsh spent several visits together at McLuhan's University of Toronto office: Karsh the sensitive, pragmatic, skillful, visually oriented lens artist; McLuhan the highly complex, philosophical, polemical student of literary and poetic metaphor. It would have been fascinating to hear these two gifted men argue their views about human communication. As long as the weapons of combat were words, McLuhan probably won. He is easily capable of producing a rhetorical whirlpool that would drown an Olympic distance swimmer.

Karsh finally drove McLuhan to the Royal Ontario Museum, where Harley Parker, one of McLuhan's colleagues, had designed a display on the development of life in prehistoric seas. The exhibit incorporated electronic devices, unusual lighting, sound effects, and tape-recorded lectures available to visitors through wall telephones. Karsh chose this background to illustrate McLuhan's involvement with electronic extensions to the human nervous system. The Karsh McLuhan portrait (Figure 35) employed extraordinary skill with both consciously and unconsciously perceived communication techniques.

POINT TO POINT EYE MOVEMENTS

The eye's fovea—an almost microscopic spot near the retina's center—jumps from point to point on a scene as we collect cognitive visual information. Fovea movements are compulsive, covering as much as 500 degrees of arc per second. Since the cell structures around the fovea are quite dense, it appears that conscious visual perception is closely related to the fovea movements and information transmitted to the brain from fovea cells. Once the fovea starts its movements from one point to the next, it cannot stop or change course but must continue until that specific movement is completed before initiating the next.

So-called peripheral vision—information picked up and transmitted to the brain from cells around the retina's periphery—appears to be registered subliminally, for the most part. Vision, however, is total and instantaneous. In microseconds, the retina transmits all the information from a total single percept into the cerebral cortex, the brain's outer layer. As mentioned earlier, an individual is consciously aware of only a small fraction, perhaps 1/1000th, of the total information which has reached the brain during a single percept. The actual operation of this system is only vaguely understood.

It appears that the incoming information does not translate simply or linearly into meaning, at least not at the conscious level. The editing process admits into consciousness small amounts of the total information perceived; the remainder is stored in the unconscious memory system for indefinite periods.

The human visual system is highly complex and poorly understood, but a skillful artist or photographer can control fovea saccades for most of his viewers, as Karsh did in the McLuhan portrait by placing the writer's head off center and using a back light aimed at the first telephone from below—as indicated by the faint telephone shadows on the wall.

For most viewers, the eye first moves to the focal point between the two telephones over McLuhan's left shoulder, then to his face, back to the shell on the wall, down to the hands, and across to the book on medieval art he holds, then back up to the phones again. There would be minor variations—some viewers might begin at a different place—but for most, this would constitute the initial primary saccade system.

McLuhan recalled that Karsh carefully posed him for the portrait and appeared to know exactly what he was doing all the time, though he never discussed it with his subject. Whether Karsh *knew* at a conscious or unconscious level what he was doing could only be answered by Karsh.

The worst insults endured by creative photographers, so several have told me, are questions involving their lens settings, speeds, lighting, camera angles, and other such technologies that are irrelevant to their pictures' perceptual significance to viewers. Once again, in photography as in all media, the name of the game is *meaning*. Technique is only the mechanical means to produce both conscious and unconscious meanings inside the viewer's head.

A CALL FROM ABOVE

McLuhan is posed looking philosophically off into space, an enigmatic, prankish, knowing half-smile on his face. His thoughts of the moment might be ironic, humorous, or both.

McLuhan's spotlighted temple suggests he is thinking. His eyes are turned upward. In portraits, subjects usually look across at equals, down at inferiors, and up at superiors. It is difficult to imagine anyone to whom the philosopher might concede intellectual superiority. He is widely known, and loved, as a man who questions and probes everything. This upward, thoughtful focus of the eyes might suggest his deep religious convictions, implicit in all his writing. He might be reflecting on the several art texts which lie before him on the table. The volume on the left is opened to a medieval portrait.

In terms of subliminal meaning, the wall background is intriguing. There appear four wall telephones, but none is being used. There are no dials on the phones, so they are presumably direct lines. McLuhan could well be waiting for someone to call. But direct lines to whom?

Carl Jung perceived groups of four as universal religious symbols—archetypes. Several specific symbolic possibilities immediately occur: the Four Horsemen of the Apocalypse (War, Pestilence, Famine, and Death), or the Four Apostles (Mark, Luke, John, and Matthew). Even the Egyptian God Horus had four sons. At the moment Karsh stopped time by clicking his shutter, however, the phones were silent, waiting, hanging inertly in their cradles.

Over McLuhan's right shoulder is a large scallop shell, a strange symbol to be so dominant in a portrait of an adventurer in human communication. And yet, the scallop is the symbol of the religious pilgrim, at least since the Shrine of St. James major (Santiago el grande), the patron Saint of Spain, was erected in the Spanish village of Compostela during the eighth century. In Karsh's portrait no one is communicating. The phones are silent. The scallop is *clammed up*. McLuhan waits.

HANDS COMMUNICATE

McLuhan's hands are perhaps the most striking feature in the portrait. They are held in a rigid, frozen, almost deathlike detachment as he leans lightly on the book-strewn table. The hands appear separated from their body and seem to float gracefully against the sweater's dark background. Both thumbs are extended from the hands. The hands appear heavy, unnatural, and quite unlike McLuhan's. The left thumb (often used in art as a phallic symbol) is gracefully erect—perhaps stretched would be a better word. The extended left thumb and forefinger on the top of the pencil form a "V," opening up above the shoulder toward the scallop's clamlike shell. Clams, incidentally, are considered not at all communicative. Considering his mischievous facial expression, there is certainly a strong suggestion here he might be thinking. "Don't worry! I'm clammed up! I won't tell!"

Karsh is widely discussed among portrait photographers for the way he uses, and retouches, hands in his pictures. Here, McLuhan's hands appear to have been extensively reworked, made to appear rigid, artificial, lifeless, although very graceful (Figure 36). The closest parallel context in which hands are posed in this fashion is in the ritual dances—Balinese, for example, in the Far East.

Once again, perhaps the statement should be phrased as a question: Could Karsh's portrait mean that McLuhan is performing a ritual, religious, ceremonial dance before a world where communication had ceased?

There are no simple answers in art (as opposed to commercial applications of art), nor in real life (as opposed to advertising representations of real life). With his McLuhan portrait, Karsh created an intensely complex intellectual puzzle. The meanings are not superficial. McLuhan, for example, appears to be holding in his left hand a pencil ready to write. McLuhan *is* left-handed, but the left hand is posed in a highly prominent position. For a left-handed person, the position would be quite unnatural for writing. Moreover, McLuhan actually writes with his right hand. He was taught to write that way as a child, though he does almost everything else with his left hand.

Karsh posed McLuhan's left hand with the pencil for symbolic reasons. As most people are right-handed, the left hand holding the pencil would subliminally appear dissonant or incongruous. The left has for many centuries been considered in art as the nonaggressive or protective hand, often symbolizing the unconscious, the irrational, even the illogical. There is neither paper nor note pad apparent upon which McLuhan could write with the pencil.

In addition to the symbology, embedding appears throughout the portrait. SEX mosaics cover the hands, face, and wall (Figure 37). A small face, similar to the medieval face in the open book, was apparently retouched into the dust jacket of the book under McLuhan's right hand.

EVEN NORMAN ROCKWELL

The SEX verbal embed is really a quite simple device. One of the earliest SEX embeds discovered in American commercial art appeared on the May 20, 1916, cover of the *Saturday Evening Post*.

This was Norman Rockwell's first cover for the *Post*, showing a formally dressed ten-year-old boy pushing a baby carriage while being harassed by other boys from the neighborhood (Buechner, 1970). The boy with the carriage wears a bowler hat. It is a very famous painting, initiating a career which led Rockwell to become one of the highest paid artists in history. Unlike so many others, he received the money before his death.

If you can find the old *SEP* cover, relax and look carefully at the cheek of the boy pushing the carriage. Lightly embedded in his facial complexion is the familiar word SEX in rather large letters. You will locate another such embed in the hair of the second boy with a baseball cap. There are many of these embeds in the painting. We can only guess as to whether Mr. Rockwell consciously knew what he was doing, but the embeds certainly helped enrich both his art and his bank account. Virtually all of Rockwell's covers contain similar embedded SEXes. From the overwhelming evidence of modern advertising, it appears that the device sells products. We must therefore assume it also sells concepts, ideas, ideologies, emotional evaluations, political candidates, and much else.

UNCONSCIOUS TO UNCONSCIOUS

When Dr. McLuhan read this analysis of the Karsh portrait, his amused comment was, "Did Karsh make fun of me?" Only Karsh could really answer this question, but I am inclined to doubt it. Certainly Karsh did not make fun of McLuhan in the way Rembrandt made fun of the six drapers. This is a very significant portrait of an important contemporary intellectual. Yet, the photographer did introduce into the portrait elements of irony, humor, and paradox. The portrait communicates a depth of meaning and significance felt subtly more than intellectually understood by most viewers.

Richard Wagner once described music as "the unconscious of the composer speaking to the unconscious of the audience through the unconscious of the musicians." The statement would certainly apply to photography or any other creative medium. Perhaps for some people the intellectual and critical examination of art is even undesirable. There are always those who need mystique as a protection against familiarity and intimacy that might breed contempt—or an understanding of reality's complexity, which might be threatening to the fantasies which prop up fragile egos.

Several important elements within the McLuhan portrait

have not been mentioned. Readers may continue to explore on their own. The fun and excitement of art lies in individual exploration and discovery. It is totally irrelevant how this writer, McLuhan, or Karsh himself might intellectually rationalize what went on in the picture. Individuals can often find unique or unusual interpretations of significant meaning in form and detail that, in turn, point the way to newer and deeper insights.

Within any given culture, there is a certain uniformity or common denominator to various aspects of meaning. Some, such as archetypes, even appear to transcend various cultures. But *meaning* and *significance* are complex interactions that may produce variations in perception among individuals.

Perhaps it is the function of art to constantly remind us of *who* and *what* we are, and perhaps *why*. If art is to make a contribution to human survival and adjustment, it should never become trite, simplistic, uniform, or one-dimensional in motivation—as it has in the commercial media. Virtually any Madison Avenue advertising artist has at his disposal a technology vastly superior to anything Da Vinci, Holbein, Rembrandt, or Dürer could have dreamed about. It is awesome to conjecture over what Michelangelo might have accomplished with a high-pressure airbrush. Nevertheless, today's technologically superior ad art is discarded after only brief exposure periods. Indeed, most modern commercial art is purposely designed to not even be noticed at a conscious level.

It is worth remembering that in spite of the current cultural propaganda man is not a machine. After thirteen years in universities, trying to teach writing and literature, I am convinced it is impossible to teach anyone to write, compose, paint, sculpture, or innovate creatively. With luck, you might get across minor techniques, or perhaps elementary craftsmanship suitable for low skill level commercial production. And, of course, you can teach *about* art and creativity and perhaps inspire self-confidence in individuals who already possess innate creative abilities. You can also teach individuals to recognize and appreciate perceptual innovation and significance. And, of course, you can teach about the importance of creativity in our cultural heritage. But no one can be *taught* to create a significant human experience in any media form. Assuming an individual has the potential, this must be learned the hard way—over years of painful experience and experimentation.

CREATIVITY HIGHLY ENTREPRENEURIAL

Rarely have I heard successful artists share their unique perceptions of reality with others, least of all with other artists. Indeed, perhaps the only thing most artists have in common is an entrepreneurial intensity that would shame even the most aggressive businessman. Each appears to view himself as being in business for himself. But perhaps this strong individualism goes beyond mere selfishness. Quite possibly, nonverbal perceptual insights cannot be meaningfully verbalized. But, for the student who may ultimately grow into we know not what, it is useful and exhilarating to expand the borders of conscious perception as far back as they can be pushed. It is certainly a part of human growth to achieve increased sensitivity, greater conscious awareness, new levels of feeling and experience, and an openness to the new and unlabeled. The most meaningful human part of us lies hidden—even from ourselves—deep in the intricate and unknown pathways of our unconscious.

5·THE REPRESSED EXPERTS

*The "nature of things," including that of
society, was so defined as to justify
repressions and even suppression as perfectly
rational. They leave no time and no space for
a discussion which would project disruptive
alternatives.*

Herbert Marcuse,
One Dimensional Man

EDUCATED TO NOT WANT TO KNOW

I have never been surprised that superb artist-craftsmen utilized subliminal techniques. Artists—perceptual engineers—have traditionally been society's most sophisticated students of perceptual subtlety. What did turn out to be surprising was the discovery that in spite of all the time, money, and effort expended to study both art and perception, virtually no one in the universities ever got wise to what was going on. If subliminal communication technique was utilized centuries ago, why—in this age of seeming enlightenment and apparently miraculous scientific-technological innovation—was it not general public information? I will venture a simple answer.

We did not know about subliminal phenomena because we individuals, our institutions, our society in general, and our media, who might have told us had their profits not been based upon keeping it quiet, simply did not want us to know. To be forced to deal with the fact that humans can be influenced, managed, manipulated, convinced, persuaded, or controlled in ways over which they have no defense is an affront to centuries of ideological orientation, especially in Western nations immersed in traditions of democratic idealism. It also

71

contradicts the entire mythology of so-called free enterprise economics.

United States culture, particularly, has a formidable built-in inability to deal with subliminal phenomena. For a century, the Anglo-Saxon-Germanic cultural tradition has resisted the idea of unconscious repression. But rarely have so many formidable barriers to the concept been built as they have in America.

Basic to the public acceptance of America's economic and governmental power structure is the belief that individuals have complete control over their decision-making, and that they can opt in their own interest for any alternative desired. The United States is a culture with a built-in need to disbelieve hypotheses that contradict the popular notion of "free will," perhaps America's most fundamental fantasy.

THE ISOLATED IVORY TOWER

A remarkable scientific book was published in England by N. F. Dixon, an experimental psychologist at University College, London. Sophisticated, complex (difficult to read for the uninitiated), it is a basic text on the apparent effects of sub-stimuli upon human behavior. Dixon painstakingly reviewed, over several years, some 500 studies from all over the world that both attacked and supported the subliminal issue. He exactingly traced the complex logic, arguments, and empirical research that had been published on the subject. One U. S. advertising agency president told me, "Dixon's book is basic reading for our creative department. We think of it almost as an operational bible." Yet Professor Dixon's book rarely mentions commercial mass media, except to assure the reader periodically that none of what he's writing about has any application in the real world. He even confidently tells the reader not to worry!

Not once does this apparently dedicated scholar even appear to suspect that what he has been studying and analyzing so precisely over so many years—as little more than interesting laboratory experiments and theoretical conjecture—is commercially applied with great intensity just outside the window of his office. British media are just as saturated with subliminally embedded material as media in the United States, perhaps even more so. Yet in all the years during which Dr. Dixon concentrated his considerable energies on the study of subliminal phenomena, he apparently never made the real world connection.

It is fascinating to study the pros and cons in research on this issue: for every paper supporting the effectiveness of subliminals, there appear several denouncing the supportive evidence and the entire concept. A small group of U.S. and British scholars found, consistently over the years, positive support for the effects of sub-stimuli, but their colleagues often viewed them as "unscientific," "paranoid," and "unconvincing."

In sorting through this material, one receives the distinct impression that much more than mere facts underlie the issue. U.S. mainstream psychology has a strong vested interest, perhaps culturally generated (it is hard to believe they are all on ad agency payrolls), in denying or putting down the issue. A national culture's educational system, prevailing philosophical perspectives, popular literatures, and standards for scientific method and proof usually follows—and is subservient to—its economic system. Science, especially, discovers whatever it is rewarded for discovering, rarely the opposite.

INSTITUTIONAL REPRESSION

Individuals do not repress information uniformly. Repression thresholds—the point at which information becomes threatening and is obliterated from conscious awareness—appear much higher among individuals in certain occupations such as science, engineering, and medicine, than among those engaged, say, in art or philosophy (Gordon, 1967). It appears that individuals rigorously trained in linear reasoning, cognitively or quantitatively oriented, have higher thresholds and also appear more susceptible to substimuli.

This *perceptual rigidity* could be caused by a rigorous education and/or a predisposition, dating from early childhood, to view the world from a tight, linear, well-organized perspective. Perhaps significantly there is probably no more rigorous a cognitive-oriented brainwashing system in the world than the American medical school. The cultural system actually defines an "effective physican" as one who resists intuitive insight.

A glance through any medical journal published in the United States will reveal scores of pharmaceutical ads heavily utilizing subliminal stimuli. Pharmaceutical corporations literally control chemically oriented American medicine via the powerful educational effect of the media they subsidize—most U.S. medical journals are supported by pharmaceutical advertising. At this level of saturation, the drug ads work both individually and collectively upon physicians, strongly orienting them toward drug solutions for virtually any symptom a patient might describe. In nations where the drug industries are neither so powerful nor pervasive, medical education perspectives and professional expectations are quite different.

AVOIDING CONFLICT WITH SOCIETY

Curiously enough, other susceptible groups would certainly include cognitively oriented psychologists, sociologists, and anthropologists. At some conscious or unconscious level, Dr. Dixon and many of his colleagues in the social and behavioral sciences must have known that subliminal embedding techniques were widely utilized by ad agencies. Unless, of course, they were oblivious to media such as television, radio, newspapers, magazines, billboards, etc. But then, I vividly remember the testimony of residents living near Nazi World War II extermination camps who swore they had no knowledge of what was going on. Indeed, it finally appeared that some were telling the truth. Knowing would have put them in dangerous conflict with the Nazi establishment. They did not know because they had *preferred not to know*—certainly an aspect of repression.

The repression process is really very simple and all of us have used it at one time or another. As mentioned earlier, we forget something has happened, then forget that we have forgotten. To our conscious minds, it no longer exists. The memory, however, remains buried in our unconscious memory system capable of resurfacing in behavior. The process is invisible, compulsive, and automatic within each individual.

McLuhan's comment that "1984 really happened around 1930, but we didn't notice," describes the general effect of subliminal media upon western society. As George Orwell predicted over thirty years ago, this could have happened only by first convincing intellectuals to restrict their efforts to the study of cognitive (what is consciously perceived) psychology, sociology, anthropology, and linguistics. And so we did.

ONLY CONSCIOUSNESS COUNTS

The heaviest opposition to the notion of subliminal stimuli originates among groups or individuals with strong predispositions to view human behavior in a mechanical-man perspective, quantitatively measurable, environmentally motivated, derived from deterministic free will, and defined by consciously knowable criteria.

When the book *Subliminal Seduction* first appeared, I anticipated a small war with advertising agencies and portions of the business community. It never occurred to me how threatening my disclosures about subliminal manipulation were to the general academic establishment, especially to the behaviorists, cognitive, and experimental psychologists who have been indoctrinated with the view that only what we *consciously* know, think, and do is of any significance. *Behaviorism* is the dominant school or perspective in U.S. academic psychology.

Most readers have probably never heard of *behaviorism*, though its perspectives permeate virtually every area of U.S. education from kindergarten to university graduate schools. It began at Germany's Heidelberg University under Wilhelm Wundt during the mid-1850's. Imported into America in 1883 by one of Wundt's brilliant students, the movement proliferated, eventually including such distinguished names as John Dewey, Edgar Lee Thorndyke, John Broadus Watson, and B. F. Skinner.

One major objection—often politically expressed—to the dynamic and humanistic psychologists, working in the philosophical traditions of psychoanalytic evaluation, was their almost continual involvement with social and economic issues—which they often viewed as the fundamental cause of mental illness. The behaviorist-experimentalists overcame that problem with a research system which, they made people believe, was "purely scientific," not concerned with moral issues, and therefore a virtually perfect "science" that never challenges the status quo, nor concerns itself with what goes on outside the laboratory. The basis of *behaviorism* is the "experimental method," dependent upon studies of rodent behavior and the quantified verbal testing of humans which presumes to demonstrate psychological realities. This resulted in the virtually total trivialization of an important field of research and study.

Behaviorists dogmatically reject concepts such as "mind," "unconscious or subconscious," "perceptual defenses," "psychotherapy," and anything requiring individual analytic evaluation. Behaviorists generally reject the heritage of philosophical-intellectual studies on mental processes, as well as the psychoanalytic-dynamic psychologies which developed before, during, and after the work of Sigmund Freud and his contemporaries. With near religious zeal, *behaviorism* looks to:

1. quantification or statistical method for "scientific proof" as opposed to insights via intellectual reasoning;

2. strict verbal definitions that invariably become mere word games or semantic nonsense since the brain's reality is non-verbal—words are never what they describe;

3. rigid control over experimental variables, which is unlikely even in the most ideal laboratory situation—never in the real world; and

4. exclusion of genetic inherited behavior considerations in favor of solely environmentally conditioned behavior.

Behaviorism generally attempts to describe *what* has happened, avoiding the more perplexing questions of *how* and *why*. Cognitive psychology looks at only the conscious manifestations of the brain which is like viewing only the portion of an iceberg that protrudes above water while ignoring the invisible six-sevenths that sinks ships. Had its methods and perspectives synthesized with other attempts to penetrate the enigma of human mentation processes, *behaviorism* might have eventually made a substantial contribution to human knowledge. Unfortunately, it did not work out this way.

CULTURAL INVESTMENT IN MECHANICAL BRAINS

The so-called "scientific" view currently compares the brain with a digital computer system. This view, published in an enormous range of commercially successful textbooks, no doubt helps merchandise the staggering array of information storage and control systems and their related industrial and commercial *hardware, software, artifacts*, and *services*— economic enterprises that constitute a large proportion of the U.S. gross national product.

When Norbert Weiner, often called the father of electronic computer systems, wrote his major book *Cybernetics* in 1932, he drew a remote analogy between his machines and the brain, comparing several apparently parallel functions. His comparison was only an illustration of how computers might someday function *in support of* the human brain. People are vastly different from machines, especially in their capacities to *think* and *will* (Arendt, 1977).

Electronic computers are machines. The sensitivity and complexity of their input mechanisms do not even remotely approximate those of the human senses. Electronic machines cannot feel, think, or evaluate multisensory inputs from tens of thousands of simultaneous sensory sources. The largest conceivable electronic computing system's memory would not even store a fraction of the data retained by a single human brain.

It has been traditionally difficult for American psychology to deal with the mentation process. This is a highly integrated technological society, dedicated from cradle to grave to proving simplistic, mechanistic cause and effect relationships. In 1973, nearly forty years after Weiner's *Cybernetics,* Wilbur Schramm, former head of Stanford University's Communication Institute published *Men, Messages, and Media* which tried to explain human communication systems by direct comparison with computers. Schramm's simplistic text even used system flow charts, viewing human brain physiology as predictable, mechanistic, and as knowable as the electronic machine used to define and describe human communication.

Clearly, American society—and those who manage it— have a strong vested interest in promulgating the fiction that a human brain is comparable to an electronic computer.

Not just intellectual perspectives, these conventional wisdoms have grown into full-fledged political movements that control national professional associations and large, influential, academic departments and schools in most state-supported universities, not to mention the preponderance of both corporate and governmental research funding. Such distinguished humanist scholars as Rollo May, Erich Fromm, R. D. Laing, and Karl Menninger would be philosophically unacceptable in a majority of U.S. university psychology departments.

I have personally watched the behaviorist majority in several university psychology departments harass highly competent *dynamic* or *humanist* colleagues into resignations. *Behaviorism* supports and reinforces the U.S. economic system in so many subtle ways that it should have made at least someone suspicious. This culturally induced compulsion to view the mind in quantitative terms has, predictably, produced a psychological testing industry. Thousands of tests which claim to demonstrate almost anything anyone might want demonstrated are profitably merchandized. Intelligence tests, for example, permit schools and other institutions to direct and redirect people in a variety of channels. The tests themselves, however, have nothing to do with "intelligence," for which there exist several dozen sometimes useful, though often contradictory, definitions. Psychological tests will tell an experienced clinician what they should already know from their personal observations; or, in a specific context they might suggest a useful diagnosis. They do not, however, produce definitive information, and their predictive potential is extremely limited.

MANAGING THE COLLECTIVE UNCONSCIOUS

Behaviorism is now even making substantial inroads within European universities, in countries where consumer-oriented economies have developed comparable to that in the United States. Cultural disavowel of any invisible system within the brain capable of subverting "free will" has often protected Americans and many others from conscious awareness of what they are really doing. This also demonstrates *collective repression* at a cultural level. If individuals can perceptually defend themselves against (repress) certain kinds of information, then societies, subcultures, and even occupational groups can certainly exercise a similar repressive potential.

Many definitions in the social and behavioral sciences, for example, could be described as avoidance or repression techniques in what they both *include* and *exclude*. Over the past few decades, the ways in which America defines itself, its motives, and its goals changed and modified constantly, far more in response to social, political, and economic pressures than to the weight of new evidence or discoveries.

The label "scientific" far too often merely supports the conventional wisdom that society or scientists wish, at some particular moment, to believe, avoiding perceptions that might force reassessments of basic assumptions. Academic jargon, particularly, confuses, diffuses, and obscures what is essentially still a highly subjective individual interpretation of reality. The social sciences, as they are practiced in the United States, are often anti-social and usually unscientific.

OBSERVERS ALWAYS PART OF WHAT THEY OBSERVE

Even more than the rest of us, those who publicly label themselves "scientists," like to believe they deal only in "truth" and "fact"; that by rigorous verbal definition, disciplined systematic organization, and strict quantified analysis, they have somehow eliminated the ageless philosophical paradox of removing the observer from what he has observed. Anyone who blindly accepts the fiction of "objective, scientific, undisputable fact" may find himself in a great deal of danger.

This "objectivity" was accomplished in the natural and physical sciences, to some extent, through higher mathematics. Bertrand Russell argued convincingly, however, that even in mathematics mathematicians' vested interests are always an invisible part of their computations, especially in their interpretations of results and applications. This is poignantly true in all of the so-called social, behavioral, and linguistic sciences.

For example, sociology's pathetic attempts to produce a language of precisely defined, polysyllabic labels to describe a complex reality has really resulted in little more than a word definition game of academic anagrams. In any word-oriented science, verbal formulations and descriptions develop from each individual scientist's unique perceptual system. No one has yet developed an objectified system of verbal evaluation, nor is it likely that anyone will do so.

CONVENTIONAL ACADEMIC WISDOM

It is foolish to blame specific groups or individuals, however, for their cultural vulnerability to repression and their self-serving blindnesses. One way or another, all of us are products of what we behold as our societies educate us in what is to be valued or discarded, considered reality or illusion, and channel our motivations for effort and accomplishment. Most schools and universities have always been controlled by states of mind at least a century behind the contemporary world which surrounds them.

University research in human behavior is very limited—both in quantity and quality and certainly in financial resources. Increasingly trivial specializations are the current rule. In psychology, there are presently some 30 areas of specialized study—not bad for a discipline of study whose subject—the human brain—is still understood in only a very primitive way. In reality, of course, "psychology" is not separated from economics, religion, history, language, medicine, geography or socio-cultural phenomena. In the real world, these subjects all overlap, integrate, and blend with each other. No psychological question can ever be isolated from the total experience and environment of the patient without distortion and misrepresention. Sadly, research in the social and behavioral sciences has had an unfortunate tendency to focus upon whatever currently acceptable (merchandisable) themes and methodologies happen to be supported by government or foundation research grants, academic journals, professional societies and university politics.

I have generally found the business world far more reality oriented than the universities. In business, both profits and survival are more critically dependent upon reality assessments. By comparison, business research focuses single mindedly upon problem solving; the problems are usually those of optimizing returns on investments, or simply making a buck. Most of my business research clients could not have cared less about conventional wisdoms, professional politics, "scientific" methods, or ideological proprieties. In my experience, business research was very open to intellectual innovation, as long as making money remained the central objective.

If it worked, it was *good* research. If it didn't work, the researcher was likely to find himself soon unemployed. Even considering the restrictions on business research—obsessive profit orientation, singleminded objectives, secrecy, anonymity for researchers, competitive strategies, and a tendency toward easily administered, fixed research systems—the work was usually exciting.

U.S. BUSINESS: TOP SECRET

The billions of dollars of unpublished research done by corporations over the past quarter century on mass behavior modification can only be speculated upon, even though it is known to have been prodigious. For example, the Schlitz Brewing Co. spends some $10 million annually on research into human behavior relative to beer consumption, incorporating an extraordinarily broad range of language, cultural, and behavioral studies. International Fragrance and Flavors (which owns 60,000 scents and 20,000 flavors) spends annually some $15–20 million on research into smells and flavors—vital sensory inputs into the brain which result in behavior relative to hunger and reproduction (see *Media Sexploitation*, Chapter 6). This fascinating and important research has gone on for several decades, but only bits and pieces ever publicly surfaced. After searching three medical school libraries for information on smelling and tasting, I discovered only half a dozen books and a small handful of articles on the subject, virtually nothing as to how these senses affect the brain and behavior. Clearly, IFF, only one large corporation out of several in the business of manipulating smells and flavors in behalf of U.S. business, has accumulated more data on the subject than are available to any university medical school.

To compete for economic survival, every major marketing-oriented corporation in the United States must finance research on human behavior as it involves new and current products, consumer utilization, competitive product and brand images, and the modification of public opinions, beliefs, and attitudes.

Several billion dollars of corporate investment are allocated annually to the study of human behavior. It is most unlikely that the findings will ever appear in scholarly journals. American business is far more secretive about what it does to compete than is any agency of government. Anyone wanting to know what the CIA or FBI is currently up to can either call Jack Anderson or spend several afternoons hanging around the Washington Press Club bar. But just try to discover what is going on at DuPont, General Motors, or Schlitz. American corporations employ small armies of so-called public relations specialists whose main job is to keep secrets, releasing only information that serves corporate objectives or strategies.

Corporations such as Coca Cola, General Foods, Howard Johnson, Kraft, and the major distilleries, breweries, and wine makers could opt for public disclosure of their research in the public interest, but this proprietary research is never likely to appear as long as it provides its sponsors with competitive business advantages, or as long as it might be embarrassing to admit.

Unless someone has worked at a very high level of corporate responsibility, there is no way he could even know such studies have been done. Corporations, like agencies doing secret government research, parcel out various projects in such a way that the individual researchers may never find out the ultimate, applied significance of what they have discovered. Anyone who has performed such research has signed contracts whose fine print threatens endless legal sanctions against unauthorized disclosure. For further information on the effects of subliminal stimuli, we must rely upon the small amount of published experiments available—developed by a handful of academicians, whose work, for the most part, does not fit into the mainstream of conventional, research-grant-subsidized university research.

6•MORE BANG FOR A MEDIA BUCK

*It may be impossible to resist instructions
which are not consciously experienced. There
would seem to be a close parallel between
these phenomena and those associated with
posthypnotic suggestion and neurotic
compulsive response.*

> N. F. Dixon,
> *Subliminal Perception*

WHAT WE THINK WE KNOW

There is an ancient philosophical paradox that an analytical instrument, such as the human brain, cannot analyze itself completely. Be this as it may, attempts to understand the human brain are replete with well-intentioned failure as researchers have labeled and described various apparent functions and anatomical structures without really understanding *how* or *why* they worked.

Several theorists have written that we may never clearly understand the brain. In spite of highly exaggerated claims to the contrary, our sciences are not yet even close to an answer. We may, indeed, never know how the brain functions. The mentation system has so far defied functional analysis, and there exists no completely validated theory of human brain processes which explains behavior and language. We do, however, have literally hundreds of theories about *how* and *why* behavior and language may work. Unfortunately, they are only theories.

I haven't the remotest idea whether Freud, Adler, or Jung—or for that matter Watson and his behaviorist disciples such as Skinner—were right or wrong. Until the minute neurological-chemical-electrical systems that make up the perceptual input system are comprehensively understood, there is really no way of knowing.

I am often intrigued by the theories about why rainbow trout bite on a particular fly. No one really knows how a trout thinks, so there are virtually as many theories as there are fishermen. The only ones worth taking seriously are the ones which work, that is, seem to help you catch fish. Similarly, theories of how the brain functions are abundant, but the only psychological theories of any value are those which help us achieve some specific objective—whether clinically treating pathology or manipulating people into the purchase of an underarm deodorant. It is merely necessary for a theory to be useful.

THE PUZZLE OF PERCEPTION

Somewhat more appears to be known about the individual senses—sight, hearing, smell, taste, touch—and how they mechanically appear to function. Most standard texts on the senses (nearly 40 differentiated input systems into the brain have been isolated and described, though there could be many more still to be discovered) provide great detail on how individual organs operate. All senses transmit information to the brain simultaneously, though the largest volume of data appears to be induced through vision. Offhand, most of us believe that our eyes edit perception, that they see some things and not others. But apparently the eye's retina transmits *everything* it registers into the brain's cortex, where the actual editing process takes place. This selective editing process is not at all understood, though again, there is an abundance of theories.

The eye's retina transmits prodigious quantities of picture image information into the brain at different intensities and speeds. As briefly discussed earlier, individuals cannot control their fovea movements. But an artist or magician (perceptual engineers) can manage fovea movements in both specific sequences and areas within any scene he controls.

Fovea movements are tracked and studied with instruments such as the *Mackworth Camera* and *Pupilometer*, dual camera devices that photograph the eye's retina and superimpose fovea movements on the scene an individual perceives. The brain's search for meaning underlies, or may even serve as the basis for, perceptual significance and/or repression. Though the conscious and unconscious levels are most frequently discussed, many other levels of meaning are quite possibly available to the human mentation process.

SUCCESSFUL ADS APPEAL UNCONSCIOUSLY

Over a ten year period I was often involved with various techniques of ad testing for large, international ad agencies. From time to time, I performed consumer recall evaluations on ads, usually to placate a client who had become nervous about the effectiveness of a large promotional expenditure. As far as I know, recall analysis was never seriously applied in the development of new, creative ad themes. Banality, not memorable (consciously memorable) dramatic content was the basic building block for sales-effective advertising. The executives who employed me often commented that any ad consciously recalled was a loser, as far as sales were concerned.

At the time, this logic puzzled me. Now, I realize the purpose of an advertisement is to motivate a purchase decision—days, weeks, or even months after it has been perceived for even an instant. This objective has little to do with conscious memory; in fact, it is entirely possible two different brain systems are involved. The job of an ad is to sell—not to be recalled. The two behaviors are not at all necessarily related. The conscious memory system may actually be incompatible with media's marketing objectives.

CONSCIOUS AND UNCONSCIOUS MEMORY SYSTEMS

Most of the vast sensory data input into the human brain are probably dumped as irrelevant, while more significant data are retained. Freud's theoretical model of the mind included three interrelated processes—subconscious, preconscious, and conscious. Memory (retention potential), he believed, operates at all three levels. Conscious memory, however, appears very limited. Unless specifically trained to expand their conscious memory systems, humans generally have highly limited conscious access to the total data stored in their brains.

The preconscious, as Freud theorized, is an intermediate stage in which information in transition between the unconscious and conscious is held available for use. As hypnosis regression experiments illustrate, the unconscious memory is prodigious and retains vast stores of perceived information going back to very early childhood. Several theorists, including Otto Rank, have speculated upon even prenatal memories stored in the unconscious.

Dr. Wilder Penfield, the Montreal neurosurgeon who first empirically demonstrated the unconscious memory mechanism during brain surgery some 25 years ago, theorized that the brain retains throughout life *every* perception it perceives. This is certainly feasible: the unmeasurable capacity of multibillions of memory cells has never been explained in terms of conscious memory, which utilizes only a tiny fraction of the available memory system.

Over many centuries various training techniques have been developed to assist an individual to increase the proportion of perceived data consciously available. For example, most individuals with strong enough motivations can be trained to enter a room for 30 seconds, leave, and then make a several-hundred-item list of objects in the room. The trick is based upon not letting the eye or brain focus consciously upon any specific object but to generally record the entire scene for later recall in detail. It has been called "learning to utilize peripheral vision." Peripheral perception appears to occur also with other senses, such as touching, hearing, and tasting. Peripherally perceived data do not usually surface in conscious awareness, but do enter the brain system and may be retained for extended periods. Such consciously unavailable data have been retrieved from brain storage through hypnotic regression, narcosynthesis (drug-induced hypnosis), dreams, and electrical stimulation of the cerebral cortex during surgery.

Artist-craftsmen can easily trick or manage the human senses into transmitting peripherally perceived data in media at this lower signal strength so that it reaches the brain without ever achieving conscious recognition. If the data are highly emotionalized (sex or death), they are likely to remain within the unconscious memory system—often described as having an enormous capacity but lacking in ability to intellectually synthesize and interpret information.

HOW TO BYPASS THE CONSCIOUS MIND

In regard to subliminal information being perceived by the unconscious memory system, the particular transmission technique or sensory input system does not appear significant. Exposure can be very brief or prolonged, via peripheral or central vision, or through hearing, taste, smell or touch. The more of the various senses subliminally utilized in a specific strategy, however, the stronger and more substantial are likely to be the behavioral and memory effects.

Several writers have theorized that *sensory dominance*—what we are most consciously aware of perceiving at any given moment—shifts continuously from one sense to another. Visual perception appears dominant over all the other senses, shifting momentarily to, say, olfaction (smell), gustation (taste), etc., but all sensory inputs continue to operate as they transmit data into the brain. An example of effective communication strategy would be to lead the dominant visual sensory input into conscious concentration (perhaps with sexual stimuli) while slipping the behavior-critical information into the brain via sound.

The unconscious system appears able to unscramble even certain kinds of distorted information without individuals becoming consciously aware of the perception. This phenomenon will be discussed in Chapter 11, "The Anamorphic Tiger," which demonstrates the use of visual distortion techniques to bypass critical conscious awareness.

A comparable effect can be accomplished with sound by changing speed harmonics in a recording. The sound is consciously perceived as jumbled—speeded up or slowed down—but the information is perceived in its undistorted form at the unconscious level. In one recent example, a rock group called Cheap Trick embedded the Lord's Prayer in the last part of the third verse of a song called "How Are You?" The prayer was embedded into the record at one-eighth regular speed (4 rpm) at a low volume level. The record appears to have a depressing effect upon audiences, perhaps because the prayer unconsciously triggers childhood memories of security and stability under parental domination that conflict with the struggles for autonomy during puberty. For whatever reason, the record sold primarily to early and mid-teenagers.

OVERLOADED PERCEPTUAL INPUT

Perceptual overload is another subliminal media strategy: bombarding individual perceptions with sensory stimuli in heavy quantities or intense volume, thus initiating some level of hypnotic trance. Overload, in effect, performs sensory anaesthesia at the conscious level, assuring that media content will reach the unconscious without ever surfacing at the conscious level. Highly enriched verbal or pictorial imagery, together with rapid changes in subject content, intense color variation, high volume, and heavy peer group reinforcement (such as occurs at rock concerts or in the Sistine Chapel) create perceptual anaesthesia. The basic imagery then bypasses conscious awareness and induces information into the unconscious memory.

An evening of TV viewing is a typical example of perceptual overload. Every five minutes or so, program content changes during commercial breaks of 30, 60, 90, or 120 seconds. Programs change every 30, 60, or 90 minutes. There is so much information coming at viewers over so short a time that they sit like somnambulists, staring blankly at the screen. This is precisely what they are intended to do. Nevertheless, they have perceived prodigious quantities of information. When they finally turn off the TV and go to bed, they have only vague and scattered conscious memories of the evening's experiences. Little may ever surface at the conscious level. By the following day, the night's TV viewing experience has become a dreamlike memory, with even more limited conscious recall. Viewers usually describe these vague media recollections in general terms of feeling, lacking any ability to deal with specific detail.

This is not the viewer's fault, but the way the system was purposely designed to optimize merchandizing effectiveness. TV talk-show host Mike Douglas once commented that he and his wife were avid Arthur Godfrey fans; they rarely missed his daily radio program. One day after they had completed their supermarket rounds, the Douglases noticed that unknowingly they had included in their purchases virtually every product Godfrey had advertised the preceding week.

Conscious, critical awareness could mean trouble for both publisher and broadcaster, and so conscious consideration of the fine details is the last thing any media technician would seek as long as he serves the advertiser. Critical awareness might lead viewers and readers to decide they don't like what is being done to them. They could decide to express displeasure by harassing their congressman, assassinating the TV set with baseball bats, or adamantly refusing to buy advertised products. These are all excellent defensive strategies.

THE SUBLIMINAL MASSAGE

The publicly available data supporting subliminal stimuli effectiveness, limited though it is, have appeared in academic journals, books, and research papers—produced largely by academic psychologists Much of this information was derived from laboratory situations, and laboratories—it cannot be overemphasized—are far removed from the real world. As it exists in human perception, the *real* world is a most complicated and untidy place—the product of individually and culturally oriented perceptions with their attendent maze of repressions. Nevertheless, there exists substantial published evidence that substimuli affect human behavior in at least ten specific areas of behavior.

1) conscious perception
2) emotional response
3) drive-related behaviors
4) adaptation levels
5) verbal formulations
6) memory
7) perceptual defenses
8) dreams
9) psychopathology
10) purchasing and consumption behavior

These are not necessarily the only effects of substimuli; but these categories represent more or less traditional areas of concentration among researchers.

MANIPULATING CONSCIOUS PERCEPTION

The high-speed tachistoscope is a projector with a shutter operating at between three and ten thousandths of a second. Its images are invisible at the conscious level, but are perceived at the unconscious level. A great many laboratory experiments with this instrument have demonstrated that substimuli can influence or change what we consciously perceive.

In a typical early study (Klein and Holt, 1960), test subjects were asked to draw human figures from sexually ambiguous descriptions. Before they began to draw, pictures of male and female genitalia were presented to them via tachistoscopic displays. The test subjects' drawings were more masculine after they had subliminally perceived male genitalia and more feminine after subliminally perceiving the female.

In another often repeated study (Smith, Spence, and Klein, 1959), words were tachistoscoped for test subjects before they were shown a picture of an expressionless human face. Descriptions of the face were significantly more pleasant when the preceding substimuli was the word *happy*, compared with a similar test when the consciously invisible word was *angry*. Just think of the possibilities presented to advertisers by such demonstrations of human vulnerability.

EMOTIONAL RESPONSE IMPACT

Subliminal stimuli can also intensify or diminish an individual's or group's emotional reaction to consciously perceived data. Emotional response has been discussed as an aspect of meaning in works of art. But, as we have seen, emotional response to seemingly neutral or inert products such as Scotch whiskey, cologne, fried clams, or a book can be intensified via substimuli. Emotionalized substimuli can even affect the functioning of autonomic systems within the body, as measured by increased brain alpha and theta rhythms on an electroencephalograph (EEG), subtle variations in heart rate (EKG), and higher electrical potentials in the skin. (GSR).

In the movie *The Exorcist* (See *Media Sexploitation,* Chapter 7) substimuli were applied to sustain and intensify levels of audience emotional excitation—"kick tripping the audience" in the movie industry jargon. Similar techniques were utilized to emotionally manipulate the audience in *The Texas Chain Saw Massacres,* which won the London Film Festival's Outstanding Film of the Year award. Producer Tobe Hooper explained, "Subliminal perception is a killer. The capacity of the unconscious to take information and run with it is unlimited. We flatter ourselves by thinking we are in control of our thinking. We must be nuts." (*New Times,* May 13, 1977, p. 62.)

MANAGING DRIVE-RELATED BEHAVIORS

Another area of psychological theory has developed explanations as to how perception and memory relate to various drive systems. Considerable argument exists over just what constitutes a drive mechanism, although sex, hunger, thirst, and aggression are usually agreed upon as drives triggered by innate mechanisms within the body. There have been endless discussions over which has the most powerful effect upon behavior. Memories of these drive stimuli affect both conscious and unconscious memory systems. When an individual is sexually stimulated, hungry, thirsty, or aggressive, drive excitation appears to act as a priming force upon the memory systems, evoking recall of similar past experiences. Several important studies, including that of Spence and Ehrenberg, 1964, demonstrated that drive systems can also be activated by substimuli that evoke drive-related memories.

Once primed by drive excitation, an individual is more susceptible to substimuli. Researchers Gordon and Spence, 1966, found hungry test subjects were more susceptible to substimuli than those who had recently eaten. Gadlin and Fiss, 1967, discovered that food recall could be facilitated by substimuli accompanied by food odor. Several other studies illustrated that priming—verbal or pictorial images consciously perceived before exposure to substimuli—sensitized the subject to later substimuli (Spence and Gordon, 1967).

In advertising, the reader or viewer is primed by the content. While watching *Charlie's Angels* or reading a copy of *Playboy*, the audience is primed for sex-drive excitation. An ad for deodorants, automobiles, or alcoholic beverages is then subliminally cued to the sex drive via embedded genitalia or via the word SEX lightly etched into a layout.

In such circumstances, the drive states would have to be consciously perceived for this to work effectively. The consumer is thereby sensitized and receptive to the substimuli, and earlier drive-related fantasies stored in the conscious and unconscious memories are evoked. This might explain why it is very unwise to shop in a supermarket when hungry. Food labels and other advertising are loaded with subliminals. In another example, the Howard Johnson Clam Orgy copy and picture could prime an individual's hunger at the conscious level while the subliminal appeal is to sex. Both conscious and unconscious memory systems would then, we can theorize, initiate the desired behavior—an order for fried clams.

But such compounding of drive-related stimuli in the unconscious memory system would have a very powerful retention and motivating effect. What disorientation, misevaluation, or even trauma such manipulation may also accomplish inside a consumer's head and value systems can only be conjectured upon at this point.

CULTURAL VALUE SYSTEM MODIFICATION

Published experimental data suggest that exposure to substimuli can change an individual's evaluation or attitude toward virtually any subject. Theoretical literatures of both sociology and psychology include a large group of experiments around theories called "adaptation level" (AL)—cognitive social scientists' attempts to quantify value judgments. For example, if a subject were to evaluate an object's weight on a nine-point scale between *heavy* and *light*, substimuli could change the evaluated chosen anchor point either upward or downward. Almost a century ago, judgments as to the heavier of two weights were influenced by subliminal differences between the stimuli (Peirce and Jastrow, 1884).

Weak electrical shocks were judged to be more intense with the introduction of a series of subliminal shocks alternating with the consciously perceived ones (Black and Bevan, 1960; Goldstone et al., 1962). Estimates of various sized round disks, as evaluated on a five point scale, were similarly changed; there were subliminal projections of a disk larger than any of those evaluated for one group and a smaller subliminal disk projected for another group (Boardman & Goldstone, 1962). Judgments of loudness were raised by introducing subliminal tones (Bevan and Pritchard, 1963; Bevan, 1964).

From these relatively simplistic laboratory experiments with loud–soft, large–small, strong–weak, and heavy–light, it is a relatively simple technological step to such dichotomies as good–bad, true–false, moral–immoral, right–wrong, good–evil, and so on. If personal value judgments—the major product of culture—can be modified via substimuli, then it is entirely possible to change a cultural value system in virtually any direction if one spends enough time and money on subliminally reinforced media.

Consider the question of pornographic material such as the Howard Johnson clam plate inserted into advertising. Millions of Clam-Plate Orgy placemats were printed during several years and utilized in several thousand restaurants all over North America. This material enters millions of people's memory systems from a high-credibility source: the prestigious Howard Johnson Corporation. Experimental evidence strongly suggests that, over a period of time, after enough exposure to subliminal data like that in the clam plate, many individuals would modify their moral attitudes toward activity such as sexual orgies, even perhaps bestiality. Reproductive behavior—not the simplistic manipulative nonsense described as *sex* in its American cultural adaptation—could also be modified.

Adaptation level theory and experimental evidence also suggest that fantasy modification would be most pronounced in individuals with strong, rigid, moralistic preoccupations— just the opposite of what conventional logic would lead us to believe. The resulting conflicts between a conservative, Puritan-Calvinist heritage and the fantasy promise of sexual promiscuity and indulgence provide irresistible sales opportunities for the ad industry.

Current U.S. cultural preoccupations with releasing sexual inhibitions and socio-legal restraints is an excellent case in point. Media, as a circulation-advertising gimmick, has for several decades pushed the notion of mate-swapping, orgies, casual sex, and perversions of a dozen varieties, etc. We have been told repeatedly by influential national media to cast loose our chains and screw. Should someone from outer space study Americans from their media, they would easily conclude the United States is one great big, violence-wracked, never-ending gang bang.

As long as these fantasies remain masturbation fantasies, the harm they do to human relationships remains hidden from sight, difficult to pinpoint. But, of course, sooner or later humans will try to accomplish *the real thing*. Most humans simply cannot act out these sexual fantasies without inflicting severe emotional damage upon themselves. True, there may be a few who can get away with it, or so it appears. But they are very few. Most people who attempt to act out American gang-bang fantasies in real life will end up in medical, psychiatric, or psychotherapy clinics, or in divorce courts. Should you doubt this, just ask your physician or attorney. Most are well acquainted with the syndrome.

So what happens to a population with traditionally strong, conservative views of reproductive behavior after several decades of bombardment with salacious stimuli at the conscious and unconscious levels? Just chat informally about "sex" with any few dozen American teenagers, from any socioeconomic background. They very quickly give you a picture of incredible confusion, uncertainty, guilt, alienation, hostility, contempt, and distrust toward the opposite sex and the entire question of mature adjustments to reproductive drives.

Of course, the primary motive for the use of such imagery is to sell products. But these media constitute a culture machine, manufacturing our value system like so much sausage through a production line, then switching the value system around again when it is no longer an effective sales stimulus.

VERBAL BEHAVIOR REINFORCEMENT

American students of language and behavior have traditionally considered *words* and *pictures* as different in the ways they affect behavior. Both dynamic and behavioral psychologies appeared to have kept the two perceptual entities separate. Research on substimuli, however, suggests that as far as can be determined, the two media can be considered as mutually reinforcing, integrative, and similar in their effects upon behavior.

A large number of research studies dating well back into the nineteenth century illustrate human response to subliminal verbal stimuli. Several early studies explored the phenomenon that subliminal stimuli can influence what we answer in response to a question, often expressed as "guesses" (Sidis, 1898; Peirce and Jastrow, 1884). These early experimenters also demonstrated the presence within the brain of an "inner self" (secondary self, unconscious, subconscious, third brain, deep mind, etc.) that perceives information of which the conscious mind is unaware.

In one intriguing experiment (Dixon, 1958), test subjects were told to respond with "the first word that comes to mind" each time a flash of light appeared on a screen before them. Unknown to the subjects, a subliminal word was tachistoscoped into the light flash. Galvanic skin response (GSR) measurements were taken during each flash of light. Readings were significantly higher for emotional than for neutral words. Subjects made lists of words they consciously associated with the light flashes. They often associated the subliminal word with synonyms, especially when substimuli had, in the researcher's words, "a Freudian flavor."

Dixon's study has been reinforced by a prodigious number of later experiments. In another (Fuhrer and Eriksen, 1960), the verbal material was presented subliminally upside down and backwards—but with similar results. As mentioned earlier, many people in a hypnotic trance can fluently read upside-down, mirror-image text, suggesting that the unconscious portion of the brain can perceive information despite seemingly incomprehensible distortions.

In another such study (Worthington and Dixon, 1964), subjects guessed numbers after exposure to subliminal numbers, producing significantly more correct than incorrect guesses. (Many of the incorrect guesses gave the next highest number to that subliminally tachistoscoped.)

Experimental evidence suggests that subliminal words and pictures have similar symbolic significance, but that their effects upon behavior or memory rest upon their emotionalized meanings. Meaning appears to exist at both conscious and unconscious levels. Meaning at one level can vary widely from, even contradict, meaning at the other. It is what these subliminal words or pictures mean that is primarily significant, not what they *say*. *Meaning, in effective communication at any level of perception, is truly the name of the game.*

The advertising industry's verbal substimuli are not really an articulate form of communication. About nine words have been found in national advertisements—SEX (the most commonly utilized), FUCK, CUNT, PUSSY, PRICK, PENIS, DEAD, DIE, KILL. Undoubtedly, the unconscious system perceives other words as well, but these nine appear most frequently as reinforcement devices for commercial art. Also found were several attempts to use phrases similar to post-hypnotic commands— U BUY, GET IT. Theoretically, they should also work, but here the risk of discovery becomes greater. Apparently substimuli will not affect behavior if it is consciously perceived.

It does not require a genius to realize that embedded substimuli like the letters SEX, unconsciously identifying the product with reproductive behavior, would significantly affect merchandizing response. Such metaphorical devices as "Dig into our Clam Plate" and "The road to success is paved with rocks, let us smooth them for you" are powerful verbal reinforcements for subliminal art. "Dig into our Orgy" might be the unconsciously perceived meaning of the Howard Johnson ad. In a sense, the clam plate becomes the price of admission.

The "rocks" are loaded with bizarre images of self-destruction, nightmarish hallucinations, self-immolation, and the like, which Johnny Walker's Scotch will presumably help the drinker overcome, or if death-wish theories have any merit—perhaps achieve.

In a poetic use of language (words and pictures) it is important to remember that symbols say very little about realities, but refer to the fantasies each of us projects, both consciously and unconsciously, throughout our lives. For most individuals, there are no clear separations between their perception of *illusions* and *realities*. The relationship changes constantly in response to often uncontrollable influences. This symbolic dimension is invisible, isolated from conscious awareness.

SUBLIMINAL DREAM PERCEPTS

Humans clearly have an ability to exclude, shut out, repress, or deny taboo or emotionalized media content, even though the stimuli can be demonstrated to have been unconsciously perceived. Taboo stimuli primarily involve sex or death—the two polarities of human existence, the beginning and the end—but they can also involve current or recently experienced neurosis or psychosis: persecution fear, self-image deficiencies, aggression, incest fear, anal preoccupations, etc. Even recent painful or anxiety-provoking events (economic or personal loss, embarrassment, death, impotence, or the fear of having to endure such experiences) can generate taboos to which we are vulnerable. Everyone fears something. Between 1948 and 1960, dozens of experiments were published on the effects of substimuli upon the perception of emotional or taboo content (Dixon, 1971). In both words and pictures, taboo or emotionalized stimuli are more likely than neutral stimuli to be repressed and go consciously unrecognized. The Kanon Cologne ad is a typical example.

Repressed and taboo imagery is likely to surface in dreams. In 1917, Otto Poetzl demonstrated that substimuli induced during normal waking hours will affect subsequent dream experiences. Poetzl's "Law of Exclusion" postulates that dream content derives *entirely* from substimuli. Later research (Foulkes and Rechtschaffen, 1964) suggested that rapid eye movement dreaming, as compared with non-REM dream content, indeed originates from substimuli, though the substimuli are often symbolically transformed. Another of many studies (Shevrin and Luborsky, 1958) also reaffirmed Poetzl's findings, but added that substimuli emerging as dreams were emotionally unpleasant. For their dreams, subjects appeared to unconsciously select subliminal material with strong emotional significance, often excluding substimuli with weak emotional references. Weak or emotionally irrelevant substimuli, though, often seem to serve as a symbolic cover for significant objectionable material.

For example, students were asked to report their dreams after viewing the Howard Johnson placemat but without being told about the subliminal content. Several reported dreams that involved groups of men and women struggling with each other. In one dream, the group was struggling to get out of a sinking boat, but the door and porthole were locked.

Substimuli tend to evoke symbolic dream responses—either directly representational (the phallic Coca-Cola bottle tended to evoke a penis identification); or indirect (the word "cow" tended to evoke images with an oral-passive-mother-related content rather than with other farm animals (Pine, 1960, 1961, 1964)). All of which makes dream analysis an extremely difficult technique for studying substimuli, even though dreams are important symbolic representations of our values, conflicts, and environmental maladjustments.

Dream research suggests "significance" is the key to involvement, at least at the subliminal level—which provides a rather upsetting paradox. Obscene substimuli, for example, should have stronger effects upon individuals with rigid, moralistic perspectives than on, say, a well-adjusted swinger—if such an individual is conceivable. Moral prohibitions or inhibitions provide "significance," thereby *increasing* vulnerability.

It was also Otto Poetzl who demonstrated that subs seem to trigger conscious behavior after a time delay and a secondary related exposure—hours, days, weeks, months, perhaps years after the initial substimuli were perceived (Poetzl, 1917). For example, a month after perceiving the Kanon ad, a man might find the bottle in a store and purchase the product with the conscious rationale that, "It's strong stuff," "It's a sexy smell," or "It will turn women on [avoid rejection or castration.]" Such cues as the bottle shape or label during the secondary exposure would trigger purchasing behavior without the consumer having any conscious memory of having seen the ad.

Poetzl's theory is only a simplified rationale of what must be a very complex system within the brain. Nevertheless, the ability of subliminal stimuli to evoke strong delayed emotional reactions appears well documented (Hilgard, 1965; Kroger and Fezler, 1976; Dixon, 1971).

BECKER'S LITTLE BLACK BOXES

Dr. Hal C. Becker has had a distinguished career in scientific research since World War II. During 25 years on the Tulane University Medical School staff, he received roughly $1 million in research funds, was granted five patents, and published over 40 scholarly papers in scientific books and journals. He frequently lectures before learned societies. A specialist in biomedical communication and clinical-behavioral engineering, Becker studied at Tulane, MIT, Princeton, and George Washington universities.

During the 1950's, Becker began experiments with subliminal stimuli. In 1962 and 1966 he patented subliminal induction devices capable of introducing information into the brain without the recipient's conscious awareness (Becker, 1962, 1966). The earlier patent included a high-speed tachistoscope that flashes images for 3 to 10 milliseconds at varying intervals.

For several years, Becker operated a successful weight reduction clinic near New Orleans. Using a twelve-week clinical program which involved a series of videotaped programs utilizing subliminal audio and visual stimuli, he sustained weight loss for hundreds of obese patients. Becker's program is recognized by the New Orleans Medical Society and receives most of its patients—many have unsuccessfully tried endless diets and weight-loss programs—by physician referral.

Becker recently developed an anti-theft program now used in a large number of Canadian and U.S. retail stores. He designed an audio (voice) input which inserts a subliminally perceived authoritative voice repeating admonitions against stealing into store music systems. The subliminal voice, 30 to 40 decibels under the music, is recorded on an endless loop tape cassette and is undetectable even with sophisticated instruments. The low volume level of the subliminal voice varies instantaneously against changes in the supraliminal (consciously perceived) music volume.

The subliminal message repeats, "I am honest. I won't steal. Stealing is dishonest," and similar phrases. In six large stores tested over a nine-month period, both employee and consumer theft losses dropped by 37 percent. This, however, was only a prototype system. Becker believes more sophisticated strategies of subliminal persuasion, or even threats, will drop losses even further. The system's success led its users to predict that 80 to 90 percent of retail stores will eventually utilize subliminals to prevent theft—or for *other* purposes. Someone should be keeping an eye on the *other* purposes.

Widespread employee theft, of course, is currently a major drain on the U.S. economy. Few would quarrel with proprietors' rights to protect inventories in any way not specifically illegal or in violation of a labor contract. But this simple induction technique could easily be used to sell high-profit merchandise, or—for that matter, political or ideological indoctrination.

During 1978, Becker designed a new videotape subliminal insertion technique. Again, the subliminal message is videotaped on an endless loop cassette. The subliminal message can be inserted easily into any program or commercial. A two-inch-videotape operates at 60 fields per second. Two fields constitute a frame. Becker's automatic electronic system inserts the subliminal message in alternate fields at roughly one ninetieth of a second flashes. Normally these would be observable by most people, but the device calculates the light intensity within each frame and inserts subs just above the light level in the supraliminal frames. The ingenious device is so simple to use, it could be operated in any living room, and—for all practical purposes—is undetectable.

Though Becker's patents were granted seventeen years ago and are available to anyone from the U.S. Patent Office, I have never met a psychologist who knew of their existence. Such is the power of the profit motive, however, that I have known over a dozen ad executives who had possessed these documents for years. There is no way to be certain that numerous such devices have not been in service for at least a quarter century. Anyone with a strong enough incentive and money to invest could construct a similar input device from Becker's patents. No one would ever know, or could prove, what was going on unless they got their hands on one of the subliminally embedded tapes. Even then, under current laws, it might be difficult to bring the issue into court.

The question is really academic at this point. Becker, often severely criticized for his anti-theft system, is doing nothing that the advertising and mass communication industry has not done for years. Unlike the advertisers, however, Becker publicly announced what he was doing, how, and attempted to follow strict ethical guidelines.

EDUCATION AND INDOCTRINATION

Dr. Bruce R. Ledford, an educational psychologist at East Texas State University, studied the effects of subliminal imagery and symbolism upon learning behavior. Using a rear-projection screen in his classroom, he projected a variety of separate sex, death, and neutral images on the screen at only one candlepower above the ambient light in the classroom. Ledford's students consciously were unaware of the images. Different groups were exposed to different images. Control groups received no rear-screen projected images at all.

After a 30-minute exposure period, classes were tested on specific lecture content that had been openly presented. Ledford reported that "significant learning differences," as measured by test scores, "occurred among groups exposed to subliminal sexual stimuli" (Ledford, 1978).

The implications of these experiments are both exciting and frightening. Ledford views subliminal techniques as potentially useful in "efficient instructional design." Substimuli have been utilized for years in textbooks and other educational media, of course, but not for educational objectives *per se*. They have simply been used to help sell the product, the media themselves. I found substimuli embedded in elementary school readers, university textbooks, and a wide variety of pamphlets, brochures, and demonstration slides sold to educators. Apparently the practice extends back over many years. Though their primary effect would have been sales, these subliminal stimuli would have had a peripheral educational effect.

In a society that produces the world's most expensively educated illiterates, Dr. Ledford's discovery may be very important, though, as he points out, substantial further research is needed. But—and the question has not been seriously asked to my knowledge—should we *sell* educational content, intellectual perspectives, visions of *truth* and *reality*, and value systems?

U.S. educators have generally ignored, perhaps quite purposely, the relationship between education and cultural propaganda. Much of U.S. education has degenerated into point-of-view or role indoctrination, rather than emphasizing basic skills and wide intellectual perspectives on the human condition.

Once again, however, Dr. Ledford's significant and promising research did not demonstrate anything that was not known and widely practiced by the media industries. The dilemma over whether to use subliminal techniques in education is *purely* academic. Media have been subliminally educating us for a very long time.

SUBS IN PSYCHOPATHOLOGY

Some of the most exciting research with subliminals has been done over the past decade by Dr. Lloyd Silverman and his colleagues at New York University's Department of Mental Health. By 1976, Dr. Silverman had published over twenty articles in scientific journals covering clinical experiments with subliminal indoctrination. Working with the New York Veterans Administration Hospital and Research Center for Mental Health, Silverman subjected mental patients in four specific areas—schizophrenics, depressives, homosexuals, and stutterers—to Becker's high-speed tachistoscope with 4-millisecond flashes of light in which pictures or verbal instructions were embedded.

Silverman used exhaustive ethical considerations: his patients were volunteers to whom the procedures had been carefully explained. The 4-millisecond displays were held to a very limited repetition duration. Indeed, the experiment's measurable effects persisted no longer than 30 minutes after the sessions.

With symptoms being measured by a variety of standard clinical tests (Multiple Affect Adjective Check Lists, Rorschach Inkblot, Paraphrase Task Assignment, Pathological Nonverbal Behavior Assessment, Thought Disorder Evaluation, Sexual Feeling Inventory, and others), Silverman and his group were able to both *increase* and *decrease* symptoms in the four areas of pathology. The experimenters *increased* the patient's chief symptom in 70 percent of the schizophrenics, 60 percent of the homosexuals, 72 percent of the stutterers, and 63 percent of the depressives. Symptom *reduction* in the respective psychopathologies appeared comparable.

Most important, Silverman's work demonstrated that subliminally perceived information can be directly linked to psychopathological behavior. Generally, you can make some individuals either sick or well by exposing them to subliminal stimuli.

I was intrigued at how the work of Becker, Ledford, and Silverman—only three of perhaps two dozen scholars in the United States and Great Britain with whose work I am familiar—has been largely unknown outside each experimenter's limited area of scholarly contacts, demonstrating the highly fragmented nature of "psychology" research. Silverman, for example, had used Becker's tachistoscope in his experiments for over ten years without being aware of either Becker's patents or his publications. Neither had Becker heard of Silverman nor had either been even remotely aware of extensive commercial developments with subliminal technique.

SCIENTIFIC AND ARTISTIC CREATIVITY

I have been privileged to know several real scientists, men who distinguished themselves in highly creative intellectual innovation, who changed the world during their life spans. All were outspoken advocates of critical, hard-nosed thought. Each penetrated the suffocating iron curtain of conventional wisdoms that dominated his field of study; each fought the prejudices of colleagues who clung desperately to safe, well-trodden ways of thought and perspective; each used the term "scientific" with restraint and caution; and each agreed that innovative science is as much a crapshoot as is art or any other creative effort.

Individuals with something to sell, on the other hand—journalists, promoters, hucksters of a hundred varieties—throw the label "scientific" around indiscriminately as though it conferred some form of indisputable omniscience or truth. Science, like art, is actually anything you can get away with in a particular place at a particular time which works or at least appears to work.

NUMBERS EXCLUDE MORAL QUESTIONS

As one ad executive told me, "We are concerned only with the facts. It is not our [the advertising agency's] fault the human brain seems to work that way."

Actually, ad researchers would rather *not* know how the brain operates. It would be a troublesome kind of knowledge, loaded with a variety of moral and ethical issues advertisers and their clients would rather not get involved with. After all, their job is only to sell products.

In business, life is kept simple; moral questions are usually resolved in terms of legality and their effects upon profit and loss. Though I personally obtained more insight and enlightenment from dynamic and humanistic psychologies (Ehrenzweig, Brown, Laing, Jung, Thass-Thienemann), experimental research provides the kind of information likely to be accepted by a business executive—one seeking hard-nosed, "scientific," empirical facts that support an engineering, mechanistic approach to behavior. It is also an approach to human manipulation in which heavy capital investments in applied research could be justified. Perhaps most important, the approach subordinates or ignores moral and humanistic considerations, classifying them as "emotionalism" or "unscientific."

In the United States, a largely invisible multibillion-dollar research industry constantly evaluates the effectiveness of media marketing investments, offering media industries a self-correcting feedback mechanism. This is a finite, measurable, knowable kind of information: *Does it sell or doesn't it?*

If media content works (that is, *sells*) then its use is continued and amplified. If not, the content is scrapped in favor of ones that do sell. It is a remarkably simple and efficient system. One of the several vague labels attached to this data-gathering and analysis is "marketing research." Utilizing advanced behavior modification technology, American marketing systems can accurately predict what virtually any group of humans will do in virtually any given situation. Individual behavior still cannot be predicted reliably, but group behavior is highly predictable via many measuring instruments. Our consumer-oriented economy is based upon this predictability.

A great many individuals adamantly refused even to consider subliminal manipulation—denying and denouncing the very idea in the face of an overwhelming body of confirming factual evidence, research, and theory. While subliminal persuasion lay within the pages of science fiction, it was respectable conjecture—non-threatening, even amusing. But to place the subject prominently in a real-life context makes it Orwellian, fearful, and loathsome.

"NORMAL" MALADJUSTMENTS

As discussed earlier, under constant substimuli bombardment of sexual imagery, an individual's moral prohibitions and inhibitions would most probably erode. Eventually, that person's attitudes toward sexual obscenity would adapt to the generally prevailing cultural norm—but without their ever realizing any change had occurred. Of course, while all this basic attitudinal change was going on, some individuals would experience seemingly inexplicable trauma and confusion in their sexual, emotional, marital, and social adjustments.

Such an insight, of course, is unlikely to make one beloved by either commercial media or university psychology departments. For this discovery of subliminal techniques was something no one really wanted discovered.

7 • MEDIA STUDY AS A SUBVERSIVE ACTIVITY

You are biting the hand that is feeding them.
Marshall McLuhan, *in conversation.*

WINNING BATTLES, LOSING WARS

Up to the time *Subliminal Seduction* was published, my relationship with the University of Western Ontario was reasonably tranquil; there were minor conflicts from month to month, but nothing of great significance. My courses were popular. From time to time I worked as a consultant to government agencies and private companies. *Subliminal Seduction* was published in October 1973. As my students described it at the time, "*Seduction* really hit the fan!" My class enrollments soared dramatically. Each semester, limited seating denied 200 to 300 students admission to my courses. Word got around rapidly. More and more of my students reported confrontations with roommates, family members, and other professors.

Such reactions continue even today. I have two dozen letters from teachers whose supervisors threatened disciplinary action or dismissal if they continued to recommend my books to their classes. The heaviest anger and hysteria derives from individuals with heavy vested interest in the media status quo.

During one early seminar, attended by several dozen faculty members in a large midwestern psychology department, roughly half my audience walked out after only twenty minutes, many not troubling to hide their anger. Over the years, the most defensive occupational groups have been print journalists, university psychologists, and physicians. I am often amused at the extreme hostility, even open agression, advertising people display toward my books. They vehemently

105

deny that anything I wrote was true, but no contradicting evidence is ever offered—only loud denials and much name calling. Ad executives repeatedly claim that my accusations are unfair, that they cannot defend the industry against my charges. Nonsense!

When *Subliminal Seduction* first appeared, ad executives in both the United States and Canada assured everyone the writer of such a book was "crazy," "paranoid," "sick," "obsessed with sex," etc. In a nervous, hysterical review of the book, Jerrold Beckerman, a research director at J. Walter Thompson, Inc. (the world's largest pre-Watergate ad agency) questioned the university's wisdom in permitting me to corrupt young impressionable students, asking, "How could anyone in their right mind so distrust businessmen?" Had he asked me directly, I would have answered, *"only another businessman."* Beckerman's vicious and insulting attack was published in the UWO Business School's official *Quarterly Journal*—which, quite incidentally I am certain, was generously endowed with JWT ads. The UWO *Quarterly* refused to print my reply to Beckerman, even though I offered to let the editor delete anything she considered objectionable or untrue. The war was on.

AVOIDING THE ISSUE

John S. Crosbie, President of the Magazine Association of Canada, wrote directly to the President and Vice Chancellor of UWO, comparing *Subliminal Seduction* with Clifford Irving's biography of Howard Hughes and referring to me as "emotionally disturbed" and "a sick man"—pretty stern stuff coming from the head of a national media trade organization. As with all the attacks launched against the book, no gesture was ever made to deal with my evidence and charges.

At the time, I couldn't believe any serious person would take such infantile name calling seriously. The ad industry's attacks upon my work were strangely ironic, coming as they did from experts at the deception, manipulation, and exploitation of consumers. Ad executives frequently charged I was ripping them off for profit. I was always flattered by this criticism, as it brought to mind my fantasy of Robin Hood—ripping off the ripper offers.

When you consider the high stakes involved, it should have been easy to disprove my books had they been untrue. I continually offered to present and defend my research before university faculty, administrators, or anyone else who was interested, but there were no invitations. I was never even invited to discuss my work with any of the UWO Trustees, the President, Vice Presidents, Deans, Department Chairmen, or any of the others involved in what was about to happen.

SEDUCTION IGNORED

Subliminal Seduction's first printing was a cautious 7,500 copies—for the publisher, a break-even edition. Even if some of them had to be sold off bargain counters, the publisher's investment could have been recouped. Bookstores accepted on consignment virtually the entire printing. Christmas, the heaviest book-buying season of the year, passed uneventfully for the book. In early January, Prentice-Hall began to receive the books back from bookstores across the nation. *Subliminal Seduction* had simply not moved. It appeared my exposé of media would die along with the first hard-cover printing. Readers buy hardcover books because they hear about them on radio or TV talk shows, or read newspaper and magazine reviews. Though a smattering of reviews appeared in book-trade journals and in a small number of print and electronic media reviews in Canada, the world of publicity had greeted *Subliminal Seduction* with stone cold silence.

Few individuals realize that media reviews are carefully planned, rarely accidental. Authors who appear with Johnny Carson, Dinah Shore, Merv Griffin, and on other such programs are carefully screened, even rehearsed before their appearances. Very little happens in the world of commercial media that is not carefully planned in terms of optimizing the advertisers' investment returns. Publishers send out hundreds of free copies of their books to reviewers and publicists. If book sales justify a promotion budget, they spend endless telephone hours trying to arrange interviews and author appearances, for which book publishers usually pay expenses. Media notoriously freeload on material certain to enhance their profits.

Both good and bad can be said about this system. If reviews come off well, publishers get their money back many times over. However, they rarely risk promotion or ad budgets on a loser. Over 40,000 books are published each year in the United States, relatively few of which are ever heard about on talk shows. Books you find out about in media are usually already successful, or at least paying their own way.

Subliminal Seduction was simply ignored by the media. One publicist told me I could probably blow up the Pentagon and the story would be lucky to make *The New York Times* Want-Ad Section—even if I paid for the ad. During that first year I often found difficulty in getting past the receptionist into the buildings of radio and TV stations, let alone on their programs.

Word apparently was circulated to several major news media to "blackout" the book. NBC and CBS, like the national news magazines, refused to discuss the book privately, let alone publicly—curious, though perhaps understandable. Had the book misrepresented the facts of subliminal persuasion in media, then it should have been widely exposed as a fake. On the other hand, if it had told the truth the scandal deserved to become a major public issue.

Publicists who worked on the book were often told that even a hatchet-job review would invite heat from the ad agencies, who move in quickly when information threatens their corporate objectives. After having been turned down for the Johnny Carson program numerous times, I was once told candidly by a member of the show's staff that "NBC simply refuses to irritate its advertisers." A conversation was reported to me between the editor and business manager of one national news publication. The editor wanted to review *Subliminal Seduction*. "Fine!" the business manager replied, "All the advertising we lose from the review will come out of your salary!" It often appeared my career as an author had begun and ended in almost the same month.

Considering the angry reactions of my university employers, if the book failed I could probably look forward to a career as a night watchman. North Americans believe, more than anything else, in success—usually measured in dollars and cents. With copies of my book flowing rapidly back to the publisher's warehouse, it seemed reasonable to conclude my chances of being shot down were eminent. I have never desired to die humbly, quietly, and obscurely. After nearly thirty years in media as a writer, radio-TV producer, director, announcer, and researcher, if my demise was about to occur it was going to be as flaming a spectacular as I could arrange.

When the big time media turn you down, there are the local media. Audiences are much smaller, but if you can appear in enough local media, it is one way to be heard.

The first step was to obtain lecture engagements. I was willing to talk anywhere, anytime, for anybody—for free, if necessary. It usually was for free—an unknown has little chance to get into the lecture circuits unless handled by one of the half dozen large agencies, who usually will not even audition unless you are a national celebrity. I went anywhere I could get myself invited—church groups, service clubs, conferences, meetings, high school and college classes—usually at my own expense. With luck, I might get $50 or $100 for my two-hour lecture. It seemed unreal that intellectual celebrities such as Buckminster Fuller and Marshall McLuhan received $5,000 a lecture.

Eventually I was invited on local radio and TV interview programs. Once I drove all night in a blizzard to Columbus, Ohio. The publisher paid for gas, the TV station offered a bed where I could sleep a few hours before the show, and I paid for my own food. The show was a disaster—a 20-minute interview at 8:30 A.M. with a rock-and-roll disk jockey who had not read the book, but was adamantly dedicated to putting it down.

There were to be many such interviewers, and many such interviews. Yet, I never ceased to be amazed at how many dedicated, thoughtful, articulate, and courageous journalists still are willing to risk their jobs by bucking the system. Most of these, however, seem to be in small-town media, less pressured by ad agencies and corporate interests than those with major big-city audiences.

Excellent, though often critical, reviews of the book were eventually published by writers such as Harry Reasoner of ABC, Paul Dickson of *The Washington Post*, Bobby Mather of the *Detroit Free Press*, John Saunders of *The Toronto Star*, Thomas Goldthwaite of *The Phoenix Arizona Republic*, Doug Yocom of *The Portland Oregon Journal*, and the editors of numerous religious publications such as *The Catholic Layman*, *The Salvation Army War Cry*, and *The National Council of Churches*.

CANADA'S GOVERNMENT NETWORK

The Canadian Broadcasting Corporation (CBC) news and special events departments were probably responsible for promoting *Subliminal Seduction* into a Canadian best seller. Unfortunately, Canada's 22 million people (comparable to California's population) buy far fewer books than their U.S. counterparts. Through 1974–75, I appeared on at least two dozen CBC network radio and television programs and was interviewed, probed, examined, and argued with. My confrontations with CBC journalists were often argumentative, but rarely unfair—in considerable contrast to my treatment by many U.S. commercial broadcasters.

Even though the CBC is government-owned, it broadcasts $200 million each year of advertising (modest by U.S. standards) and thus CBC, not unlike the privately owned U.S. networks, is highly sensitive to advertiser pressure—except perhaps in their news and special events departments. Behind the scenes, of course, the ad industry was fighting to ridicule and keep me off the air. A detailed dossier on me was circulated to every ad agency in Canada. A barrage of critical letters and phone calls was aimed at the university trustees, and administration.

One example of ad agency censorship power came when CBC paid my expenses to videotape three 30-minute shows on subliminal advertising. Eventually the series was to be distributed as an educational film. A CBC producer explained they had decided to tape the programs in Edmonton, Alberta, rather than Toronto, Ontario, because there was likely to be less advertiser pressure.

We spent two days taping. At least twenty technicians were involved. I was impressed with the quality of the work— direction, thoughtful questions, lighting, camera shots, editing, and care used to reproduce the subliminal ads. The production must have cost the Canadian taxpayers a substantial amount of money.

Several weeks later, I discovered the entire production had been erased from the tapes via the efforts of a CBC advertising executive. Only 15 minutes of the one and a half hour videotaping ever appeared on the air, and that over a local Manitoba newscast.

I suspected many CBC journalists took a personal delight in my attack upon the advertising industry.

Most journalists who have been around any length of time, and who do their job aggressively, have been bruised by advertiser pressure, especially the high-level heat generated by the large, international ad agencies. In any respect, within a short time *Subliminal Seduction* was a best-selling book in Canada.

THE BIG GUN MISFIRES

At the time, the ad industry's major lobbyist was Robert E. Oliver, President of the Canadian Advertising Advisory Board. *Subliminal Seduction* had caused Bob Oliver more than a few sleepless nights, or so he once admitted to me. We debated on numerous TV shows. Ours was a strange act. We would be friendly before and after going on camera, once even sharing a long taxi ride. On the air, though, Oliver was a tiger, trying to talk incessantly so I couldn't interrupt or answer, calling me a "liar," "a madman," "a fool," an "irresponsible rabble-rouser." He did everything he could to keep me from showing examples of embedded ads on camera. Once he even refused to appear if I insisted upon using my slides.

Our road-show TV debates finally led to a public forum sponsored by the Ontario Committee on the Status of Women, held in Toronto's large St. Lawrence Center. Well over 2,000 packed the lecture hall. People were even sitting in the aisles. Several hundred watched on closed-circuit TV in the lobby. This was far different from a broadcast, where the audience had limited time to study my examples, many of which reproduce badly on TV. I lectured for 45 minutes, projecting a series of subliminal ads on the screen, many with content highly demeaning to women. The audience responded angrily, though enthusiastically, to the presentation.

For the first time since I met him, Oliver was shaken. He had to confront a live audience who clearly perceived the subliminal advertising skulls and genitalia. He complimented me on my "wild imagination," and told the audience he had seen nothing of what I was talking about. He called my presentation "disgusting fantasy," adding half a dozen or so other insulting phrases.

Oliver had taken the wrong strategy. Almost unanimously, the packed audience booed and jeered for several minutes. I almost felt sorry for him. His hands shook, he paled, and he was visibly hurt, almost like an overconfident boxer struck by a blow he didn't anticipate. This was the last time Oliver and I met.

THE VIRGIN AUDIENCE

Later, for example, on a TV show in London, Ontario, where my university was located, Oliver and several articulate corporation presidents were interrogated on "honest advertising practices" by a roomful of high school students. The skilled executives easily handled the students' naive questions, making the ad industry to be a major public benefactor comparable to Albert Schweitzer and Jonas Salk. The program's skillfully developed conclusion was that anyone not grateful for advertising was subversively un-Canadian. The students' passive questions surprised me. For several years I had often lectured in local high school Consumer Affairs classes. Many local high school teachers had taken my evening and summer courses; and *Subliminal Seduction* was widely used as a text in the local high schools, junior colleges, and universities.

Several months later the TV station manager inadvertently let slip to me how difficult it had been to find an "uncorrupted student audience." The students on Oliver's program had been bussed in from a small, rural community some 200 miles away.

Several close friends in the ad industry cautioned me to be careful. Reportedly, large agency executives were worried the subliminal issue would get out of control. Already several Canadian Parliament members and U.S. Congressmen were known to be exploring the subject.

THE BATTLE STRATEGY SURFACES

In the meantime, UWO had been in the process of finding a new Dean for their planned Journalism School. The new Dean made his position clear from our first meeting: "I think subliminal embedding is hogwash," he told me, "It would be a pity if you became known solely as the dirty pictures man."

The other three tenured faculty, all former employees of the local *London Free Press*, soon got on the bandwagon and agreed wholeheartedly with the Dean. Curiously, perhaps, the publisher of the local *London Free Press* also owned the principal local radio and TV stations, was deeply involved with large ad agencies, served on the UWO Board of Trustees, and supplied part-time employment for the department faculty. By this time, I could see how the battle would be fought.

For the next two years I was often astonished at the resourcefulness applied in digging up new harassments in an attempt to force my resignation. Simply firing a tenured professor could have been a messy business. Through students, stories began to filter back that I was being ridiculed and attacked in the classes of other professors in the department.

My small research budget was eliminated, as were my several teaching assistants. My office space was reduced to the size of a closet. I was assigned to teach only large classes, 500 to 600 students per year, and ordered to submit daily lecture outlines to a one-man "committee" who would decide appropriate lecture content, textbooks, assignments, examinations, and would conduct periodic course evaluations. The electric typewriter was even removed from my office.

I had no doubt from the beginning that sooner or later they would win. The only question was when and under what circumstances. But I was extremely careful not to give them what they wanted—a show of anger, insubordination, confrontation, or an even minor problem with my students.

One of the Journalism Department's stranger accusations against me, I thought, was that the whole scandal was my fault. Had I not such a dirty mind, none of the subliminal business would ever have come out. I was personally blamed for the hidden obscenities in newspapers, in magazines, and on television. Defensive logic does not have to be reasonable.

One investigative reporter on the *London Free Press* was assigned to research my private life. He actually went around campus asking co-eds whether or not I was sleeping with any of them, and he once confronted me with what he alleged to be a student's charge of sexual misconduct. His story was never printed, however. Once, I was actually threatened with dismissal by the President of the university over a ridiculous minor incident—a charge quickly withdrawn when the Faculty Association made it clear the matter would end up in court. To keep the heat on, I was repeatedly accused of flunking students who disagreed with me.

FUN IN COVENTRY

For over two years, the other three tenured journalism professors did not speak to me. They silently passed me in the halls, rigidly holding their heads away. In the British tradition (which Canadian Anglophiles still fantasize they are part of) this is called "putting one into Coventry." Their performances quickly became the subject of considerable student humor.

I was often denounced by the ad people—and by now, an unsettling number of people in the university (many in the politically powerful Psychology Department—as "emotionally unbalanced," "crazy," "paranoid," "sick," "sex-crazed," even "dangerous." I shall always be grateful for the kindness of a handful of distinguished scholars, many of whom placed their own careers in jeopardy by being openly supportive. Marshall McLuhan wrote several letters in my behalf to the UWO President. In a thoughtful note at the height of the battle, McLuhan reminded me how Louis Pasteur was kicked out of the medical-scientific establishment of his day for discovering germs. It wasn't really funny, but we often joked about Soviet intellectual dissidents ending their careers in mental hospitals.

After returning from a Mexican Christmas vacation in 1974, I discovered that all the courses I had taught for six years had been cancelled and removed from the following year's catalogue. Course changes in large universities are rarely looked at carefully; it was only by chance that one of my friends noticed the deletions. The action had been engineered secretly over several months, passing through various committees as a "routine matter."

This turned out to be an expensive mistake. You can harass a professor with minor nuisances and there is not much he can do about it, but secret course deletions moved the whole thing into a larger ball park. I retained John Judson, a lawyer with heavy experience in civil rights litigation.

In a letter to the President of the university, Judson documented six specific areas of harassment:

1. Denial of merit ratings and related salary increases.
2. Attempted intrusion and attempts to control the daily content of my class lectures.
3. Secret cancellation of courses I had successfully taught for six years.
4. Denial of promotion and earned sabbatical leave.
5. Assignment of excessive teaching load—one-third higher than other departmental faculty.
6. Exclusion for two years from departmental faculty and committee meetings.

I initiated a barrage of appeals to faculty grievance committees, wrote memos to university officials, groups involved with freedom of information, and provincial officials. It is very difficult for an individual to fight the resources of a large public institution, but nevertheless, it may be important at least to go down fighting.

THE TOWN HALL ARENA

While all this was going on, I became involved with a public debate sponsored by the Ontario Alcohol Research Foundation in the Town Hall of Stratford, a small city near Toronto. Ontario Town Hall meetings have much the democratic flavor as those in New England and frequently receive national press coverage. A local member of Parliament, Hugh Edighoffer, and I were to debate two ad executives—Kellogg's Vice President, Ralph Davis; and Arthur Lennox, Advertising Vice President of Labatts', Canada's largest brewery. The debate: "Should Canada Ban Alcohol Advertising?" This is not a subject likely to endear anyone to publishers and broadcast station owners.

I arrived in Stratford to discover a small army of gray-flannel-suit types, employees of Labatts', setting up an assemblage of dual slide projectors and synchronized audio equipment, the latest, most expensive of its kind available. As it turned out, they had easily spent several thousand dollars on their presentation as well.

As their production began, a picture of *Subliminal Seduction* appeared on the screen. Then a red lettered bannerhead slowly superimposed over the book: "The Big Lie!" As the slides faded dramatically in and out, Davis solemnly and self-righteously denounced the book as "pornographic," "irresponsible," "untrue," and on and on.

Into the small meeting hall a large group of press, television, and radio reporters were jammed. This debate was intended to be something special. The subliminal issue was to be destroyed once and for all, and me along with it.

Edighoffer and I performed our portions of the debate; I demonstrated a series of subliminal ads. Compared with the slick, expensive production that preceded us, we were probably undramatic, certainly technically unimpressive. One of my students, who had scouted the auditorium, reported half the audience appeared to be employees of the local Labatts' Brewery. Edighoffer remarked that we were going to need a lot of luck on this one. But after over two hours of heavy argument, the audience voted 75 percent in favor of a total ban on alcohol beverage advertising. Another 13 percent voted for at least a partial ban. The admen's expensive hard sell had apparently backfired.

Considering the number of journalists who attended, the media only lightly covered the event the following day. Most stories emphasized what the ad executives had said. Edighoffer's and my part of the debate were presented briefly and unconvincingly. The audience vote was generally omitted—not surprisingly when you consider the massive Kelloggs and Labatts' ad budgets. Had the admen won, the debate would have been front-page news throughout Canada.

THE NEGOTIATION

After the debate Judson cautioned me to be careful. You just don't take on North America's richest and most powerful lobby without expecting fireworks. For a week, nothing happened.

Then Judson was casually invited to lunch by a wealthy corporation lawyer. The university employed a small army of regular lawyers, but this man had been hired as a "special consultant," so he said, "just for this one problem."

Through Judson, he offered a cash settlement for my resignation.

I merely laughed, but the man persisted. Over the next few weeks, three additional, increasingly generous, offers were made, finally reaching $64,000. Judson was jubilant. There was no record of any cashiered professor ever receiving such a settlement; most were lucky to get a month's severance pay. I was angry at the prospect of being bought off.

Judson believed $64,000 was the highest the school would go outside of court. The alternatives he outlined were grim; continuing the fight would be expensive and could keep me in litigation for years. UWO could fire me, he emphasized, since tenure has no legal significance, but is primarily a device for controlling professors. As a contractual obligation, there are a dozen ways it can be circumvented. I could sue for damages, of course, but might lose on some technicality after years of litigation. Based on precedents, a court settlement might even be less than the $64,000.

In the inexorable logic of business, law, and practical reality, Judson was right. Every good poker player has to know when to walk away from the game, no matter how much it hurts.

JUST DON'T TELL ANYONE

The UWO President tried to include a paragraph in our

agreement that I was never to discuss the settlement publicly. I laughingly refused. Presumably, the $64,000 was public funds. If neither of us had anything to be ashamed of, why keep the transaction secret?

Had he not made an issue of his secrecy clause I might have left quietly, but the challenge was too great. Since the polemic began, I had written down almost every significant event. I sent them as memos to several Deans, Vice Presidents, the President, and other executive administrators. Every so often these memos were answered. The file ended up with an almost day-to-day account that now included some 75 letters and memos. Several university executives had said and written things about me that some might find shocking or, at the least, amusing. One, for example, had told the Faculty Association Director, "I would fire Key if I could, but the man's too competent."

One of my former students, now the student newspaper editor, had been after me for months to let him look through the file. After the $64,000 was safely deposited, we copied the entire folder. He wrote a meticulously factual, detailed story, publishing it in the next three issues of the student newspaper. The student called it, *"The $64,000 Question!"* I replied that the $64,000 was not the question, it was the answer. The question was, "How Much Is Academic Freedom Worth?"

Though slightly bruised by the publicity, the university executives knew that the real power was theirs as long as they served local business and political interests. All they had to do was wait and make no foolish comments that might further embarrass the university. When the professor who caused the whole problem was out of the country, and the students who supported him graduated and scattered across the nation, the issue would die a natural death.

A year after I left the university, the President who had so clumsily engineered my resignation retired, and was immediately appointed Chairman of a Royal Commission Investigating freedom of information.

Though the book was widely read and discussed across Canada, when I left the country in the fall of 1975, *Subliminal Seduction* was still virtually unknown in the United States. Canadian media are isolated from United States awareness. The battle began all over again.

8 ◆ THE MEDIA IMMERSION

> *It took me a long time to discover that the key thing in acting is honesty. Once you know how to fake that, you've got it made.*
> Actor in TV commercials

ALL THE NEWS THAT'S FIT FOR ADVERTISERS

Subliminal Seduction was published in late 1973. During its first year, the book was generally ignored by media in the United States. One of the unpredictable events—without which the whole subliminal advertising scandal would have disappeared from print in the United States—occurred in early 1975. An editor told me that black readers appeared to be buying the book in heavy quantities. I was surprised. I had not yet explored the devastating implications of subliminally programming minority populations into WASP value systems.

It took several months to finally track down what had happened. Wallace Muhammad, leader of the Black Muslims, had told 25,000 Muslims at a Chicago convention that his father Elijah's dying words were, "Read *Subliminal Seduction!*" Several Muslim publications reviewed the book. I met one young Muslim who had purchased 72 copies of it, carrying them around in a shopping bag to give away to people he met on the street.

Then, *The National Enquirer*, which has the largest circulation (7 million) of any newspaper in the United States, did a full-page review of *Media Sexploitation*. Say what one will about this sensational tabloid, it is virtually the only national publication in the United States free of advertiser control or pressures. It publishes no advertising. It was the first U.S. newspaper to achieve national circulation—a remarkable accomplishment when you consider it was done without advertising income. Many of the *National Enquirer* staff appear to be British graduates of Fleet Street. And, they are extraordinarily good at what they do—whether or not you approve of what they do.

Tony Brenna, who wrote the full-page review of *Media Sexploitation* for the *Enquirer* (July 6, 1976) researched the story over several weeks, interviewing dozens of people. His first draft was over 5,000 words, his research file on the story several inches thick. By the time he completed the final draft, edited down to some 500 words with pictures, he could easily have written an entire book on the subject.

Having once been a newspaper writer, I was impressed. But one detail in Brenna's capsulized final story troubled me. He was fascinated by the Benson & Hedges cigarette ad with the word CANCER ingeniously embedded on the back of a hockey glove (see *Media Sexploitation*, Figures 41, 42).

Each time an ad is reproduced photographically, it loses 10 to 20 percent of the detail. Though we achieved fair legibility with the B & H ad in the book itself, the word CANCER would not reproduce readably on the *Enquirer*'s coarse newsprint. So, demonstrating their ingenuity, artists simply retouched the word, bringing it out in the picture like a neon sign. When I first saw the reproduction, I was certain we would all end up in court. But the New York ad agency responsible for embedding the word CANCER in a Benson & Hedges cigarette ad apparently decided discretion would be the better part of valor.

"WE DECIDE" WHAT IS NEWS

Over several hundred radio and TV interviews, I probably received the worst treatment from two Westinghouse Broadcasting Corporation TV stations. Westinghouse stations are often accused of negative policies toward anyone who criticizes nuclear power (they manufacture reactors), pollution (they create a good deal of it), or any other subject threatening corporate business objectives. When you consider that most Americans claim they receive their information about the world primarily from TV, such policies are malignant.

On July 1, 1975, I did the first of two interviews at WBZ-TV in Boston, a Westinghouse station. The two disk jockeys (neither of whom had read the book) and their production staff had been very friendly up to the instant the videocamera was switched on, whereupon nothing I could say was taken seriously. They rudely ridiculed both me and the book.

Another confrontation with Westinghouse "news" policy occurred at KPIX-TV in San Francisco, July 29, 1977. An interview about *Media Sexploitation* was to be tagged onto the evening news broadcast. This time, however, the interview was videotaped. In the studio, I chatted briefly with the two newscasters who were to do the interview. Neither had read my books, but both were cordial, agreeing to use several ads to illustrate the interview. They cautioned me to be careful because of their large family audience.

We did a ten-minute, very relaxed interview. Considering their unfamiliarity with my subject, their questions were excellent. We even managed to include quite a bit of humor.

As I thanked the interviewers and prepared to leave, the studio door suddenly burst open. In charged a nervous, hysterical woman shouting, "We're throwing that out! We can't put crap like that on the air. Do you all want to get fired?"

She was the producer and apparently had been in the control room during the interview. Almost everyone on the set, including cameramen and technicians, appeared embarrassed and tense. All I could think of was to get the hell out of the place before I made an ass of myself in a fight I couldn't win. Later in the afternoon, having become increasingly angry, I called the KPIX-TV news director and complained about the rude treatment. After all, the publisher had paid my expenses for the interview. It had cost KPIX-TV nothing.

He laughed at me. When I reminded him that the interview involved legitimate news information, especially to consumers, he said, "We decide what news is going to be!"

THE ACTOR ROBOT

August 3, 1977, just after paperback publication of *Media Sexploitation*, a Signet publicist arranged another WBZ-TV interview in Boston. Because the interview was to be on their 6:00 P.M. *First Four News* (a jazzed-up, so-called "action news" version of the day's events), I expected I would be dealing with professionals who, even if critical, would be fair.

I arrived an hour early. The news staff were very friendly, chatting, joking, kidding around. Several technicians who had read my books complimented me and looked at the examples of subliminal art I had brought. When the producer finally appeared, I invited him to select whichever of the visual material he thought would best support our interview.

"No," he said, "we won't have time for that! This will be only a quick one-minute interview. We'll just talk about the book in general terms."

The news program dramatically began. Each actor, playing the part of journalist, performed the news script typed onto the teleprompter. This remarkable device has been called "a professional lying machine" and is rarely understood by audiences. A large glass plate is positioned just a few inches from the camera lens. The announcer appears to look directly into the lens, maintaining steady eye contact with each individual viewer. Actually he is reading the news script as it is reflected on the glass plate and acting out the role of journalist. The camera lens is focused many feet away on the set. The words are not transmitted to the audience as they pass across the plate. The device produces a high-credibility illusion of the journalist-actor-reader's experience, knowledge, and wisdom about the events of the day. In America, you cannot successfully lie to anyone unless you are looking them straight in the eye. This is not necessarily true in other cultures.

I had seen this machine operate many times, but I marveled at the acting skill displayed by the attractive young WBZ-TV "news team." The teleprompter reduces the on-camera reader to an actor robot, completely controlled by the script, written hours earlier by writers unknown to the audience and sometimes even to the announcers.

FAKED SINCERITY SELLS

Finally, it was my turn. The sincere-voiced anchorman sat down next to me on an expensive imported chair. Before the camera turned on, he told me casually, as though he had just thought of it, "I'll talk about the book briefly, then we can discuss it." The red camera light flashed. We were on the air.

For over five minutes, the anchorman lectured in a rapid, well-modulated voice in such a way that any interruption I might have made would appear offensive to the audience.

He called my evidence about subliminal advertising ridiculous, and charged me with unfairly attacking advertisers who, after all, provided an essential public service. He assailed items such as the Ritz Cracker SEXes (*Media Sexploitation*, Figure 4) as "ludicrous." He carefully avoided any reference to the easily perceived, blatant examples of obscene embedding reproduced in the book—such as the Liquid Plumber TV commercial reproduced (*Media Sexploitation*, Figures 28-32) which had been broadcast many times over WBZ-TV, as well as over most TV stations across the nation.

THE MONSTER WHO ATTACKS ADVERTISERS

Like an idiot, I just sat there waiting for my turn. On the studio TV monitor, I could see the camera switch from the anchorman—handsome, casual, relaxed, conversational—to me in facial close-ups. Now I discovered the reason a technician had spent nearly 15 minutes adjusting the overhead lights before the show. The effect, called "monster-lighting," made me look like someone who had spent the afternoon raping six-year-old girls. Even so, I could not help but admire the reviewer's articulate presentation. At least, he appeared to have done his homework.

I finally caught on to what was happening. The anchorman faced a camera over my left shoulder, appearing to be looking at me while he spoke. But there in the Teleprompter were his carefully written lines as they rolled across the glass plate. Later, when we were off the air, he admitted he had not read either of my books.

When he finally finished reading the script, I was given less than a minute in which to reply. I am not certain what I said, though angry as I was I probably stumbled around like a damned fool. I had been drawn and quartered skillfully before the audience of Boston's "most watched"—at least so WBZ-TV claimed—news program. There was nothing I could do about it.

Later the *First Four News* team passed me in front of the station while I waited for a cab. None would make eye contact with me. I suspect the "news" interview production was written with the help of Boston's leading ad agencies.

Should I ever again fall into such a trap on a live show (videotapes can always be edited or erased) I would simply hold up something in front of the camera, blocking the Teleprompter. Then, all the interviewer could do is *wing it*, and depend upon his or her actual knowledge of the subject. Forced to face an alternate camera, without a Teleprompter, most TV anchorpersons would be rendered instantly speechless.

SNYDER'S INSOMNIAC SEMINAR

I am still awed by the audience of 7 million of NBC's *To-morrow Show*—a 1:00 A.M. early morning program hosted by Tom Snyder. Our interview was taped in January 1977, and I was grateful it was in the late afternoon. That single interview reached more people than all the 150 interviews on local media I had done the preceding year. It was the funniest and most chaotic interview I had ever done.

Snyder's producer said they first spent two weeks calling Manhattan ad agencies whose work had appeared in my books. It is simple for anyone in the business to find out who is responsible for what. The ad executives were invited to appear in a face-off with me on Snyder's program. The producer reported that all those contacted had sworn my books were all nonsense. Every one of the executives contacted, however, begged off—claiming they had to be out of town the afternoon of the taping. All had the same excuse. I was not really surprised. For several years ad executives, when invited to appear on numerous radio or TV programs in the United States or Canada, frequently replied with identically worded excuses, as though they had memorized a script on how to deal with situations involving either me or the subject of subliminal advertising.

During the commercial breaks in our interview, Snyder carried on an increasingly angry dialogue with an NBC censor assigned to supervise the program. The woman insisted brand identifications in the print ads I showed be deleted—labels, names, identifications of any sort. She continually threatened to stop the tape if we mentioned brand names.

At first Snyder tried to accommodate her, holding his hand over the secret identifications. But, as he held the ads up before the cameras, his hand kept slipping off, exposing the names of Benson & Hedges, Kraft Parkay, and so on. After trying to accommodate the censor and conceal the brand names, Snyder blew his cool. "This is no . . . way to run a . . . TV program. Get off my . . . back . . . ." he shouted. As his frustrations increased, he finally hurled a stream of profanity at the poor woman that would have done justice to a stevedor. Everybody in the studio broke up laughing, everyone except the censor. I kept thinking there was no way NBC would ever let this program go on the air.

I was surprised when the Snyder interview was broadcast

about three months later. My considerable respect for Snyder increased when I later heard he had also fought with several NBC executives who attempted to cancel the interview as a favor to ad agencies.

THE MEDIA TREATMENT

As time went on, media reviews of the books appeared in Boston, Cleveland, Chicago, Baltimore, Detroit, Edmonton, Atlanta, Montreal, New Orleans, New York, Minneapolis, Houston, Los Angeles, Phoenix, Portland, Philadelphia, San Diego, Salt Lake City, St. Louis, Seattle, Toronto, Vancouver, Washington, Winnipeg, and other cities. The books were also eventually reviewed in dozens of smaller communities across the United States and Canada.

During July and August 1977, shortly after the paperback publication of *Media Sexploitation*, Signet sent me on a three-week, 17-city, 72-interview tour—known in the publicity world as "the treatment." My last interview was with Allan Hamil, whose Vancouver TV show is syndicated to some 300 stations across North America. I have no conscious memory of what transpired during the five-minute interview. I was numb from the three-week ordeal. After the show, Hamil—a gracious and articulate host—gave a party for the guests, including Dr. Laurence Peter, author of the best-selling *The Peter Principle*. When I described my 72-interview marathon, Peter laughed, saying he had once done 192 interviews in six weeks. Such is life for anyone who wants to write books.

TIME FOR SUBLIMINALS

November 1977 I was contacted numerous times by *Time* correspondents from Los Angeles and New York. I spent three weeks doing almost nothing but talking to *Time* staffers. Guy Shipler, a highly respected *Time* correspondent in Carson City, Nevada, spent two afternoons with me studying dozens of subliminally embedded ads, many of which had appeared in *Time*. He had apparently read my books and was intrigued with the illustrations. I gave him twenty slide copies of embedded ads (many used as illustrations in the three books) with detailed explanations of their subliminal content. *Time* had the ingredients for an explosive exposé of advertising chicanery.

Over subsequent weeks, I spoke quite often with *Time*'s New York office. A staff writer for the *Behavior* section admitted that the subliminal embedding of obscene pictures was well known in the media business. He needed help, however, finding independent confirmation on the use of word embeds like SEX in print media. I named several individuals I thought might discuss the technique on a strictly confidential basis; I also suggested he check with the *Time* art departments, as some most ingenious word embeddings have appeared in *Time*'s covers and news pictures.

A personal friend at *Time*, who saw the subliminal story file, told me its size alone was impressive. Apparently the magazine had done an exhaustive research job. My contact reported on having read a draft of the story which, so he said, complimented both my research and books. A publicist at Signet reported the piece had been scheduled three times for publication and was withdrawn just before deadline on each occasion.

Finally, I received a brief note written on *Time* stationery, dated February 20, 1978, returning my twenty slides, thanking me for my help, and saying—without explanation—the story had been killed.

THE HIDDEN POWER BEHIND MEDIA

This, and similar situations over the past eight years, told a great deal about news media's control by the advertising industry. It should be relatively simple for an organization with the resources of *Time* or *Newsweek* to prove conclusively, once and for all, whether I am right or wrong. Such conclusive proof, one way or the other, might permit everyone involved to get a good night's sleep. In either case, it would make a first-class news story.

There is obviously a great deal of money, public confidence, and power threatened by my research and writing. These subliminal manipulation techniques, frighteningly, involve even worldwide human survival probabilities over the next few decades. If individuals can be so easily controlled and manipulated, indeed, this is a most dangerous world. This public scandal is of far greater significance than Watergate or oil company greed.

If anyone is ever to act in behalf of the U.S. public against advertiser control over media, it probably will be one of government's so-called Federal regulatory agencies, but only after someone finds a way to make them do what they are already supposed to do under the laws of the land, as will be explored in Chapter 9. I do not easily advocate placing media control in the self-serving hands of government bureaucrats; but, at this moment, at least, there just does not seem to be anyone else available. Commerce, industry, and media are so deeply involved in the media rip-off that they certainly could not be further trusted to manage U.S. media in the public interest.

The FCC's public image, sustained by both advertisers and the media, is that of a guardian angel, protecting citizens from the avaricious broadcasters and advertisers. Nothing could be further from the truth. With the notable exception of a small group of individuals who include Newton Minnow and Nick Johnson, the FCC and its staff have spent most of the past couple of decades—and our money—working in behalf of broadcast industry profits, very rarely representing the average consumer.

THE FLASHER IN THE ICE CUBE

My most exasperating and unsettling media confrontation occurred, however, with my own publisher—The New American Library. It emphasized again that nothing media related can ever be taken at face value, for granted, or safely ignored. Several months after *Subliminal Seduction* appeared as a Signet paperback, a student questioned me about the book's cover. He claimed there was something profoundly troubling about the martini-on-the-rocks-with-a-twist pictured on the cover and the question printed in red letters, "ARE YOU BEING SEXUALLY AROUSED BY THIS PICTURE?" He felt the martini was "a little too real to be real."

I studied the cover photograph for a moment (see Figure 38), concluding that the drink with its ice and lemon peel was much like any other martini. I assured the troubled young man there was nothing to fear. Signet was a highly respected paperback publisher, a subsidiary of the Los Angeles-based Times-Mirror Corporation, a large communications conglomerate. Certainly they would not resort to subliminal trickery to sell a book that exposed advertising agencies' perceptual skullduggery. I hoped to restore the student's confidence in at least one small portion of the mass communication industry. To think that a photograph of a martini on a book cover could sexually arouse anyone was absurd.

Several days later, while relaxing after dinner with a martini-on-the-rocks-with-a-twist, I again thought of the student's comments. Signet had not discussed the cover with me before publication, but authors are rarely consulted on jackets and covers. Still, it was curious. Why a martini? The book pointedly attacked the alcoholic beverage industry for using subliminal advertising that can hypnotically induce individuals into addictive syndromes. Logically, it just didn't make sense. Why would a martini be used as a device to sell my book?

As we have seen, one of the more common subliminal techniques is to hide various taboo or obscene images in paintings or retouched photographs. These images are repressed by viewers, not consciously perceived, but instantly registered at the unconscious level. The next time you look at an advertisement or illustration, study such design elements as clouds, water, waterfalls, ice cubes, mountains, or any portion of the work that appears diffused, unnatural, or unreal—that is, if you can still determine what *is* real.

Book advertisements, jackets, and covers, today include some of the most ingenious subliminal artwork ever created. The consciously perceived message is often banality in its purest form, but the hidden message, designed for the subliminal perception, may be exquisite. The name of the game, of course, is sales. Books are merchandised with an intensity and technical skill not at all unlike that used to sell soap, deodorants, cosmetics, booze, hygiene products, laxatives, politicians, and the rest of what is sold and bought in America—which includes just about everything.

As I relaxed with my martini one evening after dinner, I began to look carefully into the murky depths of the Signet martini. Now, several years later, I have still not completely recovered from the shock. Once again, before reading further, carefully scrutinize Figure 38 for anything the average bartender would not put into a martini-on-the-rocks-with-a-twist.

Standing boldly in the center of the glass on top of the lemon peel is the figure of a man about one-half inch high on the actual cover. He wears a hat, an overcoat pulled back, and is exposing his erect genital. As time passed, my students referred to him—with affectionate humor I always hoped—as "Flasher" (see Figure 39).

Above Flasher on the ice cube appears the face of an older woman (see Figure 40), her mouth open, finger pointing as though she were scolding someone. If your grasp on reality is steady enough to permit you to perceive a story line within a paperback cover martini, the ice cube portrait could be Flasher's mother, perhaps scolding her naughty little boy.

To complete the family circle, in the lower right-hand corner of the glass appears another face—bald head, moustache, eyes peering darkly out of the shadows at the bottom of the glass. Dad, relegated as usual, to an insignificant role in family life, is in the dregs at the bottom of the martini.

Just beneath the lemon peel, slightly to the right of Flasher, appears the letter "X," about one quarter inch high. Slightly to the left of Flasher, below the peel, is another larger though crudely drawn letter, an "S" roughly three quarter inches high. Distorted markings appear between the two letters "S" and "X," which the brain will read unconsciously from six feet away (as it appears on a bookstore shelf) as SEX. A smaller "S" also appears just beneath the letter "X," followed by a very light "E" and "X."

A final, subtle, detail involves a lightly etched oral-genital situation occurring in midglass. This more exotic example of subliminal art may be consciously available only to the more advanced student of merchandising art.

One of the more sophisticated perceptual strategies painted into the martini glass I have saved for Chapter 11. "The Anamorphic Tiger." Pictures are worth thousands of words, but only if you can perceive around your repressions.

THE "MARTINI BOOK"

This Signet cover has had peculiar effects upon people, even those who did not purchase or read the book. Many distinctly recall the martini on the cover, even though they cannot remember the title or author's name. I am often identified as an author by "Yeah, I remember, you wrote the book with the martini on the cover?" What really hurt were the doubts created in my mind: did the book sell well because of the text, over which I had labored two years, or because of the subliminal content within the cover? Had the fine Madison

Avenue hand of the alcoholic beverage advertisers infiltrated the Signet art department, who had slyly turned the book into an insidious appeal to popularize martinis? I recall how, after years of loyalty to vodka Bloody Marys, I had inexplicably switched to martinis-on-the-rocks-with-a-twist about the time the book was published in paperback.

Or, on the other hand, had some ingenious market researcher discovered that my books appealed strongly to flashers? Could all those millions of socially concerned individuals who bought the paperback be secret genital exhibitionists?

There is one other disconcerting possibility for an author who likes to think he performed a public service by exposing the devious wiles of Madison Avenue. Perhaps the artist was making fun of me. I had exposed his beloved advertising industry, and to get even, the artist subliminally portrayed the author as a maternally dominated dickie waver.

BRIGHT LITTLE PACKAGES OF DUZ

After my discovery of the Signet martini, I began to study other book jackets and covers. The most sophisticated subliminal art usually appeared on paperbacks. Many of the top paperback art directors, it turned out, learned their craft in advertising agencies. While reviews still sell hard-cover books, it is the cover that sells paperbacks. Vice President and Art Director James Plumari of New American Library said, "I think of these [the books] as bright little packages of Duz soap out there on the supermarket shelves."

To this day, Signet's art director claims all he did was put a martini on a table and take a picture of it. Shortly after an article I wrote on the *Subliminal Seduction* cover appeared in the *Book World* section of the Sunday *Washington Post* (September 18, 1977), the *Post* published the following exchange of notes between Plumeri and myself.

> Dear Dr. Key:
> I am shocked that you, the expert on subliminal art, missed the images completely in the cover art of our Signet paperback edition of your book. Why not read more closely the images in that martini glass you claim I worked on so cleverly?
> The flasher, as you and your students affectionately

call him, is not a man at all, but a woman—you sexist! Although you label the coat *she's* wearing "just any coat," I'll have you know it's a specially designed Calvin Klein. The hat is by Adolpho.

Now let's talk about the older woman image to which you refer. Shame on you. For such an experienced person in the art of subliminals, you certainly missed this one. It isn't an old woman with her mouth open, finger pointing in a scolding pose. Not at all. It is a *man, not a woman*, a midget to be exact, wiping his mouth with an extended finger showing off his newly acquired pinky ring containing two round diamond stones surrounding a long sapphire.

And, Dr. Key, the mustachioed man you assume to be "Dad" is really The Flasher's dog, Barf, a rare species occasionally spotted on the asphalt wilds of Madison Avenue.

Look again, Dr. Key. The "S X" below the lemon peel does not suggest the word "sex." The "S X" represents our photographer's (Sam Xavier) initials. He always tries to sneak them in whenever he can. . . .

Indeed, Dr. Key, as I've told you before, we simply photographed a martini glass with *no* "subliminal retouching." In this case, "subliminal seduction," like beauty, is to be found only in the eyes of the beholder. Besides, I'd never get any paperback book covers done if I spent all my time retouching photographs.

Sincerely yours,

Jim Plumeri,
An Exasperated Man,
Vice President and Art Director,
New American Library

Dear Exasperated Plumeri:

Your letter is a vivid and touching example of what can happen to anyone who hangs around Madison Avenue too long. Flasher is wearing, clearly, neither Bonwit Teller nor Saks. The coat and hat are distinctly GI issue, probably out of the WWII surplus now surfacing in the Iron Curtain countries. And, anyone who mistakes the subliminal man on the lemon peel for a woman should be designing record album covers for Alice Cooper and David Bowie.

With both *con*fidence and *sin*cerity,

Bill Key,
President and Director of Fantasy Analysis,
Mediaprobe, Inc.

THE HARD-SELL LION

Hard-cover book publishers occasionally indulge in sophisticated subliminal book jacket art, but this is rare. Expensive art work of any sort is still considered a frivolous investment by many publishers. One superb example appeared on Robert Ardrey's most excellent book *The Social Contract* (Figure 41). The book jacket was designed for the Atheneum Publishing House. Subliminal merchandising art usually involves content about sex, the origin of life, and the end of life or death in some taboo manifestation. The unconscious appears highly sensitized to anything dealing with these two polarities of human existence.

A small horse—an animal considered with much affection in America—is placed within the lion's mouth. The horse is dead, of course, as the predator's teeth have penetrated its body. By now, alert readers may have consciously noticed the lower jaw of the lion, *an erect, black, male* genital, perhaps subliminally symbolizing Ardrey's thesis that man originated in Central Africa. The lion's left jaw closely resembles a female genital.

On the jacket's back plate are painted numerous deer. You can easily observe the dark, large male deer about to jump on the little female deer. It is easy to perceive what is going on in these pictures when someone tells you about it, but repressed content is rarely recognized consciously by consumers shopping in bookstores. Indeed, if you know what to look for, jackets are sometimes far more interesting than the books they cover.

My hard-cover publisher, Prentice-Hall, appears to take great pride in book jackets not designed to attract book buyers by subliminal means. This at least gives the author the illusion that his book is selling because of its content, not because of devious art work. As an author, however, I think I would rather have the money.

9 ⋅ THE REGULATION OF DECEPTION_____

> *We are well along on the Icien road*
> *where man must not only not believe or trust*
> *or love or hope, but must not think.*
> *Good government regards those with minds*
> *and the will to express themselves as a*
> *nuisance, to be destroyed if they cannot be*
> *made to conform. They have replaced*
> *human society with a mere survival system*
> *that does not take human emotion into*
> *account.*
>
> Colin M. Turnbull,
> *The Mountain People*

THE UNCONSCIOUS WAS TO BE MANAGED, NOT TALKED ABOUT

The notion that people may be affected by stimuli of which they are not consciously aware could have begun around 400 B.C. with Democritus, Plato, and Aristotle. Each described in his writings how small, unnoticed perceptions appeared to affect behavior. Over the centuries, these "small, unnoticed perceptions" resurfaced in the writings of such philosophers as Montaigne and Leibniz. Many of the late nineteenth century physicians and philosophers—Schopenhauer, Nietzsche, Freud, Jung, Rorschach, etc.—were preoccupied with the phenomena. But with the ascendancy in the United States of behaviorism and experimental psychology, through the 1950's, 1960's, and 1970's, concern over unconsciously perceived information became increasingly dormant.

Vance Packard's widely read 1957 book *The Hidden Persuaders* revealed American industry's research into the use of subliminal stimuli for marketing objectives. As a result of Packard's book, six state legislatures and the U.S. House of Representatives considered legislative action to ban subliminal techniques. By the early 1960's, however, public discussion on the subject virtually disappeared; the proposed legislation was never enacted.

During a brief period during the late 1950's, several broadcasters and numerous ad agencies openly offered subliminal techniques to their advertisers. But media industries backed off in the face of hostile public attacks. Almost universally, the media denounced substimuli as a violation of the public trust, un-American, and highly immoral. Numerous public demonstrations of subliminal technique were staged. Quite predictably all failed to demonstrate the effectiveness of substimuli.

Subliminal advertising surfaced as a national issue during the fall of 1957. The FCC had numerous inquiries about subliminals from the TV networks: from WTWO, a Maine station that had experimented with subliminals; from the TV Code Board of the National Association of Radio-TV Broadcasters (NAB); and from two leading commercial exponents of subliminal technique. The NAB requested its members to submit "any proposals to use TV in the process called subliminal perception," (NAB release, January 23, 1958).

ANOTHER NEVER-COMPLETED STUDY

In response to a letter from Senator Charles Potter (October 24, 1957), the FCC detailed a possible basis for regulatory authority over subliminal broadcast techniques. They stated that in addition to the Communication Act, the FCC had rule-making authority under Section 303, subparagraphs a, b, and c. However, this authority has never been invoked to this day on any matter even vaguely related to subliminal broadcasting.

A curious *Memo on Subliminal Advertising* from the NAB (November 6, 1957) recognized the federal government would eventually be interested in subliminals. The memo discussed research effectiveness and industry implications, noting "the very serious possible public reaction to subliminal advertising." The memo also considered the possibility of prior broadcast announcements informing audiences that subliminals would be used and the need for monitoring equipment to detect subcontent, concluding "the industry should anticipate these contingencies and devise a systematic policy to deal with them." Unlike the FCC and FTC, the NAB appeared fully aware of the profit potential in subliminal broadcast techniques.

Congressman William L. Dawson of Illinois urged the FCC to request networks and stations not to use subliminals until a study was completed. This study was never initiated, however. On November 27, 1957, the FCC wrote Representative Dawson that such a warning would be inappropriate, though the FCC did then issue a public notice stating that "caution in using the new technique would evidence proper regard for the public interest" [FCC Public Notice, 57-1289 (1957)].

In May 1958 the NAB TV Code was revised to ban subliminal projection: "Any technique whereby an attempt is made to convey information to the viewer by transmitting messages below the threshold of normal awareness is not permitted." This NAB Code, of course, has no legal significance whatsoever. Individual broadcast stations are supposed to review ads in relation to the NAB Code. However, only slightly over half of U.S. commercial TV stations are NAB members. Code violations may lead to warnings, suspensions, hearings, or revocation of memberships, but rarely do. The NAB is little more than a public relations agency for the industry.

MYTHOLOGY OF SELF-REGULATION

The myth of industry self-regulation is worth looking into. Ad agencies create and produce most television and radio advertising, though a small proportion of the total—usually locally sponsored ads—are produced by stations themselves. Ad agency internal production controls may include legal staff opinions, client approval at various production stages, and advice from industry and regulatory agencies, such as FCC, FTC, FDA, ICA, and BATF (Treasury).

Broadcasting networks screen scripts and review some ads at normal audio and video speeds. Certain ads, such as those directed at children or pushing drug products, are reviewed somewhat more carefully. These reviews (and I have personally participated in many) are made not in terms of what you cannot or should not do, but in terms of what you can get away with. Infrequently, public pressures may make an ad agency back off and develop an alternate approach, but the game is played primarily in terms of not making waves. After all, sales effectiveness is the real issue to which ad agencies are ultimately accountable.

Infrequently and ineffectively, the National Advertising Division (NAD) of the Council of Better Business Bureaus reviews national advertising and offers "guidance" for ad agencies and clients. The group has, on rare occasions, responded to specific complaints as to the "truth and accuracy" of ad claims. To handle complaints the NAD cannot resolve, a National Advertising Review Board (NARB) composed of advertiser, agency, and public representatives appoints a five-member panel.

Supposedly, the self-regulatory framework prevents deceptive and excessively offensive advertising, but the machinery was designed to work in support of industry, not consumer, interests. When the NARB was first established, a regulatory framework similar to that used in Great Britain was proposed, but this involved an agreement not to use ads that were found unacceptable. The NARB unanimously rejected the British model.

The NARB's very superficial analysis involves only supraliminal ad content—what is consciously and obviously perceived—only the tip of the iceberg. While the Code formally prohibits substimuli, the NARB has never looked for them and is unlikely ever to do so without specific, enforceable, legislative imperatives.

As one advertising agency spokesman commented, "Agencies don't get paid for sticking to principles. If a company wants to go haywire in its claims, the agency either goes along or loses the account. Agencies need the moral crutch of Uncle Sam's regulations to resist the pressure of clients in this Darwinian jungle." (Howard and Hulbert, 1973, p. 61.)

Government regulatory agencies have played an extremely passive role in enforcing advertising standards. Both advertisers and agencies have strongly opposed meaningful intervention of any sort—either public or private.

During early 1958, bills were introduced into the House of Representatives to make unlawful the use of subliminal advertising (HR 10802 and 11363, Representatives Wright and Hosmer). Reintroduced the following year by Representative Wright (HR 1998), the anti-subliminal bill was again shelved in committee. The bills provided fines, imprisonment, and other penalties for violators.

In 1962 the FCC received numerous complaints after the program *To Tell the Truth* announced that subliminal ads were inserted during the program's credits. The announcement turned out to be a hoax, and CBS reported it had acted to prevent a recurrence of such references.

CONVENTIONAL WISDOMS RULED THE HEARINGS

Ten years later, in 1971, the FTC conducted hearings on "modern advertising practices," presumably as defined by the ad industry (Howard and Hulbert, 1973). The report's treatment of the subliminal issue was excluded in a classic example of intentional naiveté. The report defined *information* as "awareness of some event in the environment" and reflected the conventional ad agency stance that "the consumer almost never, if ever, takes in useless information"—a mis-statement that casually sidestepped at least a century of psychological theory, experimental evidence, and clinical practice.

The subliminal issue was described in the report as an "unfortunate folk myth," a product of popular speculation! One ad executive who testified at the hearing later laughingly described to me industry testimony as "A sympozium of conventional wisdoms. Everyone told everyone pretty much what everyone wanted to hear and believe. A few of us were worried some bright young FTC hustler might ask a few sophisticated questions. No one ever did. Our industry presentations were very well rehearsed and the responses were predictable."

The FCC Report depicts the consumer as "aware of everything he perceives and unaffected by that which he does not consciously perceive"—a picture of the human perceptual system quite in opposition to that presented in most elementary psychology texts. Strangely, the authors of that report clearly appreciated the importance of "impact advertising" and offer lengthy discussions of optical manipulation, editing, lighting effects, fast- and slow-motion techniques, animation, and music—specifically in the context of techniques *not* consciously perceived by consumers.

NONCOMMERCIAL SUBS AUTHORIZED

An FCC *Information Bulletin on Subliminal Projection*, February 1971, stressed that Section 317 of the Communications Act would effectively prohibit unidentified commercial sponsorship through subliminal techniques. The Bulletin noted, however, that FCC rules made "no provision . . . for the announcement of purely sustaining program material," which was apparently exempted from the subliminal projection definition. The Bulletin actually *authorizes* the use of noncommercial subliminals in program content preceding and following commercials.

After a period of extremely effective lobby effort, the subliminal issue was locked up in Congressional committees, sidetracked into the generally ineffective FCC, and left to be managed by an industry-controlled NAB. Most people believed a law had been passed to prohibit subliminal projection. The entire issue lay dormant until Christmas 1973, when both the FCC and FTC received complaints about a TV commercial for Husker-Do, a children's game, which contained four tachistoscopic displays urging viewers to "Get it!"

The NAB Code Authority had learned of the toy commercial in late November and had received assurances from the ad agency responsible, Low & Associates, Inc., that telegrams had been sent to all stations, authorizing them to cut the frames with subliminal content out of the ad. Many stations, however, continued to broadcast the uncut commercial, some later denying they had received the telegram. Low & Associates explained that although it had "advised against this procedure on the general grounds that such practices were not acceptable, our client insisted and the single frame cuts were included." (Letter from Low & Assoc. to Lloyd Francis, M.P., House of Commons, Ottawa, Oct. 10, 1974.)

After Christmas, of course, the commercial was no longer in use. On January 24, 1974, the FCC distributed a public notice to all broadcasters: "Broadcast of Information by Means of Subliminal Perception" (FCC 74-78, 29RR 22 395). The notice reviewed FCC policy on subliminals, mentioned the Husker-Do case, and stated, "We believe that use of subliminal perception is not consistent with the obligations of a licensee, and therefore we take this occasion to make clear that broadcasts employing such techniques are contrary to the public interest. Whether effective or not, such broadcasts are intended to be deceptive."

THE INFALLIBLE SYSTEM

During January 1974, I wrote the FCC, requesting their policy on subliminal techniques in broadcasting. My letter was answered by William Ray, Chief, Complaints and Compliance Division—the citizen-handling department within this federal bureaucracy. Ray cited Section 5 of the FTC Act which "prohibits unfair or deceptive acts or practices in interstate commerce," and explained the FTC "had primary responsibility for regulation of advertising in this country."

However, he wrote, "this commission has stated repeatedly it expects its licensees, as part of their obligation to serve the public interest, convenience, and necessity, to exercise reasonable diligence to prevent use of their licensed facilities for false and deceptive advertising." Ray also cited Section 326 of the 1934 Communication Act, which prohibits the FCC "from exercising censorship over any broadcast matter." A strange letter: the FCC expects its licensees not to deceive the public, but cannot itself investigate or censure deceptive or false advertising.

Ray further explained the FCC "looks to the FTC which has primary responsibility and special expertise in this field to determine whether an advertisement is false, deceptive, or otherwise contrary to federal law." Ray requested I report to the FCC any instances where subliminal techniques had been used in broadcasting.

I immediately sent Mr. Ray a copy of *Subliminal Seduction* and wrote him (on February 9) a detailed description of subliminal technique—the Liquid Plumber ad (*Media Sexploitation*, pp. 71–73), a large group of TV ads for Shell, Chevrolet, *NBC Nightly News*, and other examples. I offered to send the FCC slide photographs of the individual video-taped frames in which the subs appeared.

No answer.

PASSING THE BUCK

I again wrote Mr. Ray on March 20, requesting he answer my February 9 letter. Finally, four months later (June 3), Ray's brief note again reminded me the FTC had primary responsibility to determine whether an ad is contrary to federal law.

I also wrote the FCC (August 30, 1976) with a research proposal to investigate the extent of subliminals in U.S. broadcast advertising. In a brief reply returning my proposal a Kenneth Gordon cited the catechism that the FCC has held "the use of subliminal technique is inconsistent with the obligations of a licensee and has made it clear broadcasts employing such techniques are contrary to the public interest, and that whether effective or not, the broadcasts are clearly intended to be deceptive."

Gordon cited Section 326 "which prohibits the FCC from censoring broadcast matter or any act which interferes with speech freedom by broadcasting." Again, I was referred to the FTC.

I began to appreciate how so many FCC commissioners and staff members qualified for high-paying broadcast industry jobs after they left the government. The FCC is on record as prohibiting subliminal techniques in broadcasting, but unfortunately cannot enter into an investigation because that would conflict with freedom of broadcasting—a position presumably backed up by the First Amendment. They then pass the buck to the FTC. I recall the old adage that it takes a considerable intelligence to appear convincingly stupid.

PATIENCE APPRECIATED

On September 20 I again wrote to Mr. Gordon, citing in a formal complaint two radio examples of subliminal technique: a California bank commercial that employed a low-volume voice track under the announcer's voice, and a widely broadcast rock-music recording—"Hooked on a Feeling," by a rock group called Blue Swede which has an obscenity embedded in the background chant (*Media Sexploitation,* pp. 117–18). (I have met five disk jockeys who were fired when they discussed this obscenity and demonstrated it on the air.)

Again, no answer.

I finally wrote Mr. Gordon, November 15, requesting an answer to my earlier letter. He replied a month later, stating that my complaint had been forwarded to the Chief of their Broadcast Bureau. "Your patience in this matter is appreciated," he concluded.

I damned well hope so! An entire year of communication with the FCC was a total waste of time and postage. I am still waiting—not so patiently anymore—for an answer to my letter of September 20, 1974.

THE FTC'S EXCUSE

My first contact with the Federal Trade Commission was in a March 20, 1974, letter to their Bureau of Deceptive Practices. I outlined some of the material in my books and requested their reaction. On May 9 I received a brief, polite reply, advising me the matter was under consideration by the FTC staff. On May 17 I again wrote the FTC, reminding them I had posed several specific questions in my March 20 letter on the use of subliminal advertising techniques in interstate commerce. Finally, four months after my inquiry (July 19), I received a letter from Bruce J. Parker, an attorney in their Division of National Advertising.

Parker advised me that "subliminal technique is not specifically prohibited or otherwise covered under any Federal or State laws"—an interesting comment when considered against the Wheeler-Lea Amendments to the Federal Trade Commission Act: "Unfair and deceptive acts or practices in commerce are declared unlawful" [Section 5, Federal Trade Commission Act, 15, U.S.C., 45 (a) (1) (1970)].

Interpretations of this law have established that unfairness to the consumer is in itself a violation, regardless of the practice's effect upon commerce [*FTC* v. *Sperry and Hutchinson Company*, 405 U.S. 233 (1972)]. Section 5 of the FTC Act, it was held, is intended "to protect the trusting as well as the suspicious [*FTC* v. *Standard Education Society*, 302 U.S. 112, 116 (1937)] as well as "the ignorant, the unthinking, and the credulous" [*Aronborg* v. *FTC*, 132 F.2d 165, 167 (7th Cir. 1974)]. These descriptions certainly describe the manipulated consumer who has been educated in behalf of the media.

In another decision, audience vulnerability is considered: "The mental condition of the audience . . . is an element to be considered in arriving at which construction might reasonably be put upon the advertisement [Doris Savitch, 50 FTC 823, 834 (1954)], [*aff'd per curiam*, 218 F.2d 817 (2d Cir., 1955)]. Were the FTC to seriously represent the consumer, they might well look into the "mental condition" of the U.S.'s 12 million alcoholics and the effects of the $800 million worth of subliminal alcoholic beverage advertising pumped into their brain systems during 1978.

DEFINITIONS OF DECEPTION

In a similar situation, the FTC examined "distinctive characteristics" that render consumers unable to protect themselves by careful inquiry or to exercise their normal care or business judgments [Funeral Industry Practices, Trade Regulation Proceedings, 40 Red. Reg. 39904 (1975)]. By the FTC definition, deceptive advertising "undercut[s] the consumer's normal judgment faculties." Subliminal ads that contain sufficiently "dangerous" emotional content actually generate psychological vulnerability.

The FTC has also described the factors [*FTC* v. *Sperry and Hutchinson Company*, 405 U.S. at 244] it considered in determining whether a practice that is neither in violation of antitrust laws nor deceptive is nevertheless unfair: whether the practice, without necessarily having been previously considered unlawful, offends public policy as it has been established by statutes, the common law, or otherwise—whether, in other words, it is within at least the penumbra of some established concept of unfairness.

The FTC is empowered to scrutinize advertisements for deception and unfairness at an *implicit* as well as *express* level. Not only is the literal truthfulness of a claim to be assessed, but also "all of the implications, innuendos, and suggestions which are conveyed in the advertising message" [Rodale Press, 71 FTC 1184, 1271 1967, vacated on other grounds and remanded, 407, F.2d 1252 (D.C. Cir 1968)].

Indeed, the judicial history of the Wheeler-Lea Amendment shows concern for advertiser exploitation of audience vulnerability. "We cannot ignore the evils and abuses of advertising; the imposition upon the unsuspecting; and the downright criminality of preying upon the sick as well as the consuming public through fraudulent, false, or subtle misleading advertisements" [HR Rep. No. 1613, 75th Cong., 1st Sess. (1937)].

VIOLATIONS OF FEDERAL LAW

All the advertisements presented in my three books on subliminal advertising and communication appear to be viola-

tions per se of federal legislation. As these ads were utilized in interstate commerce, they clearly qualify for judicial sanctions under the FTC Act.

Parker's letter, however, went on to explain subliminal technique "was considered more of a 'gimmick' as opposed to having any real potential for useful application to commercial advertising." He then alluded to the difficulty in defining *subliminal*, a problem which was done very nicely by the Canadian Radio-TV Commission (discussed later).

Parker reported that the FTC staff's interest was focused upon commercial advertising where a "tachistoscopic message is projected"—fascinating information! The FTC has limited its consideration of subliminals to the simplistic use of tachistoscopic technique. In 1969 a Coca-Cola research executive told me tachistoscopic displays had been obsolete for over a decade in advertising. He described to me several subliminal embedding techniques (including low-intensity light) that were far superior to the tachistoscope and much more difficult to detect.

In short, the FTC could, if it were doing its job, assert authority to prohibit subliminal manipulation from several perspectives: (1) manipulation of vulnerable aspects of consumer mentality; (2) violation of public policy as enunciated by the FCC Public Notice that "subliminal techniques are contrary to the public interest"; (3) employment of a technique held deceptive in itself.

A FOLLOW-UP TO THE FOLLOW-UP
TO THE FOLLOW-UP

On September 9, 1976, I proposed a research project on subliminal advertising to the FTC to determine in a legal context how widespread the use of subs was in U.S. broadcast media. It was a modest proposal, utilizing only five researchers over a one-year period. My letter was not answered.

I wrote a follow-up letter (November 15) requesting that my September 9th letter be at least acknowledged. Again no answer. Finally, by telephone, I obtained a December 14, 1976, appointment to present a large variety of subliminal advertisement examples to the FTC. I paid my own expenses to Washington for the meeting, arranged by a Richard B. Herzog, Assistant Director for National Advertising. My two-hour presentation was attended by only a half dozen young attorneys on Herzog's staff, who listened attentively though noncommittedly. I was surprised: usually my presentations are followed by at least a two-hour question-and-answer session. The small group appeared friendly, but extremely uncommunicative. Herzog did, however, invite me to submit a brief outline on a method to study subliminal ads as the basis for further research.

On December 16 I wrote Herzog, briefly outlining the research procedure. Like the earlier ones, this letter went unanswered. As so many have discovered before me, federal regulatory agencies are far more interested in industry's problems and in avoiding controversy than in consumers, citizens, and politically unpopular questions. How do you get Civil Service employees to do the job for which they are paid? The game goes on and on, according to the script written by the ad industry and performed by obedient federal regulatory agencies.

One FTC attorney commented privately that they had sent one subliminal (the ad for Johnny Walker Scotch, Figure 6) back to the agency that created the ingenious ice cubes, requesting an explanation. An agency executive replied that "they couldn't figure out what he was talking about."

"So," the attorney said in exasperation, "what do we do now?"

What he does now, if he is really interested in finding out about the Johnny Walker ad, is take a sworn deposition from the artist, the creative and research directors, the agency's president, executive vice president, and anyone else involved with the ad—a relatively simple and inexpensive procedure which both the FTC and FCC are empowered to utilize. Presidents, executive vice presidents, and creative directors should know what their staffs are doing and how their client's money is being spent. Certainly no one in the industry I ever met would chance a prison sentence by lying under oath. It should be very simple—*if anyone really wanted to find out.*

The FTC clearly has the authority to suppress the use of subliminal techniques as an unfair (deceptive) commercial practice. The FCC could utilize its rule-making authority but has relied upon its 1974 Public Notice to Licensees, deferring questions on enforcement back to the FTC, which in turn defers questions back to the FCC or to the industry organizations—an incredibly well-organized system that assures no one ever does anything of significance, especially institute an active investigation to publicly explore subliminal techniques. They also resolutely continue to ignore a sizeable quantity of published research available on the subject of subliminal effects. Federal agencies have not exerted pressure of any sort on the subliminal issue, except perhaps in what I assume are inept, amateuristic, and incompetent efforts such as their response to the *Husker-Do* commercial. In short, the communication industry stance on subliminal communication appropriately has been, simply, *Don't Get Caught!*

ELSEWHERE ON THE PLANET

Reluctance to deal with subliminals is not uniform among other nations. In 1972, Belgian legislators designated subliminal techniques as an *invasion of privacy*. Anyone convicted would be punished by one year in prison and a 1,000 to 10,-000-franc fine, penalties applied to "anyone who by any means whatever projects images or sensations which, though not consciously perceived, are capable of influencing behavior" (Draft Legislation, January 26, 1972).

In Great Britain, subliminal messages of any kind are explicitly banned by the Television Act, 1964, Section 3. The Independent Television Authority (ITA), the government agency that supervises commercial TV, is given responsibility to ascertain that broadcasts do not include "any technical device which, by using images of very brief duration, or by any other means, exploits the possibility of conveying a message to, or otherwise influencing the minds of, members of the audience without their being aware, or fully aware, of what has been done."

The BBC is also specifically prohibited from using subliminals. Britain's ITA reviews over 8,000 scripts annually, rejecting about 15 percent. They also view all finished ads before broadcast, passing on their accuracy and overall cultural acceptability. But curiously, British *print* ads are as saturated with subliminals as those in the United States. So far, at least, the government has avoided a confrontation with newspapers, magazines, billboards, and so on.

THE ONLY LAW ENACTED

Lloyd Francis (MP for Ottawa West), a member of the Canadian Parliament, submitted three bills that would have comprehensively banned subliminal techniques from the nation's broadcasts: Bill C-333, to provide substantial penal sanctions for commercially motivated violators who utilized subliminal and similar ad techniques; Bill C-276, to establish a Canadian Advertising Council, a mixed-constituency monitoring group; and Bill C-314, to amend the Broadcasting Act to prohibit the transmission of subliminals.

Introduced October 15, 1974, for the first reading, the three bills were in response to the Husker-Do "Get It!" episode, which had also triggered the FCC inquiry in the United States, as well as to a growing public response to *Subliminal Seduction*, widely read throughout Canada at the time.

Industry response to the proposed legislation was subtle but well organized, reminiscent of the earlier industry response in the United States. Direct confrontation with legislators on the issue was carefully avoided, but, one ad executive in Montreal told me privately, "They really hit the panic button on this one!" In public all appeared serene and confident, but never in a quarter century had he observed such a frightened industry-wide reaction: "The ad agencies couldn't have been more scared if the Prime Minister had decided to nationalize them."

Officially, Canada's National Association of Advertising Agencies stated in a letter to MP Lloyd Francis that if his proposed legislation was the will of the Parliament, the industry would not oppose the issue. This was a carefully conceived strategy: industry acceptance made it impossible for investigative hearings to be conducted. As there was no opposition to the proposed legislation, even depositions could not be justified.

Privately, however, the ad industry moved forcefully to have the legislation withdrawn—as it eventually was. This was an issue neither the ad industry, nor media, nor government wanted aired in public. Nor, as it turned out, did the university where I was employed as a Professor—which appeared to be under pressure from almost everyone.

ANOTHER REGULATORY LOOPHOLE
CUSTOM DESIGNED

The Canadian Radio-Television Commission (CRTC) is similar to the FCC and equally as ineffective. On June 27, 1975, the CRTC came to the ad industry's rescue by issuing an Amendment to the Television Broadcasting Regulations—which are not in themselves laws but could become judicial precedents after a successful prosecution against a violator. These simple regulatory directives function more in the interest of the industry (as in the United States) than on behalf of consumers, and are addressed only to broadcasters, totally ignoring ad agencies and production houses.

The CRTC Amendment stated:

9.1 (1) No station or network operator shall knowingly broadcast any advertising material that makes use of any subliminal device.

(2) In subsection (1), "subliminal device" means a technical device that is used to convey or attempt to convey a message to a person by means of images or sounds of very brief duration or by any other means without that person being aware that such a device is being used or being aware of the substance of the message being conveyed or attempted to be conveyed.

The definition of "subliminal device" in paragraph 2 was well written and could serve as a model for other nations. Paragraph 1, however, was a Machiavellian masterpiece.

The Amendment's initial draft had said simply, "No station or network operator *shall broadcast* any advertising material that makes use of any subliminal device." In response to heavy complaints from the ad industry, an alternative wording was suggested that required knowledgeable action. "Shall *knowingly* broadcast" was inserted into the amendment, thus deftly making the CRTC amendment unenforceable.

The ad industry representatives involved must have known that in 1943, the U.S. Supreme Court observed "as a practical matter, the licensee cannot determine in advance whether the broadcasting of any particular network program would or would not be in the public interest" [*NBC* v. *U.S.*, 319US

190, 205, 1943]; that is, it is impossible for a court to know what anyone *knowingly* or even *unknowingly* broadcasts.

Consider what the public response would be if a law were written, "Anyone who *knowingly* commits homicide. . . ." But, for all practical purposes, the issue was closed. Industry representatives went back to Parliament, stating that as the CRTC regulation protected the public, the three proposed bills were now unnecessary.

At the time, another Canadian ad executive cynically asked me, "Who can conceivably complain, now that the public interest is protected by the CRTC?"

The Canadian Advertising Standards Council (an industry-controlled public relations group) administers the "voluntary" code of ethics for Canadian advertisers. In a curious action, one year after publication of *Subliminal Seduction*, the Council, in response to growing concern over the subliminal issue among civil libertarians, parliamentarians, and public groups, very quietly included a new provision in the code which "prohibited subliminal advertising techniques in children's advertising."

This was a roundabout admission that such techniques *were* feasible, but no one should worry: children's advertising would be protected! These codes of ethics, dozens of which relate to the communications industry, are fascinating documents to study. They constitute a virtual inventory of what's going on in any respective industry, though under the table and disguised under different labels. Anyone curious about the grimmer realities of commercial communication can simply interpret the codes inversely.

SUBLIMINAL EDUCATION FOR DISASTER

The Council of Europe's Consultative Assembly included "subliminal advertising and propaganda" among techniques inconsistent with the rights and freedoms of individuals, recommending a study on the adequacy of current legislation among member nations [Texts Adopted, 18–19 (1966–68), Recommendation 509].

In 1974, a task force report signed by Dag Hammarskjold, The United Nations Human Rights Commission recommended that "provisions be adopted which would prohibit the use of subliminal messages in broadcasting and make such use subject to penal sanctions under national laws." (31st

Sess. 7 October 1974, E/CN.4/1142/Add 2). The UN Report attempted to deal with subliminals conveyed by satellite and other broadcasting that crossed national and cultural borders, citing specific examples discovered in television broadcasts and in ultrasonic waves.

The political and cultural implications of subliminal indoctrination was called "a major threat to human rights throughout the world." The report cites the modification or elimination of traditional cultures through substimuli as realistic and technically feasible. For example, anyone with sophisticated broadcast equipment could insert substimuli into any broadcast signal without fear of discovery.

With so many governments knowledgeable about subliminal techniques, it would be foolish to assume the Soviets have not developed a potential in the area. Quite likely they are doing it to us—as we are probably doing it to them. One Israeli intelligence officer asked me simply, "Are they [the Arabs]? And, how do we?" I answered, "Most probably. I assumed you were." A great many governments in the world appear to have someone to whom they want to do it.

A ranking Canadian diplomat confidentially expressed to me his belief that the United States has, for many years, employed subliminal techniques in its *USIA* and *Voice of America* overseas broadcasts. Compared with international media power struggles, the U.S. merchandizing flim flam with substimuli looks like a children's game.

According to Robert Scott, a USIA Deputy Director, Mexico's giant *Televisa* commercial television and radio network refused to accept USIA films or video and audio material for broadcast because of suspected subliminal content. Strangely, Mexico's *Televisa* is known to have experimented extensively with subliminal broadcast techniques as far back as 1959; its problem appears only to be *whose* subliminals are going to be broadcast in Mexico.

Possibly even more important is the continued international scope of U.S. advertising agencies, who control media to a great extent throughout the noncommunist world. Whoever controls the money controls the content. They have exported commercial subliminal media techniques throughout Western Europe, the Far East, and Latin America. The effect of hypnotically programming large populations—especially in economically underdeveloped nations—is already apparent. Consumer advertising media-educates the poor into the acquisitive value systems of the rich, and there is no way for most of the populations in these underdeveloped nations to participate significantly in the never-ending orgy of conspicuous consumption for which they have been subliminally programmed.

Commercial media, therefore, assure an ever-intensifying succession of protests, insurrections, and attempted revolutions, countered by military suppression unfortunately supported by the United States. The United States is today the leading trainer and supplier of internal security forces for Latin American, Far and Middle Eastern, and African dictatorships—which include most of the nations in these areas with close U.S. ties.

10 ♦ THE SECRET OF LINCOLN'S BEARD

> *The almighty dollar,*
> *that great object of universal devotion*
> *throughout our land. . . .*
> Washington Irving

ADVENTURES IN POLITICAL MEDIA

The media are controlled by the ad agencies, who are controlled by their clients, who are controlled by . . . This is the establishment: layers upon layers upon layers of mutually reinforcing power structures.

My first of several encounters with the use of subliminals in political advertising happened during late May 1974. A national Canadian TV network (CTV) invited me to appear on *W-5*, a one-hour special broadcast a few days before the national election. The Prime Minister candidates were Trudeau (Liberal Party incumbent), Stanfield (Progressive-Conservative), and Lewis (Socialist). Over preceding weeks Canada had been inundated by advertising and promotional media supporting the three candidates.

The *W-5* staff and I spent the weekend searching through a small mountain of campaign posters, pamphlets, and circulars from all three political parties. Subliminal embeds of one sort or another were in virtually every piece examined. I selected several from each party's advertising where the engraver had clumsily allowed one or more embedded SEXes to reproduce clearly.

We assembled a mosaic of the examples on a large background screen, using a picture marked to illustrate the SEX next to an unmarked version. The camera would zoom in on the detailed examples during the interview. The ten-minute segment was filmed rather than videotaped so the fine details would more likely reproduce readably on TV screens. The *W-5* staff was ebullient. "When this hits, Wow!" the producer remarked. "This is a national scandal!"

The broadcast was scheduled for 10 P.M. Sunday night and the audience was expected to be about 1.8 million—very large for a Canadian program. My interview on the embedded political posters was the final segment. The SEX embeds reproduced well during the broadcast. On the program, I made serious allegations against the major advertising agencies for all three political parties. In both the United States and Canada, the winning parties or candidates reward their ad agencies with heavy government advertising contracts. During the interview, I had named these agencies and their presidents, inviting these powerful and influential men to explain how the SEX embeds had found their way into the campaign materials. I waited the next day for some reaction.

CTV received heavy mail about the interview. But otherwise, the silence was deafening. As far as I could determine, not a word was ever printed or broadcast anywhere in Canada on the issue I had raised. No Parliamentary investigatory committee or regulatory agency ever looked into the subliminal issue. During this period, nevertheless, several tax-supported multi-million dollar "studies" of the mass media, campaign practices, and information freedom were sponsored by the Canadian Federal Government. None even touched upon the subliminal issue.

Also during 1974, at the request of one of the candidates, I analyzed subliminal content in election campaign promotion materials used in a Congressional election in Arlington, Virginia. One of the embedded posters was later reproduced in *Media Sexploitation*, Figure 3. I discovered extensive subliminal embedding in the posters, pamphlets, and other material of every candidate except the man who had invited my analysis—the only candidate not to use an ad agency.

I presented my findings, along with an hour's lecture on subliminal phenomena, to a Washington, D.C., press conference attended by at least sixty journalists from both electronic and print media. It was a good session, I thought. Most of the journalists clearly perceived the embedded subs, and many appeared sincerely angry that such practices were going on.

When their stories appeared in print the next day, however,

I nearly went into shock. For example, Donna McKevion Hilts, a writer for the *Arlington-Fairfax Journal*, wrote, "Sex Stunt Bombs—Candidates Get Laugh Out of Subliminal Ad Charge." Sheilah Kast of the *Washington Star* termed the press conference, "a bit like a scene from the Emperor's New Clothes, with no one quite willing to admit he did not see the embeddings." The Virginia Globe's full-page editorial quoted my faculty superior at Western Ontario University, Journalism Dean MacFarlane: "If you want to know what I think of the thesis, it's horseshit!"

The Washington area press generally had a field day ridiculing the whole idea. In all fairness, however, several small newspapers and the *Washington Post* ran objective though brief reports of the press conference.

The next day, the candidate who had invited me filed a complaint with the Virginia Fair Campaign Practices Committee on the use of subliminals in political campaign literature. The FCPC refused even to consider the allegation. Most area papers gleefully reported the refusal. The *Washington Post* quoted Samuel Archibald, FCPC Committee Director, as "punning," when he said, "We're going to send [the protesting candidate] a letter acknowledging the complaint about subliminal sex and explain that the committee does not get involved in primary functions."

The whole attempt to look into sub techniques in political campaign media was, to put it mildly, a bruising experience for me and my colleagues. To my knowledge, none of the journalists who wrote the attacks had either read my book or taken the trouble to reach the numerous scholars and experts on the subject I had cited during my presentation.

The night after the articles appeared, there was a message left at my hotel that Philip S. Cook of *Newsweek* wanted an interview. I was tired, angry, and in no mood to tolerate another journalistic sycophant. But, Cook surprised me, appearing genuinely interested in what I had stumbled into. I spent over two hours showing him several dozen original examples of embedded ads and illustrations, some of which, he remarked, had been published in *Newsweek*.

A critical and sensitive listener, Cook appeared to put the story together quickly, often adding his own comments on theory and technique. I was intrigued with the man. He appeared to know things about subliminal technique I was unaware of at the time. I couldn't help wondering, however, what *Newsweek* could do with such a story without indicting itself and its advertisers.

Finally, Cook appeared satisfied with the legitimacy of what I had shown him. "I'll write the story for our Media section," he said. "Some of it may get in, but it's more likely to end in a wastebasket when the New York editors get their hands on it. Don't hold your breath," he concluded, "waiting for the story to be published."

Luckily I did not: Cook's story never appeared.

THEY SELL PRESIDENTS TOO

During early 1977, a San Diego College professor discovered a portrait of Jimmy Carter—one widely used in his campaign to have citizens call the White House—heavily embedded with SEXes. I received mail from a dozen college students who also found the portrait embeds. The professor carefully photographed the embeds in a series of seven slides and sent them to the White House. Several months later, he received only a polite thank you note from a Deputy Press Secretary.

Early one morning during August 1978 a Congressional candidate from Augusta, Maine—Hays Gahagan—called. Very upset, he reported that the words SEX, FUCK, PRICK, etc., had been discovered lightly embedded in his campaign portraits used on various brochures, posters, etc. He said the lettering was quite similar to that used on the campaign poster shown in *Media Sexploitation.*

Gahagan also claimed that similar words had been discovered embedded in one of his opponent's campaign portraits. Students at a Maine University had discovered the embeds and notified the press. Investigation revealed that Gahagan and his opponent had employed the same nationally known photographer. When queried, the photographer adamantly denied knowledge of the subliminal embeds.

I spoke at a Gahagan press conference in late October 1978 in Augusta, Maine. A large group of Maine journalists attended. I demonstrated the Howard Johnson Clam-Plate Orgy, the Johnny Walker Rocks, the Parkay Softie, and several other examples of sophisticated airbrush technique. I displayed original copies of the ads so the journalists could examine them close up. I then demonstrated what appeared to be airbrush work in the campaign literature of the incumbent Senator William Hathaway and several of his opposition candidates, including Gahagan. (Virtually all political campaign materials are produced by advertising agencies. A thorough study of their image manipulation techniques could open up a fascinating new insight into attitude and opinion engineering in North American politics.)

Georgette Bennett of NBC's Nightly News, who also covered the conference, commented that my lecture and illustrations were "clear, specific, and factual." She said it should have been difficult for anyone to leave the room without at least acknowledging the embeds were in the campaign literature. Her story was later killed by NBC. Indeed, most Maine journalists crowded around the display table were seemingly convinced about subliminal embedding techniques.

The next day the *Portland Press Herald*, supposedly quoting an Oregon academic psychologist said: "Key's theories are just a bunch of crap, ridiculous, and are scorned in academic circles. For all practical purposes, subliminal perception does not occur—a concept like sex has to be implanted cognitively, that is, the mind must be attending to the stimulus. If you can't see it, then it won't affect your behavior."

SCORNED AGAIN

Nancy Grape, a political writer for the *Lewiston Evening Journal*, tried to prove I really didn't exist: "We can report he is not counted among Reno's best-known citizens. His name, for instance, is not listed in the Reno phone directory. Reno's daily newspaper questioned, 'What kind of doctor is he?' Both city room reporters and the business desk said they hadn't heard the name before. Two leading Reno ad agencies said Key's name was unfamiliar. The University of Nevada showed no record of him as a faculty member in payroll data since 1970." Curiously, she did not simply call phone company information; our new address and phone had been listed for over six months. Even Gahagan in Maine could have given her my vita. Or, she might have called my two New York publishers.

In all fairness, however, the *Bangor Daily News* and the Associated Press did publish creditable, objective reports on the news conference. Gahagan wrote the *U.S. Senate Committee on Ethics,* requesting an investigation of subliminals in U.S. campaign literature. So far, the Committee—like so many others—has not answered.

THE SUPER PRODUCT

Money is omnipresent, often believed omnipotent, taken for granted, paid little attention to, and yet a universal preoccupation. Few people will acknowledge there is anything they don't know about money, except perhaps how to get their hands on more of it. Yet almost everyone appears a little strange about their money—which turned out to be easily the most difficult communication medium of all to study. The Yankee Dollar has acquired an almost iconic, quasi-religious symbolic significance throughout the world. And yet, after a search through several large libraries, it appears that money has rarely been studied as a psychological phenomenon.

The few research papers on money available insisted on describing it merely as a functional convenience in exchange. It has an obviously powerful effect upon the human psyche, far beyond mere purchasing values—yet the specific details of money as a medium are very difficult to pin down.

Money can be described as a nation's super product—only one brand to a country. The mint or printing office is a perfect business, a total monopoly, an institution based upon the ultimate economic fantasy of power and security, a fundamental criterion for value, a supreme authority before which humans willingly subjugate themselves, a metaphysical force against which both kindness and cruelty are measured.

Money, nevertheless, is a creation neither of God, nor of biological evolution. It was quite recently invented by man, and is constantly modified by nations to meet changes in technology and culture.

In September 1972 the Associated Press in London, England, transmitted a story on the 50-rupee notes issued by the British Crown Colony of the Seychelle Islands, 600 miles northeast of Madagascar in the Indian Ocean. A new issue of the notes was withdrawn from circulation because the word SEX was discovered in the palm leaves behind Queen Elizabeth's head (see Figure 42). These 50-rupee notes are now collectors' items. The British Colonial Office and Exchequer issued vague press releases alluding to a mischievous engraver, hoping—I suppose—that the incident would be quickly forgotten.

A glance at an earlier issue of the 50-rupee notes, however, revealed that the SEX embed had been in earlier issues of the notes for decades, very lightly designed into the palm fronds so that discovery was unlikely. In the 1972 issue, apparently, an engraving error had permitted the three-letter word to reproduce legibly.

Such hidden, embedded symbolism in currency is not unusual. In the United States, an engraving of an eagle appears on the back side of the Legal Tender Notes of 1869, 1875, 1878, and 1880. These were years during which the Republican administrations of Ulysses Grant and Rutherford Hayes ran the United States. But hidden away somewhere in the U.S. Mint was a loyal Democrat who sneaked a subversive engraving into the Notes. When viewed upside down, the eagle becomes the head of a jackass. Whether the reference was to the Democratic donkey or Republican ineptness is difficult to determine so many years later.

During 1954, the Bank of Canada issued paper currency with the devil's face embedded in the curls behind the right ear of Queen Elizabeth II. The "devil in her hair" portrait appeared on all denominations of the 1954 issue. It was never officially acknowledged that a member of the Irish Republican Army had infiltrated the Canadian Banknote Corporation, but widespread public protests forced the government to reissue the currency with a cleaned-up engraved portrait of the Queen.

The SEX embed can be described as a *media enrichment* or *subliminal trigger* device. Such subliminally perceived words as SEX, SIN, FUCK, SUCK, DIE, KILL, and DEATH are regularly embedded in visual stimuli by the advertising media. These embeds have been discovered in magazine covers, news pictures, television commercials, newspaper photographs and illustrations, movie and record sound tracks, billboards, package designs, and—perhaps the ultimate indignity—on Ritz Crackers (*Media Sexploitation*, pp. 10-11), in fact everywhere merchandising space is sold to sell. Justifications for the use of subliminal embeds in advertising mediå appear obvious. But for someone to go to all that trouble—and risk—to embed currency is difficult to rationalize until one's entire perspective toward money becomes more flexible.

VALUE IS PURELY PERCEPTUAL

It has been a very long period in human history since money carried any intrinsic value, such as a stable and easily obtainable equivalent in gold, platinum, silver, other precious minerals, or commodities.

Money today is a psychological invention, having far more to do with *perceived* rather than with *real* values. Any nation's currency is worth whatever you can convince anyone to believe at any given point in time.

Because a currency's value is "on paper" only, nations are compelled to merchandise their money with the same intensity and dedication applied to other artifacts of commerce like toilet paper or tobacco. Like most products with competing brands, money is merchandised competitively—bought, sold, borrowed, traded, leased, rented, saved, collected, advertised, and incessantly promoted. Endless campaigns are sponsored by governments, corporations, institutions, business, and industry—all with something both to gain and lose.

Marketing "success" or "failure" can be measured rather easily by comparative inflation rates or international exchange rates.

In economics (perhaps the most repressed of all the pseudo-social-sciences), there is a vested interest in wanting to believe that currency gymnastics are clearly understood—that if only this or that were accomplished, currency fluctuations would stabilize. In governmental, banking, and business institutions, well-elaborated monetary dogma tells everyone what they want to hear.

Citizens are usually educated to believe that currency value fluctuations are a reasonable and logical by-product of evolution and growth. It is normal, even desirable, that values universally erode over time as a natural consequence of "progress." Economists rarely admit that monetary inflation or deflation is simply a direct consequence of someone's manipulating perceptual instabilities for profit. In money, as in so many other psychological phenomena, every change means both a profit or a loss for someone somewhere.

It may be unsettling to think of money involved in the same marketing strategies as a can of beans or a mouthwash, but the analogy is easily observable. Each nation supports small armies of statisticians and economists who propagandize for their respective currencies. They compare each other's products in scores of ways, applying the most advantageous perspectives, interpreting values, and minutely evaluating competitive money markets. The precise nature of these payoffs, however, are often repressed by both those who lose and those who win.

SYMBOLIC AND PURCHASING VALUES

You can acquire things with money—so much of this or that in return for so many dollars. This obvious exchange value, nevertheless, may be money's *least* important potential for affecting human behavior. Exchange value, of course, is the obvious conscious preoccupation, but is of limited significance in psychological terms.

The paper currency and coinage of most nations, including the United States, are worthless in themselves; their only value is symbolic. This, of course, is why a medium such as money must be precision designed to modify and control human behavior. Money communicates as a fundamental symbol of national strength, authority, and identity—usually far more powerful in its effect upon behavior than flags, seals, and other more obvious symbols of a state's authority. Money is an advertisement for a nation, aimed at both internal and external markets.

There is no more vicious way to insult anyone than to denigrate his money. When tourists or soldiers abroad light cigarettes with another nation's paper currency, the profound insult is quite unlikely ever to be forgiven or forgotten. Even between such usually amicable neighbors as Canada and the United States it is not unusual to hear citizens of each insult the other's currency with references such as "funny money." Even people whose currency has been virtually wiped out by inflationary manipulations or mismanagement persist in the hope that somehow their currency will regain its former value—something that has rarely, if ever, happened in world history. Bankrupt currencies are reissued or reevaluated, but never achieve their former values.

Obviously money has a purchasing value that changes from day to day. Instability actually *increases* its psychological significance. Individuals are admonished to spend (or "invest") quickly before prices increase—or, more accurately, as the money's value decreases. In America, this is interpreted symbolically as a major motive to justify increased consumption (which, curiously, also increases inflation).

In a world preoccupied with economic disaster (a state of mind sustained to enhance monetary value by those who manage currency) perhaps it might be called natural for individuals to assess the world around them with the question, "How much is he, she, or it worth?" It might be difficult to determine whether money or sex constitutes America's most powerful obsession. Reproductive drives biologically evolved over several million years, of course. Money is quite recent by comparison. But it is a most visible phenomenon that sex and money closely relate in modern man's symbolic behavior—and it is also unlikely this relationship is accidental.

THE INVISIBLE MEDIUM

There is heavy resistance, especially in the United States, to consider money outside the culturally accepted sets or labels, to explore money itself as a merchandisable commodity, or to probe it as a symbolic medium of communication. Most individuals really don't want to deal with the subject. In fact, Americans know little about the designs actually printed on individual bills.

Several hundred American university students were asked to record the number of $1, $5, $10, and $20 bills that passed through their hands during a specific week. The recording task was merely a device to make them consciously aware of the paper bills they handled; presumably they looked at them for brief moments during those seven days.

Later, over 90 percent identified Washington's portrait on the $1 bill; about half identified Lincoln on the five; roughly 30 percent identified Hamilton on the ten; but less than 5 percent knew that Jackson was on the twenty. All those surveyed had handled all four denominations during the week. None of the several hundred students had the slightest idea as to the design—on *any* denomination—of seals, buildings, ornamental borders, and signatures.

Once again, when something significant has been ignored, there is usually a reason: No one wants to deal with it. When asked about slogans printed on the bills, slightly over 20 percent mentioned "In God We Trust," but virtually all were uncertain as to *which* bill or bills included the slogan. (All denominations, of course, carry the words conspicuously printed on the green side.) It is strange that such a slogan was included on U.S. currency. It could be a warning not to trust money but to place faith or trust only in a higher being; or, on the other hand, perhaps the value is meant to be enhanced via an identification with God—the ultimate ad testimonial. Indeed, many Americans often act as though they believed money was somehow a gift from God.

The description developed from the survey strongly suggested that money was another of the invisible (repressed) media of American society—unnoticed and taken for granted. Throughout one's life the bills are handled on almost a daily basis; yet they are strangely unseen, at least at the conscious level. During transactions, only denomination numbers are consciously acknowledged. Someone went to a lot of trouble and expense to decorate the world's most sought after and cherished icon of acquisition, yet few individuals comprehended, seemed aware of, or even recalled the obvious design features.

As in any media study, what individuals do *not* appear to know is usually more significant than what they are consciously and obviously aware of.

THE FINE PRINT

We have all seen Lincoln's engraved portrait thousands of times, but for just a few moments take one more careful look at the famous engraving. This portrait may have more significance to your daily life than you recognize. Find a $5 bill as new and unwrinkled from folding as possible. Because some of the detailed engraving work is quite small, a magnifying glass may be helpful.

Under a bright reading light, relax as you begin to study the portrait of Lincoln. A couple of deep breaths may help your perception of the details. Remember, humans consciously perceive more information when relaxed; tension increases vulnerability to subliminal stimuli.

Allow your eyes to drift across the engraved lines that guide perception into Lincoln's kindly eyes, his large Romanesque nose, the delicate curvatures of his lips. Remember, even though the microscopic lines which make up the engraving appear deceptively photographic, you are not looking at a photograph. Perceptual indoctrination insists we perceive the engraved lines as Lincoln's countenance, not as lines precisely engraved to resemble Lincoln's face.

Study Lincoln's face, especially the area around his mouth, for a few seconds before proceeding further. Try not to strain, become tense, or concentrate too intensely upon the portrait. Permit your eyes to casually observe the small details. Assuming you are now relaxed, follow the line leading from the corner of Lincoln's mouth, on your left, diagonally down toward his chin. This line disappears just before reaching the top line of his beard.

A short distance from where the diagonal line ends (perhaps 1/32nd of an inch below) a heavy, dark, horizontal line—forming the top of the beard—begins and continues to your right, parallel with the lips. Follow this horizontal line from left to right, roughly 1/8th of an inch. Stop where the line appears to end. At this point, just below the dark heavy line, a thin white line appears. Follow this white line back to the left as it curves down, forming the letter "S."

Allow your perception to consciously assimilate the letter for several seconds. You should perceive what appears as a white letter on a black background—the thin white line curving down from right to left.

The letter "S," embedded in Lincoln's beard, will become more strongly apparent after several seconds of relaxed viewing. Do not attempt to rush or force your perception of the letter. Wait until the "S" becomes clearly apparent before proceeding further.

Adjacent to the letter "S" appears the capital letter "E." The thin white vertical line of the "E" appears bent in the middle, bulging out slightly to the left. The upper and lower horizontal lines also appear bent. The letter "E" was crudely constructed.

The letter "X" can be found next to the "E." The "X" is somewhat lighter and may be slightly more difficult for some to perceive. Again, relax and take your time, permitting each letter to register clearly in your conscious perception. Incredible as it may appear at first thought, the word "SEX" has been ingeniously embedded in Lincoln's beard.

SYMBOLIC DEMYSTIFICATION

Once you clearly perceive the three letters in Lincoln's beard, you can hold the $5 bill several feet away and the tiny letters stand out like a neon sign. The word becomes the dominant focal point of your perception. Further, from now on throughout your life, whenever you look at a $5 bill your eyes will immediately focus upon Lincoln's beard. The tiny SEX almost jumps out at you. Perception of the word, or the inability to consciously perceive it, often initiates strong emotional reactions within some individuals. You might write down your feelings about the embedded word for later reference.

Of several thousand university students who were shown the SEX in Lincoln's beard, roughly 97 percent were able to perceive consciously the three letters—though some required more time than others before the letters became recognizable.

Roughly 3 percent of this sizable group could not perceive the three letters. They appeared to block—or repress—conscious perception of the SEX. In other words, they perceptually defended themselves from perceiving the word much like another 3 percent of test subjects refused to deal consciously with the Clam-Plate Orgy (see Figure 1). Canadians consciously perceived the SEX in Lincoln's beard easier than did Americans and *vice versa* for similar phenomena in Canadian currency; older adults had more difficulty than younger adults; men more difficulty than women.

One journalist told me I had "really flipped out" on the Lincoln's beard embed, responding initially that I should immediately talk with a psychiatrist. He was incensed, outraged that I would even suggest such nonsense. At the time I first explained the SEX embed to him, he could not perceive the letters. The tension that his anger produced had inhibited his conscious perceptual ability.

Several days later he called to apologize. After considerable effort, he had eventually perceived the SEX in Lincoln's beard—even though, he said, "I still don't want to believe the damned thing exists." His wife and son easily perceived the word SEX, however, and he described the whole experience as having produced for him "profound anxiety."

A month later the journalist called again. He had shown the Lincoln beard embed to a neighbor, who erupted in rage and had not spoken to the journalist and his family for several weeks. His editor also scoffed at the whole idea, refusing even to look carefully at the engraved portrait. The editor, he reported, curtly ordered him, "Forget that story on subliminal perception. Drop it! We haven't time for such nonsense."

In most people, the perception of SEX in Lincoln's beard appears to provoke strong feelings ranging from rage to humor. Those feelings are often accompanied by inexplicable agitation and depression. Reactions to the discovery are sometimes intense—angry, annoyed, defensive, sometimes as though an individual were being persecuted. Often this anger has been directed at me for "making us see dirty things," "hypnotizing audiences," and frequently "having a filthy mind."

These engraved SEX embeds will not reproduce in low-definition media such as television and newspapers. The *Washington Star*, May 22, 1974, unsuccessfully tried to reproduce the SEXes in U.S. currency on their front page. The failure of the letters to reproduce on coarse newsprint was their "proof" that the whole idea was a hoax. Several TV stations also tried to broadcast a slide reproduction of Lincoln's $5 bill portrait, but videotube reproduction, like newsprint, is low-definition. The fine engraving lines do not legibly come through.

For over a year I included a discussion of the $5 bill in my university lecture tours. During virtually every lecture, a small group within the audience became outraged, several times shouting obscenities or inviting me to fight. I still use the material in small classes and seminars, but I finally concluded that Americans generally are not yet ready to deal with the secret of Lincoln's beard.

Microphotographs reveal that the letters—which appear as more or less straight white lines—are actually very irregular, created by leaving spaces in the black lines which form the beard. An additional embedded SEX appears in Lincoln's forehead. Another SEX appears in the lower portion of the bow tie, the "X" being the most easily apparent letter. Again, a magnifying glass may be helpful as the letters in the tie are very small.

HONEST ABE SELLS

Should anyone cynically believe that knowledge of the secret of Lincoln's beard does not have a practical application consider this: After attending one of my lectures in San Diego, a naval Chief Petty Officer headed for the nearest bar. Within an hour he had won over $100 by betting he could prove there was something sexy in Lincoln's picture.

The word SEX was designed into Lincoln's beard at least sixty-five years ago, as it appears in the engraved portrait of Lincoln on the 1914 series of $5 bills. As far as could be determined, no one outside the *U.S. Bureau of Engraving and Printing* ever consciously perceived the embedded SEX.

At one time or another, almost everyone in the world has viewed this portrait of Lincoln. Every detail has been recorded in the brain systems of literally billions of individuals. Yet, most of the students interviewed during the money survey considered the engraved designs and portraits of "no significance."

The U.S. bills, of course, seem to have always been around. The designs rarely change. As with most media, nevertheless, perception is both *total* and *instantaneous*. Especially considering the emotionalized context in which money is perceived throughout life, the fine details of currency design are recorded in every individual's unconscious memory system. Americans apparently repress their memory of currency design, forgetting the details and then forgetting they had forgotten.

As we have seen, the repression of media is not an uncommon phenomenon, justifying the question: *Are we using the medium or is the medium using us?* The latter appears far more likely. With no conscious awareness of repressed information, we have no way to comprehend or intellectualize the medium's power or significance. It is thereby taken for granted, consciously ignored, becoming another of the invisible forces that manage our lives—quite often not in our own best interest.

THE VALUE EFFECT

It is relatively easy to find the word SEX hidden in Lincoln's beard. It is much more difficult to explain why someone went to all that trouble to engrave it there. One retired engraver, who had worked with Canadian currency, estimated that a highly-skilled technician might require a month or more of full-time work to complete each of the letters in the beard. This type of engraving was once considered an exacting art form. He described the SEX as "an old engraver's trick."

Had the embed merely been intended as protection against counterfeiting, a less troublesome noun could have been selected—perhaps GOD, LOVE, or possibly even JOY. Almost any other word could have been more consistent with America's Protestant-Calvinist heritage—more consistent, perhaps, but neither as effective nor as predictably repressive as the word SEX in the beard of Honest Abe.

The SEX embeds hidden in engravings on most denominations of U.S. currency actually increase the money's symbolic value. Subliminally, these embeds relate the currency to sex, often considered the most powerful human drive system of all. Sexualized currency would be far more valuable than mere printed paper.

It is highly doubtful the Treasury Department would have made such decisions on its own, considering the nature of low-echelon Federal bureaucracies. Such a decision, with the implied risk of eventual discovery, must have been based upon research and study. As this was apparently accomplished with public tax funds, the research should be available for examination. Data of this kind would be priceless for the light it could shed upon human motivation, perception, and behavior.

Yet, as far as could be determined, there has never been information on such techniques published anywhere in the Western world. During 1974, I wrote the Secretary of the Treasury for an explanation of the SEX embeds in U.S. currency. The answer, from a Deputy Director, denied that SEX or any other word had ever been hidden on the currency. In a condescending manner, he mentioned how fascinating he found the strange array of things people believed they saw in currency engravings. The U.S. Treasury Department had better take a more careful look at what they are communicating to the American people, but then—assuming they are competent at their jobs—they already have. I admit to being old fashioned, but I find it highly disturbing—even in this very disturbed world—to discover that even the Yankee Dollar has been sexualized along with toilet paper, underarm deodorants, and paperback books.

SEX NEVER SETS

After the Seychelle Island 50-rupee note discovery, further investigation revealed that SEX embeds appear on much of the British, British Commonwealth, and British Colonial currency in use throughout the world. The word is embedded in the engraved folds of clothing, hair, water, or background vegetation. Numerous examples, some quite hilarious, were discovered in Canadian currency.

The green side of a Canadian $1 bill issued several years ago portrays the nation's western prairie region—an endless horizon of rich, flat farmland crossed by a single highway. Telephone poles stretch out across the skyline (see Figure 43). Currency is designed and printed in Canada by the Canadian Bank Note Corporation, a Crown Corporation that operates much like the U.S. Mint.

Draw a vertical line from the silo up through the clouds to the top of the picture. Just to the right of the line, a half inch below the top of the picture on the actual currency, a light horizontal cloud formation appears which bends around to the left forming a large capital "S." Just to the right of the "S" appears a smaller "E." The final "X" streams off in the cloud formations to the right.

Attempts to discuss the SEX embed with Canadians often produced angry and outraged disbelief, even among those who easily perceived the SEX in Lincoln's beard. So be careful unless you happen to be talking with someone from Quebec, who will likely find the whole thing a hilariously funny confirmation of Anglo-Canadian hypocrisy.

It may not be at all peculiar that most people are a little funny about their money.

11 • THE ANAMORPHIC TIGER

> *There is nothing more dangerous to the health*
> *of a society than to build devious routes to the*
> *unconscious and pretend that evil is really a*
> *form of virtue.*
>
> Lionel Rubinoff,
> *The Pornography of Power*

DA VINCI'S EXPERIMENT

For anyone who wants to embed media with taboo subliminal
sex and death imagery, their major current problem is discovery. The techniques are now widely known and discussed, especially in universities. A good deal more research on the
subject is certain to be published. Sooner or later this will be
highly damaging to an industry whose survival depends upon
deceit, manipulation, and control of the consumer culture. It
is only a matter of time until public pressure leads to legislative and governmental intervention. Demonstrating a resourcefulness that would have done credit to Horatio Alger, one
ad industry response was to make substimuli more difficult to
discover and, certainly, to prove in court.

Anamorphosis is a technique of visual image distortion
which can be perceived at an unconscious or non-conscious
level. One simple example of anamorphosis is a picture that
when viewed conventionally, from the front, appears unintel-
ligible. But, when viewed from a raking angle on either side,
or reflected in a curved mirror or other special optical instruments, the distorted picture becomes clear and distinct, appearing to stand out three-dimensionally from its surface.

Anamorphosis is not a random scrambling of an image,
but conforms to precise geometric and arithmetical relation-

ships. A familiar example is a single frame from a 35-mm motion picture film processed for wide-screen viewing. When you look at the transparent films, the picture appears vertically elongated, compressed, distorted, and incoherent. A wide-screen projection lens spreads out the image and it is perceived by audiences in familiar, proportionate relationships.

Anamorphosis is believed to have been discovered by Leonardo da Vinci. Since early in the fifteenth century, artists and students of optics had been experimenting with perspective and foreshortening problems in painted images, attempting to create credible three-dimensional illusions (height, width, and depth) on a two-dimensional surface. The earliest anamorphic representations to survive are two experimental sketches produced by Leonardo da Vinci around 1470 as a young artist not yet twenty (see Figure 44). These crude drawings of a child's face and an eye assume their proper proportions when viewed with one eye at a narrow angle from the right side of the page, whereupon they appear to rise and float free above the page.

Da Vinci painted at least two anamorphic pictures during his lifetime: one depicting a dragon fighting a lion (1478), and a drawing of horses that Leonardo presented Francis I of France some time after 1516. To provide correct distance and angle perspectives—the intersection of observation and vanishing points for viewers—these paintings had to be viewed from a peephole built into their frames.

MORE REPRESSED MYSTIFICATION

Anamorphic drawings and paintings were well known throughout Europe in the early sixteenth century. Perhaps the most famous painting to have combined normal viewing perspective and anamorphic projection is Hans Holbein the Younger's *The French Ambassadors*, completed in 1533 (see Figure 45). This lifesized portrait, one of many painted by the German artist while a guest at the court of Henry viii, now hangs in London's National Gallery.

To further illustrate the way art "experts" have built a mystique around their subject, the following is a typical, widely reprinted commentary by Helen Gardner from a standard text on art history. She described Holbein's work:

Holbein belonged to Renaissance Germany. But in his greatest work, his portraits, Holbein alone of his nation had the selective ability, the capacity to extract from the total visual impression a definite linear motif to which he subordinated whatever detail he used. . . . His lines are clear-cut and sustained, not broken, indefinite, and restless, as in many Northern painters. . . . The surfaces of his paintings are as lustrous as enamel; flat, for he used shadows sparingly; and highly decorative. Holbein's keen vision, his control over line, and his ability to select a pose, a costume, and a motif of composition that will emphasize characteristic aspects of personality are evident.

All of which says absolutely nothing about the artist or his work. The description is even inaccurate in its allusion to shadows, detail subordination, and unbroken lines. As vaguely generalized as the message in a fortune cooky or daily horoscope, it could have been written to describe a Mickey Mouse cartoon. If anything, it obscures the work of Holbein, leading the reader down the path of cultural repression via meaningless jargon. The mystique descriptions used in art and many other verbalizations of mass communication media tend to camouflage meaning, programming the reader with a diffusing, formalized preconceived value system that conceals more about the human condition than it expresses. Such repressive mystification is difficult to attack or contradict, as it often has behind it the support of the society or culture. Culture, in turn, often appears organized around collective repressions.

Why couldn't the commentator on Holbein's truly ingenious work have grappled with the various parameters of what Holbein *meant* by what he painted? What was the effect of his work upon viewers, upon his society, upon behavior? What was he doing to whom for which reasons? The same questions we earlier asked about ad art. . . Once again, the name of the game in art (i.e., communication) is *meaning*. Media content becomes significant because of what it *means*, not because of the pigments and perspectives used.

Probe, briefly, the work of this skilled German artist-craftsman who made his fortunes and found immortality of a sort in the court of a British king. The canvas portrays Jean de Dinteville, the French Ambassador, and his friend Bishop

Georges de Selve as two young noblemen surrounded by rich artifacts of commerce, science, art, and philosophy. Or so it might appear at a superficial level.

The ornate and expensive costume of Jean de Dinteville (left), French Ambassador to the court of Henry VIII, reeks of wealth, power, and indulgence. The Ambassador is posed dominantly to the foreground, a worldly, sophisticated leader in the affairs of men. His hand casually rests on his dagger scabbard, upon which is engraved his age of 29 years. The French Bishop Georges de Selve, wearing his robes and cap of office, was posed in a contemplative posture and expression, his arm resting upon a Bible inscribed with his age of 25 years.

The double portrait was painted life size—over 6 feet high and wide. When approaching the canvas, viewers have the feeling that the subjects are real and in the same room with them. The bookshelves hold beautifully leather-bound books, musical and mathematical instruments, and scientific devices used by learned men of the day. There is much for the eye to savor: the positioning of the stringed instruments, the rich furs, silk brocade, expensive wool textures in their clothing, green damask curtains, and a plethora of minute details.

The articles on the shelves were reproduced in natural light, in meticulous detail. Notice these shelves are also slightly off center. Holbein must have labored long and patiently to place each article painstaking in a different perspective.

The artifacts on the bottom shelves are of earthly concern. The lute, an instrument of popular music in that period, together with the music book suggests light and frivolous amusements. The lute was often symbolic of consonance, agreement, and peace. The lute's broken string, however, suggests an underlying discord. At the time the portrait was painted, England, France, and the Italian principalities were united in one of their interminable alliances against the Holy Roman Empire. A corner of the green curtain is turned back, revealing a crucifix which portrays the omnipresent eye of the Church, probably the Roman Catholic Church as Henry VIII was then in the process of breaking with Rome to found the Church of England.

There is an obvious contrast between the earth globe on the left and the globe of the heavens above. The upper shelf, upon which the two men are leaning for support, contains the

figure 1

figure 2

figure 3

figure 4

figure 5

figure 6

figure 7

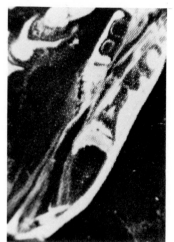

figure 8

figure 9

figure 10

figure 11

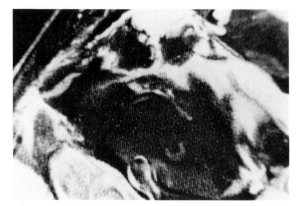

figure 12

figure 13

figure 14

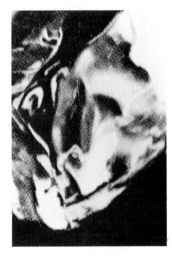

figure 15

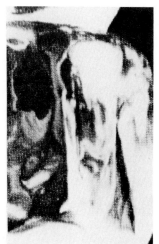

figure 16

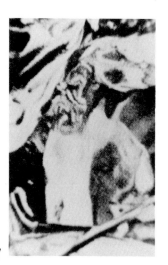

figure 17

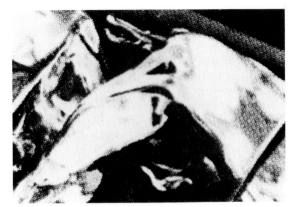

figure 18

figure 19

figure 20

figure 21

figure 22

figure 23

figure 24

figure 25

figure 26

figure 27

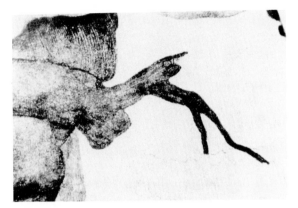

figure 28

figure 29

figure 30

figure 31

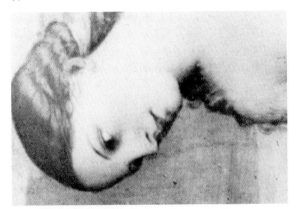

figure 32

figure 33

figure 34

figure 35

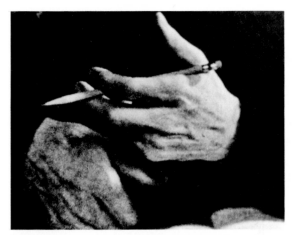

figure 36

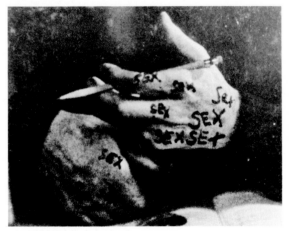

figure 37

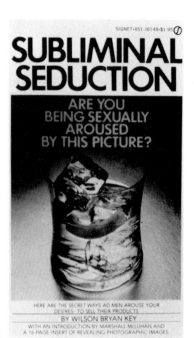

figure 38

figure 39

figure 40

figure 41

figure 42

figure 43

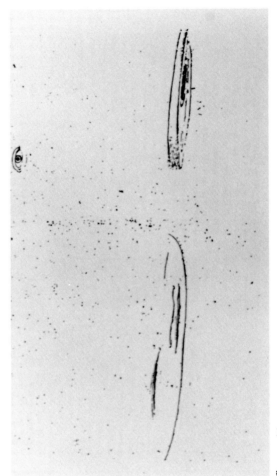

figure 44

figure 45

I.W. HARPER
**A famous American in Denmark
and around the world.**

figure 46

figure 47

figure 48

figure 49

figure 50

figure 51

The Yago wine cocktail. It's a natural for the holidays.

Brisk. Bright. Cool and light.

Yago is naturally refreshing because it's natural all the way. It's made from fine Spanish wine blended with fresh natural oranges and lemons. Nothing artificial.

Red or White, Yago's the perfect natural wine cocktail.

For the holidays, try something sensationally different: a delicious Yago daiquiri wine cocktail! You'll wish you had discovered it years before.

**Yago Daiquiri.
Another holiday natural.**

1. Eight oz. of Yago.
2. Add one pkg. dry daiquiri mix. Mix in a blender or shake.
3. Serve over ice. Makes two servings.
4. Enjoy! It's a great wine cocktail.

figure 52

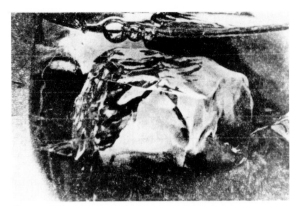

figure 53

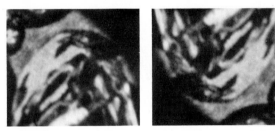

figure 54   figure 55

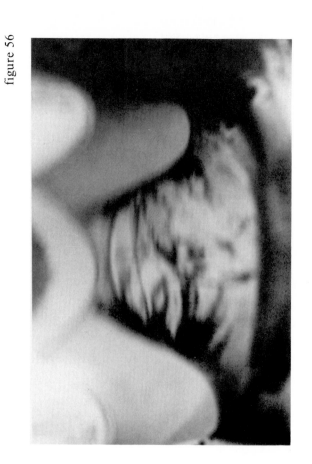

figure 56

globe of the heavens and numerous scientific instruments used to regulate time and determine the position of the stars—basic instruments of navigation which made possible both the commercial and military conquests of the day.

Francis I, the French king for whom the two ambassadors worked, had utilized the heavenly and earthly globes in a royal seal upon which was inscribed his motto, *Unus non Sufficit Orbis* (One World Is Not Enough). There are, of course, at least two ways in which this can be interpreted. You might consider the *other* world as the world of God, or the phrase might be interpreted similarly to Hitler's "Tomorrow the World." The widely traveled Holbein would certainly have been familiar with the French king's seal. The use of the globes could have been flattering to the two young nobles, or the globes might have been viewed as a threat from the British point of view.

AN UNCERTAIN FOUNDATION

Curiously, the tiled floor design—called Cosmate—is placed off center in relation to the picture's central axis. The erratic asymmetry of the painting is not an error of technical design, but appears to relate to *meaning*. The artist could just as easily—perhaps more easily—have painted the floor symmetrically. The tile mosaic is similar to that used on the floor of the choir in Westminster Abbey, except this pattern has been clumsily designed—the left circle is below the central diamond shape while the right circle is above. This asymmetrical, faulty design certainly suggests instability; the floor on which these two young men arrogantly pose appears precarious and uncertain, not the firm, solid, dependable, strongly crafted floor upon which one might expect to find these two noble members of a Royal Court. Though few viewers would consciously consider these specific details, the general nonverbal feeling transmitted is one of precarious instability.

At the conscious level, all that most viewers of Holbein's *The Ambassadors* would perceive is an ornate portrait of two young noblemen of the sixteenth century. But across the painting's foreground, Holbein placed an anamorphic projection—one consciously indecipherable to the viewer. When viewed from the upper right or lower left, from a narrow angle—5 to 10 degrees—the distorted streak of light compresses into an ominous human skull.

HIDDEN DEATH IMAGERY

Nearly four and a half centuries later, it is impossible to know how many of Holbein's contemporary viewers were consciously aware of the anamorphic skull. From the early 1400's, artists and philosophers wrote about and experimented with problems of central perspective. But this was not general knowledge; it would have been known by only a few of the most highly educated. Recall that in the first half of the sixteenth century a vast majority of Europeans, even noblemen, were illiterate. The painting was completed 78 years after Guttenberg's invention of movable type and 41 years after the discovery of America.

The Ambassadors was designed to be approached from the right. The anamorphic skull would be apparent for only an instant to anyone approaching the painting from the right side. Perception, as mentioned several times, is instantaneous at the unconscious level. The hidden skull would be perceived by everyone momentarily as they approached the painting—a phenomenon not unlike that which occurs when readers viewing an ad in a magazine or newspaper turn the page. When *The Ambassadors* is printed on a page, as the page is turned the skull—in its consciously understandable form—would be perceived for an instant.

Even without the diagonal anamorphic skull, the double portrait resonates with subtle negative meanings and significances. In the red satin right sleeve of Dinteville appears the face of the devil—his mouth curved downward in a sinister grimace. The broach pinned upon Dinteville's cap is intriguing, as it is engraved with a skull on a shield, an emblem hardly appropriate to a French Ambassador. The anamorphic skull across the portrait's foreground appears as a gigantic replica of the cap emblem and seems the central, even though covert, theme of the portrait: *All ends in death.*

Once the skull is consciously perceived, it becomes the central, highly dramatic theme of the portrait. Unconsciously perceived, it forms a subliminal attitudinal influence through which a feeling of doom inexplicably permeates the portrait.

Whether the two subjects consciously knew about Holbein's hidden skull is impossible to know, though they did personally pose for the artist. No records or reviews of the work at the time of its completion survived. But considering the suspicions, distrust, hatred, and insults common between the French and the British of the period, it appears unlikely the influential subjects would have tolerated a German artist's overt allusions to death, vanity, and temporary power. One thing is certain, however: very few who perceived *The Ambassadors* during the subsequent four and a half centuries were consciously aware of the disguised symbol of death. Had the anamorphic skull been known, critics would certainly have denounced it as a cheap trick which marred the otherwise superb portrayal of the French statesmen. *The Ambassadors* has been included in numerous anthologies and several works dealing exclusively with Hans Holbein the Younger's art, yet no mention of the anamorphic skull appeared. Even famed art authority Sir Kenneth Clarke pretentiously discussed Hans Holbein's *Ambassadors* without alluding to the skull. This is strange, indeed. Interviews with numerous art students both in England and in the United States who were familiar with the double portrait disclosed that few were conscious of the anamorphic skull. These interviews were made prior to the popularization of anamorphosis by the book *Hidden Images* (Leeman, 1976) and its lengthy review by *Time* magazine in which a reproduction of the Holbein portrait appeared.

It is, of course, possible that Holbein intended some bizarre sixteenth-century form of private joke. Jurgis Baltrusaitis, a modern French authority on anamorphosis in fine art, believed the skull was meant to be a "hollow bone" (in German, *hohle bein*) and thus a rebus that played upon the artist's name. Indeed, humerous puns and word games were widely indulged in during the period, but the anamorphic skull cost Holbein dozens of hours of work and was installed conspicuously across the foreground of a commissioned painting, for which the artist received a large fee for his labors. The huge portrait of two powerful French noblemen was no casual undertaking to which a few amusing afternoons might be allocated by the highly skilled, busy, and rich artist. Had Holbein merely wished to symbolize mortality in the portrait, there were numerous ways in which it could have been done without fear of discovery, many requiring far less time, skill, and effort.

In the early sixteenth century, anamorphosis was used to camouflage themes containing double or forbidden meanings.

Often pornographic details were included anamorphically in what was consciously perceived as only a normal landscape. The seventeenth and eighteenth centuries have been described as "the golden age of anamorphosis" (Leeman, 1976). The technique was widely used in books, paintings, and prints by many of the leading artists of the period. During the nineteenth century, however, anamorphosis was almost entirely discarded—demonstrated infrequently even as an art school exercise.

The twentieth century virtually forgot about anamorphic phenomena, at least as it relates to the world of fine art. In the early decades of the twentieth century, perceptual psychologists described and defined anamorphosis, though characteristically they avoided the issue of effects upon behavior. Once defined, labeled, and described, the technique was dismissed as an artistic curiosity—dismissed, that is, by virtually all except the merchandizing artists and hustlers, ever alert to new manipulative potentials.

A NEW MIND CONTROL FRONTIER

Holbein utilized *perspective anamorphosis* in *The Ambassadors*, in which the distorted image can be perceived from a sharply angled perspective off to one side. A modern example of similar *perspective anamorphosis* appears in the widely reproduced I.W. Harper Whisky ad (see Figure 46).

Ostensibly the ad shows a middle-aged businessman reading a newspaper while he holds a whiskey glass in which, we are led to believe, there are ice cubes and IWH. As the readers can see for themselves, the airbrushed contents of the glass are very indistinct (see Figure 47). But view the glass from an angle of roughly 5 degrees from either side of the picture. The anamorphic vagueness of the contents coalesce into a very recognizable tiger (see Figure 48), apparently intended to be perceived as the page is turned. At the unconscious level, perception would be instantaneous, much like when approaching the Holbein painting.

A tiger, of course, is an archetypal symbol of inexhaustible virility and strength. But here, instead of a tiger in our tank, we have an anamorphic tiger in our I.W. Harper. The tiger's symbolic significance is instantly and invisibly induced into the reader's brain system. It *must sell* the whiskey, however, as anamorphic projections are time consuming, expensive, and require special equipment. To paint such a design, the artist would probably use an anamorphic lens or variously curved mirrors.

In reality, IWH—or any other alcoholic beverage for that matter—may promise virility and strength, but delivers just the opposite. Alcohol in any form is the royal road to impotence. But, such is the patent nonsense upon which multibillion dollar distilling, brewing, and wine-making empires— and, of course, the gullibility of the American consumer— are founded.

Stock 84, the so-called "Smoother Brandy," is bottled by Schenley Imports of New York and, so the company advertises, is imported. Of course the label does not explain what percentage of each bottle is imported, or from where, but these questions are probably insignificant for the consumer who accept labels at face value (see Figure 49).

The copy line proffers the usual meaningless nonsense: "Finding the right brandy can be rough. Unless it's this smooth." Comprehensible definitions of "right," "rough," and "smooth" are also absent, but then American consumers of media have been well trained not to ask embarrassing questions about such pap.

The ad is an innocuous piece of banality, at least on the surface. Very few readers of *Time* magazine (October 10, 1977) would spend more than a few seconds viewing this picture, which ran in the book review section

If the ad appeared in the national edition, the two-thirds of a page display space would cost Schenley something in excess of $60,000 per issue, but it would be seen in over 6 million copies of *Time* by some 24 million readers. Roughly four people read each copy of *Time*. Several other national publications also ran the ad. The purchasing potential is staggering—if, and only if, the ad sells.

Considering the sizable investment, what makes the ad work? Its effectiveness simply cannot be explained in conventional terms—the copy is flat, meaningless, and might be read by only 2 percent of those who consciously perceive the ad. The brandy glass and sealed bottle display little creative ingenuity. At the conscious level, it is not supposed to be interesting. And yet, there is much more in this ad than meets the conscious eye (see Figure 50). Tilt the ad at a sharp angle. In the bottom of the glass is a figure praying to the heavens—a priest, perhaps, or someone who has just found salvation at the bottom of a brandy glass.

Now, turn the ad upside down. Painted very lightly, at the point where the stem connects to the glass, is a reflection of the praying figure. The body down to the genital area appears slim and muscular (see Figure 51). The head appears to have horns. The arms are raised upward in a welcoming gesture, not in prayer. This figure in the base of the glass appears to be the devil.

That is one awesome image to slip into the minds of all those nice people who read and implicitly trust *Time* magazine. Maybe some, who were forced to carry the ad around inside their heads for a lifetime, did not even like brandy.

As a technique of artistic deception, anamorphosis can be far more complex than simple perspective manipulation. To consciously perceive the projections in the Holbein portrait or the I.W. Harper ad, all you need do is read the paintings from a 5-degree angle. Anamorphic projections, however, can also be painted *inside* or *outside* of cones, pyramids, globes, boxes, and other geometrical shapes so that the information cannot be consciously perceived without a complex of mirrors and lenses.

These other, more complex forms of anamorphic projection also have been discovered in advertising. It appears the brain can unconsciously perceive certain forms of systematically distorted information. The phenomenon can be demonstrated with the *Los Angeles Times Home Magazine* (November 21, 1976, page 6) ad for Yago Sangría (see Figure 52).

VAMPIRES DRINK BLOOD

Yago Sangría is a juiced-up wine, produced by Monsieur Henri Wines, Ltd., of New York. The ad utilizes common-virility-fertility symbolism—lemons and oranges—but the layout's focal point is the large wine glass full of ice cubes and Sangría (see Figure 53).

Were you to seriously tell anyone there was a rather flat, stretched-out face painted inside the glass just below the surface left of center, he would probably smile patronizingly and suggest you switch to soft drinks. Most people would accuse you of having an overactive imagination: "You can see anything you want to see in ice cubes!" or "What you can't see can't hurt you!"

If you turn the ad upside down, however, and stand a tubular mirror just above the light pink ice cube, a rather strange image will reflect back at you. The flattened, vague face coalesces into a most repulsive vampire bat with wings (see Figure 54 and Figure 55)—hardly an image that would send you rushing out for a bottle of Yago once you consciously perceived it.

Yet, as in so many other alcoholic beverage ads, subliminal images of death or self-destruction appear to direct brand preferences. A bat is utilized in the Bacardi trademark (see *Subliminal Seduction*, Figure 17). In the Indo-European cultures, bats symbolize black magic, darkness, madness, rapacity, peril, torment, evil spirits, death, misfortune, witchcraft, blood-sucking, ghosts, discontent, or suicide (Jobes, 1962). In Spanish, *sangre* means "blood." The blood-colored Sangría in the glass ties in quite nicely with the bat symbolism.

As the Yago Sangría copy line advises, "The Yago wine cocktail. It's a natural for the holidays." Indeed, perhaps it goes well with the traffic fatalities. Such education could have shattering long-term effects upon human survival and adjustment. Such anamorphic projections have been found in a wide range of alcoholic beverage advertising.

A bloody vampire bat in a wine glass may be an overly grim way to end this chapter on media's anamorphic manipulations. Let me add one more example of deceptive flimflam which upset me far more than it probably will the reader. By the time I was ready to write this chapter, my office was littered with a collection of curious visual devices—distortion lenses, eyeglasses which turn the world upside down, kaleidoscopes, and an assortment of variously curved mirror anamorphoscopes. Anyone can construct an anamorphoscope by simply paper-clipping a sheet of silver-mirror Mylar around a 3-inch pickle jar.

Looking through a collection of pictures with the anamorphoscope, by chance I picked up the Signet paperback edition of *Subliminal Seduction* (Figure 38). I casually placed the mirrored tube just above the lemon-peel twist in the middle of the glass.

A very distinct man's face with a cap on his head appeared in the reflection (Figure 56). The murky shadows in the bottom of the martini were anamorphic distortions of the face.

Moreover, cylindrical anamorphosis cannot be read in its un-distorted form without a special instrument. To work as a sales stimulus—in order for the significant investment of talent, time, and money to be justified—the brain must have an ability to perceive and decode the picture, even though at a nonconscious level of perception.

The Flasher in the Ice Cube, his scolding mother, and dad down in the martini's dregs have been hard enough to live with all these years. But now, an anamorphic man . . .

However, as NAL Vice President Plumeri keeps saying, "All we did was put a martini on a table and take a picture. We didn't touch it." After all, who am I to question a vice president?

12•HUMAN SURVIVAL AND THE MASS MEDIA

Only now, at the edge of the precipice, is it possible to realize that everything we are taught is false. We live entirely in the past, nourished by dead thoughts, dead creeds, dead sciences. And it is the past which is engulfing us, not the future.

Henry Miller,
The Time of the Assassins

EVERYTHING CHANGES—ALWAYS

Subliminal Seduction, two years in the writing, was published in 1973; *Media Sexploitation* followed in 1976; and the present *Clam-Plate Orgy* in 1980. I began with the hope the books might initiate constructive change of some sort in American mass media—the sort of ego indulgence that often affects new authors. In the beginning, numerous academic colleagues warned me that my books would change nothing, least of all the media. Though their sour-grape comments often were intentionally malicious, they were wrong—totally, absolutely wrong. Much changed!

Since publication of my first book, the use of subliminal techniques in U.S. mass media has proliferated. Embedding techniques have become more technically refined, much more intellectually subtle, and likely more devastating in their dehumanizing effect upon the American public.

During the past few years, ad people have avoided public confrontations with me as though I carried typhoid. Top agency executives, repeatedly invited to confront my charges publicly on lecture platforms and national television, are consistently "out of town" or reply "no comment." But by now, the communication industry is generally well acquainted with my subject. My books, at least so I am told, are required reading in many U.S. ad agencies. They are utilized as textbooks in universities across America in a wide diversity of courses, such as public health, media and consumer education, fine arts, anthropology, literature, political science, family life studies, law enforcement and even psychology. I am often invited to lecture at marketing and sales executive meetings, seminars, and conferences. There have been several financial offers to found an international consulting firm that would specialize in subliminal media technology.

Over the past few years my university courses on subliminal persuasion included many students who were advertising and communication professionals whose employers paid their tuition. Of the some 90 students enrolled in my 1977 UCLA course in Subliminal Communication, roughly half were ad agency employees; several were highly skilled artists and copywriters. A few admitted quite candidly they were in the course to pick up ideas on how to rip off the American consumer more efficiently.

It appears my work is successful—at least in terms of the American criteria of success. However, I cannot escape the uncomfortable feeling this was not the way I intended the whole thing to work out. The books were intended to be devastating critiques of the mass communication industry, exposés of how Americans are being manipulated and exploited. Instead, the books have turned out to be ad industry training manuals. I sometimes wonder how Karl Marx (odiously remembered as the founder of communist philosophy, but virtually forgotten as a quite able economist and intellectual entrepreneur) might have felt had he ended his career as Chairman of the Board of General Motors.

NOBODY REALLY WINS, BUT EVERYONE LOSES

Perhaps thirty or forty years ago the first media adventurer who figured out how to embed a sexual orgy in a bowl of breakfast food held a momentary marketing head start. It is extremely doubtful, however, that any individual corporation could obtain a competitive advantage today. Virtually all major U.S. advertising agencies employ similar subliminal techniques.

Anyone familiar with marketing data knows that once a brand's share of the market has been established, it will usually shift from year to year only in small percentages. Above a certain optimum saturation level, for example, increases in media expenditures will not significantly increase market shares. Optimum marketing investments are presently evaluated by highly sophisticated computer programs.

Brands produced by smaller corporations tend to behave more erratically. True, once in a while, due to some clever but usually unpredictable marketing strategy, a major brand or product may rise or fall significantly in its market share. But this is relatively rare and, because of the variables involved, extremely difficult if not impossible to predict. In numerous studies I produced for large companies, major jumps in brand market share most often occurred because of incompetent executive decisions, inappropriate expenditures, misinterpretation of consumer dynamics, or ignorance of new product effects upon consumers.

In competitive media, there are no secrets for very long. Corporate survival depends upon knowing what is going on in the industry. As the reader has seen, subliminal techniques are quite old. In today's media systems, they are simply *available technology*. Any agency or corporation who refused to use subliminals would be at a substantial competitive disadvantage in media marketing investments. Ironically, today's ad agency *must* use subliminals just to get into and stay in the game.

Subliminal advertising probably has only sporadic, marginal effects upon changing brand market shares, but the widespread use of the technique programs the society for dramatic annual increases in product consumption. Increased consumption, of course, is a widely accepted, even advertised, definition of "progress." Progress is a notion which now must be redefined and updated in relation to the exhaustion of unrenewable world resources, ecological damage through pollution, and the frightening prospect of mankind's vulnerability to persuasion in virtually any direction desired by avaricious power structures—the modern apocalypse brought about by amoral and unrestrained economic exploitation.

Maybe this is the crux of the dilemma: American consumer affluence has come to depend upon perceptual manipulation rather than actual need. In his book *The New Industrial State*, John Galbraith explained how the survival of American corporations depends upon their management of the consumer, which of course depends upon their control of media. The consumer-media dependent industries have done their job well by first convincing Americans they have *freedom of choice* and the inherent *good taste* to decide what's in their best interest. Once these self-flattering platitudes are blindly accepted, the rest of the job is easy.

SATURATION MEDIA EDUCATES

This patronizing reality anaesthesia, resulting from the massive proliferation of marketing media, has much more to do with our lives than merely selling us products. It is *educational* in its most sophisticated sense and *cultural* as it provides a foundation for an entire structure of national values.

The U.S. federal government, intensively over the past several decades, has used similar media strategies. Media manipulation experts, of course, provide policy-making input at every level of local, state, and national government. With the help of the marketing media, they first convinced Americans they could not be controlled. Once this assumption was generally accepted, culturally disseminated, the population could be easily manipulated in virtually any desired direction. It was, then, easy to persuade people that the few rules or controls that exist are in everybody's best interest, helping them remain free and uncontrolled. Naturally, as these controls proliferated, they were accepted as normal, natural necessities for the betterment of life. Concepts of *truth* were replaced with *credibility*.

Much unlike the crude, brutish systems of totalitarian governments, this control system is highly sophisticated—and far more successful. The total advertising expenditure for 1979 was well over $50 billion, certainly enough to purchase a large amount of control over what media says or thinks about almost everything. U.S. citizens at the moment are probably more brainwashed and controlled by government and economic institutions and by the mass media-generated culture than any other population in the world, they are manipulated and managed in behalf of the consumer economy.

It may be important to remember that individuals cannot be conned or manipulated unless they can first be convinced they will benefit. Americans are endlessly entertained and are exhorted to seek out constantly even more entertainment. So-called entertainment is a major industry which sells extremely well, but also blinds. Unobtrusive media education, often disguised as entertainment, is far more significant in our total life experience than anything ever acquired from a formal educational institution. In a consciously unnoticed way, media educates us as to who we are, where we are going, why we should go there, and how we should value both people and things.

The media cliché, as Dr. McLuhan wrote, is never looked at critically, or even consciously (McLuhan and Watson, 1970), but is accepted at face value, without question or careful evaluation, remaining unseen. Social critic Wyndham Lewis once commented that "To ignore your environment is eventually to find yourself a slave to it." And, as Jacques Ellul wrote, "It is the total culture (media) in action that is propaganda teaching—environmental, invisible, and extremely dangerous" (Ellul, 1973).

WHO DEFINES REALITY?

Basic to the question of subliminal manipulation is modern society's dilemma over who will define reality—individuals themselves in their own interest, or the commercial media in the interest of the mass merchandisers? For most Americans, definitions and conscious meanings are carefully managed. Ad agencies literally run the game. News publishers and broadcasters, working under advertising agency sponsorship, define what we will consider "news" and the perspectives with which we will perceive the "news" and the world around us.

Total appropriation of media to commercial motives assures the waste of millions of hours of audience's daily lives through the dissemination of meaningless mind-dulling pap. Former FCC Commissioner Nicholas Johnson computed TV hours for the average male in the United States at 3,285 entire 24-hour days between the ages of 2 and 65—roughly nine full years of each individual's life. Media hype after media hype discredit and distort everything of human value within the society. People in the United States are often justifiably criticized as "knowing the price of everything but the value of nothing." Few any longer critically challenge media definitions for good and bad, beautiful and ugly, worthy human aspirations or goals, individual or group images, stereotyped behavior, or morality.

Like most of the general population, educational and governmental institutions usually subscribe to media definitions. Psychology, as a science, began with attempts to intervene clinically in psychopathology. But the last half century's growth in behaviorism and experimental psychology in Western nations became focused upon prediction and control of individuals and their environment, usually in behalf of perpetuating and elaborating the commercial status quo. Increasingly less attention has been paid to mental illness. Many large universities now consider *clinical psychology* a minor area of study.

Indeed, a former student of mine recently received his Ph.D. in psychology from Columbia University without, he complained, ever obtaining firsthand contact with mental patients and their illnesses. He had spent years working with rats and administering verbal tests. He was finally compelled to spend another three years of post-doctoral study gaining the needed clinical experience, and was sadly disappointed to conclude that his clinical experiences invalidated most of what he had learned in the university courses. The game continues, sometimes destructively, most often wastefully.

THE MEDIA APOCALYPSE

In our modern world, widespread anaesthetization by the mass media is a dangerous indulgence. As Barry Commoner pointed out in his exhaustive critique of U.S. economic policies (Commoner, 1976, pp. 234–235), "In all recent reports on the capital shortage, echoed in a crescendo of statements by the Secretary of the Treasury and a number of industrialists: *"Consumption must be reduced in the U.S."* Americans simply must save more and consume less. Similar, though often more elaborate, sentiments were expressed by James J. Needham, President of the New York Stock Exchange; Gaylord Freeman, Chairman of the Board, First National Bank of Chicago; and the Council on Trends and Perspectives, U.S. Chamber of Commerce.

Robert Cirino, in his book *Don't Blame the People*, asks the rhetorical question, "Can democracy survive the mass media?" There may well be much more at stake than democracy. This artificial creation of demand, especially in the

United States, is rapidly exhausting many of the world's irre-
placeable natural resources. The present highly publicized apparent energy shortages are only the tip of the proverbial
iceberg.

Perhaps curiously, leading U.S. bankers and at least three
U.S. Presidents have stated that the U.S. economy will face a
severe shortage of available investment capital over the next
few decades. There are only two places where such massive
capital is likely to be found. You probably guessed it—one is
from the government (i.e., taxpayer) in the form of low-in
terest loans or subsidies such as the current agricultural hand-
outs and those given Lockheed Aircraft by ex-President
Nixon. The other source would be private investments from
within the U.S. economy generated by savings and retained
investment earnings. But each year, media marketing investments increase, initiating a further exhaustion of savings,
investment capital, and the depletion of unrenewable resources—not even to mention the resulting ecological damage and pollution that must be corrected at public expense.

At this moment, there are enough factual data on media's
participation in what appears to be a pending national disaster to fill several books. Yet, the U.S. population, with substantial help from its mass media, continues to ignore where
it is going and who is taking it there. Survival of the world's
most economically and militarily powerful nation is endan-
gered by media's encouraging of public indifference toward
the realities that might disturb profitable marketing behavior.

CAN THE REPRESSED SURVIVE?

It would not be an exaggeration to describe contemporary
America as *a highly repressed culture*, blinded by the narcissistic indulgences promised by its mass media, in virtual total
conscious ignorance of the grim social and economic issues
that embroil the world around it. The result—a dehuman-
ized, cynical society of alienated, often desperate individuals,
each viciously competing to get his or hers.

Anyone naive enough to think that altruism is intrinsic in
man should read *The Mountain People*, Colin Turnbull's
frightening saga of a Ugandan people with no apparent humanistic qualities. The *Iks*—bordering upon extinction
through their own selfishness, greed, and indifference to the
human suffering surrounding them—most uncomfortably par-

allel many North Americans. No nation has ever survived when its people became strongly oriented around self-indulgence. When material acquisition becomes an end in itself, as it clearly has for so much of the United States, the society is in deep trouble. But then, maybe this one will continue to flourish; perhaps it will be the first to refine human and corporate greed into a viable philosophical, even pseudo-religious perspective. But, I would not bet on it!

The question should be seriously considered: Can America afford, in long-range-survival terms, to be at the mercy of information screened through powerful commercial profit motives?

MEDIA'S UNIFORM PERSPECTIVE

Scholars once theorized that a proliferation of media would also spawn new, competing ideas—innovative concepts, principles, and ideological perspectives. The public would thus be exposed to the many sides of every issue, from which they could make informed decisions. At least in the United States, this simply has not occurred. News and feature information are highly uniform in their perspectives; the same stories that appear in *The New York Times* usually appear in the *Los Angeles Times* and all the papers in between. The only major difference is in reader slant—the presentation of material aimed at specific demographic or psychographic audience characteristics.

NBC, CBS, and ABC present almost identical programming, differing only in the way they jazz up programs to attract specific audiences for their advertisers. The so-called "action news format" utilized in major markets through America is an excellent example—lots of "action," homey chatting between the actors, but very little information. Radio across the nation is even worse, as stations compete with television and each other through *Top 40 News* and *Top 40 Music* programming. Very little *Top 40* information has anything remotely connected with what is going on in the real world. In addition, U.S. print and electronic media have both achieved unprecedented banality in their content. They pander openly to advertisers' self-serving interests. Profit motives have forced them to abandon their vast potential leadership role as public benefactors in favor of babysitting their audiences, telling them what they wish to hear about themselves as an inducement to buy advertised products.

I have no quarrel with competitive retail merchandizing per se, only when it corrupts the informational integrity of public communication systems.

MYTHOLOGY OF ADVERTISING

For decades, ad hucksters have claimed that advertising results in better, more competitive, less expensive products. This is one of the least defensible mythologies in American business. If anything, the large corporations' massive ad expenditures restrain competition, establishing virtual monopolies among small groups of giants who often produce poorly manufactured junk dependent upon media for its quality image. Their ads invariably look better than the real thing.

U.S. consumers are not more naive than anyone else, but they have not been informed that they pay dearly for this torrent of banality. The more than $50 billion invested in advertising during 1979 was added to the prices for virtually everything consumers bought—a communication tax, in effect—a costly and inefficient marketing system in terms of price and quality, though, as mentioned, it is effective in increasing overall consumption. During 1980, ad expenditures are expected to reach over $60 billion.

A substantial proportion of each retail dollar spent pays for media advertising, even though the cost is hidden. All those obnoxious billboard, TV, radio, newspaper, and magazine ads were paid for by consumers, the cost being added on to the price of food, clothing, housing, medicine, and so on. With many products today the cost of *packaging* and *selling* actually exceeds the value of the merchandise. As is hammered out repeatedly in every basic consideration of economics, *There is no free lunch!*

Consumers subsidize the media in the same way they subsidize government institutions through taxes. Anyone who pays the bill has a right to demand responsible accounting for what they have paid.

THE UNHEARD CONSUMER

The FCC has never taken action against any broadcaster for using subliminal techniques, even though these have been in constant use for at least 25 years, certainly qualifying under the law as "deceptive advertising." Regulatory agencies do a superb job of serving the industries they are supposed to regulate. They respond quickly and sensitively to industry lobbies, but the consumer is usually unheard. There are only a small handful of organized pressure groups which have had important, though limited and sporadic success. All this demonstrates the almost desperate need for a U.S. Consumer Agency, or someone at least who might pressure other government agencies to represent *all* the public.

What could a concerned public institution reasonably do to challenge the use of subliminal media techniques? First, initiate an exploratory investigation by a Senate subcommittee. Advertising and media production technicians and executives can be carefully selected and interrogated under oath. These witnesses should be offered protection against industry dismissal and blacklisting. Confidential testimony could possibly serve as a basis for publicly interrogating top ad executives at policy-making levels.

In January 1979, a U.S. District Court ordered six major cigarette companies and twenty ad agencies to provide the FTC with all their research on consumer beliefs about health and smoking. A similar order could be sought on the research and development of subliminal techniques. The millions of dollars worth of research on unconscious perception sponsored by media and their related industries could be eventually made public.

Perhaps most important, however, consumers and the general public should be made cognizant of how mass media utilize subliminals. Educational institutions could incorporate this information into curricula which deal with language and behavior. Eventually, disclosures of media technology should lead to widespread public discussion of the long-term effects of media potentials for brainwashing and mind bending.

COUNTER-MEDIA INTELLIGENCE

Secondary school courses aimed at providing Americans with the critical faculties necessary to live in the media society autonomously as individuals, rather than as mass programmed shoppers, could be developed and incorporated with language studies. I pointedly do not mean courses in the kind of intellectual soft soap currently offered as journalism or mass media studies. These media appreciation courses include endless lectures on how lucky we are to live in a society with such wonderful TV, whereby, if hooked up to the right cable, you might see Lawrence Welk or *Charlie's Angels* three times weekly; pointless slogan-oriented seminars on the glories of a free press, which avoid any mention of how advertisers and publishers walk all over news editors and writers; pleasant, relaxed hours learning about the romance of Hollywood film rip-offs; or the fascinating perversities of the music industry, where corrupt, obscene rock stars popularize self-destruction as a road to wealth, status, and power. One U.S. university even offers courses on The Philosophical Challenge of TV Guide and another The Folklore of TV soaps.

DEVELOP THE INDIVIDUAL—AS ONE

Courses could be developed which might turn some incipient consumers into hard-nosed, questioning, and demanding critics of the media that will engulf them throughout their lives—consumers who can assess, in their own interest, media-engendered hypes, fads, rip-offs, pseudo-information, fakes, pap, misrepresentations, and just plain lies. They might also be encouraged to get mad, even furious, when they find they have been flimflammed.

Americans—the world's most expensively educated consumers—generally lack the education in language and media necessary to become much more than passive recipients destined to spend their lives on the treadmill of mindless consumerism as they are routed endlessly from one shopping center to another—buying, buying, and buying, in order to save money; consumers who permit themselves to become absorbed in the pursuit of media-popularized roles or fashions in the vain hope of becoming loved, respected, rich, socially popular, or sexually desirable; sheep who venerate compulsive, neurotic behavior as normal, desirable human conduct; or pathetic, helpless individuals integrated into the uncontrollable consumption of drugs, tobacco, alcohol, or other addictive substances designed to make corporations rich at enormous expense in human suffering.

It is time someone began to fight back. Individuals do not have to do, accept, believe, utilize, consume, buy, or participate in anything that does not serve their own individual interests. If, that is, they are able to differentiate between their individual interests and those of some heavily advertised corporation. Most, apparently, are not. I am always fascinated at such slogans as McDonald's "We Do It All for You!" It is still hard for me to believe anyone is simple minded enough to believe such nonsense. But, as someone who used to be paid for writing such trite, though profitable, lies, I am well aware many people will accept the line uncritically. At least for the moment, perhaps surprisingly, we still have an enormous amount of individual freedom and autonomy as humans should we wish and be able to exercise it.

For example, except possibly to buy a handful of place-mats, who would take their families into a restaurant that sold food via subliminal sexual orgies, bestiality, etc? Who would continue to drink alcoholic beverages after becoming aware of liquor company appeals to innate self-destructive tendencies? Certainly, not people in possession of their wits and concerned for their human rights, dignity, and personal well-being. They must, of course, be able first to psych out the con.

NEW TARGETS FOR TECHNOLOGY

Public health officials have frequently commented upon the total subversion of health education by advertising (Spratt, 1974, 1978). On the basis of published experimental research, there appears little question that advertising is directly linkable to lung disease ($350 million for tobacco advertising in 1978) and alcoholism ($800 million for alcoholic beverage advertising in 1978). Apparently, subliminal technology has the power to drive many individuals into pathological behaviors—compulsive eating and drinking, preferences for nutritionally deficient foods, alcoholism, smoking, a variety of sexual maladjustments and dysfunctions, and a myriad assortment of psychogenic illnesses. Additional such pathological media effects would certainly surface in response to further research.

Numerous arguments have been published on possible justifications for judicial sanctions against subliminal media techniques—common law, nuisance doctrine, trespass, Constitutional notions of privacy and due process, health considerations, and existing federal regulatory authority (Kozyris, 1975; Reed 1967, 1975). These justifications would, under FTC authority, cover both print and broadcast media, but would probably require specific legislation directed at media and the advertising and production agencies who now manufacture media content.

Ad executives have privately told me the media industry—much like the pornographers—might defend its use of subliminals with the First Amendment, guaranteeing freedom of speech. Should any such defense be initiated, however, it would be an open admission of advertising techniques in violation of FTC and FCC prohibitions, long concealed from gullible consumers. Public reaction would likely be intense. Furthermore, subliminals may not constitute "speech" in the usual First Amendment context; there is no opportunity for conscious communication. Moreover, a large proportion of subliminal content involves *obscene* or *threatening* reinforcement imagery, communicating little specific information relevant to the product.

COULD ADMEN GO STRAIGHT?

I often lecture at business and professional meetings, conferences, seminars, and conventions. Most business leaders appear very angry when they discover subliminal techniques are utilized to sell their products, in an overt violation of what are generally perceived as *business ethics*, one that even further discredits so-called free enterprise economics. But, at present, even though an individual corporate executive might find the use of subs repugnant, he could do little to end the practice without risking his career.

The ad industry is one of the least altruistic economic activities in America. Their executives tend to be cynical, hard-boiled, totally profit oriented, and sensitive to advanced concepts of behavior modification. They must survive in an extremely competitive business, constantly pressured to maximize returns (measured in profits) from media investments of their client's money.

Stephen Jones, in his excellent Yale Law School study (Jones, 1978), argues that legislation would deter ad agencies and their clients from using subliminal techniques. Once new legislation has been developed which would help Madison Avenue to go straight, Jones concludes, the use of subs will diminish or perhaps even disappear.

This is impeccable lawyer's logic, but Jones underestimates American ingenuity in getting around legislation when heavy profit is the reward. And, of course, this ingenuity can be financed by well over $50 billion of annual media ad expenditures. Subs can be insinuated into media in a variety of ways that make them, for all practical purposes, undetectable. The costs of careful screening would be substantial, and the ad industry will certainly oppose public financial support for efforts that act against their interests. Besides, I personally find objectionable the vision of a Pentagon-sized building full of bureaucrats carefully studying every page of *Playboy* magazine and every frame of TV soap commercials with magnifying glasses at taxpayer expense. Under the American system, substituting governmental bureaucratic control over media for advertiser control might produce a far more spectacular failure in trying to preserve democratic principles and freedom of information. There appears no other reasonable course than to teach individuals to take responsibility for media abuses upon themselves. This will not be easy.

The sad reality, however, is that the United States can probably do nothing about its media outrages until a major disaster, such as severe economic depression, forces power structures to accept new directions and priorities. No one has ever voluntarily relinquished power except in bits and pieces to accommodate minor changes in social and political pressure. The media have already generated enormous public support for the social damage they perpetrate. They endlessly reiterate *what they are doing for us.* "After all," the media establishment reminds everyone constantly, "what are you complaining about? Look what we have, compared with . . ." The notion, constantly reinforced by media operating in their own interest, is that the system is the most free and perfect that could have been devised.

This nonsense has been swallowed at face value by so many that criticism is rare. Somehow questions about *what they are doing to us* rarely come up.

A great many people openly admit they enjoy advertising more than the so-called information content. After all, it is the "good" news. For example, how would sports addicts react to losing their favorite game because beer commercials were prohibited? Any attempt at meaningful intervention with media will be instantly countered by tidal waves of public indignation.

Innovative solutions to the media dilemma might well develop if the subject was open for debate. Unfortunately, it is not.

SUBLIMINALS ARE HARD TO BUY

It is difficult, even impossible, for many Americans to deal with the subliminal issue. Publicly acknowledged use of subliminal manipulation would invite corporate disaster, threatening investment capital in consumer-oriented segments of the economy. Several business executives have argued, sincerely I assume, that my research and writing has already caused grave damage. They argued that such knowledge, publicly disseminated, could disrupt or destroy a more-or-less efficient economic-political system based upon the management of consumers and their consumption; such knowledge might also devastate totalitarian dictatorships as well as the commercially motivated, so-called "popular" cultures of Western society; such knowledge could force a critical reassessment, not only of institutions but of virtually everything people have been taught to hold sacred.

These arguments appear based upon one of the oldest fears of democracy, first discussed by Plato in his *Republic* around 400 B.C. Can humans deal with the realities of power and politics which surround them? Or must they be constantly nourished with slogans and fantasies which tell them only what they want to hear? The French author Voltaire once ventured: "If humans were compelled to look into the mirror of their truth, they would instantly be rendered insane." Friedrich Nietzsche, who wrote nearly a century ago on society's unconscious influences, described *history* as, "the lies through which human societies survive." Nietzsche wrote about how desperately humans avoid dealing with the truth about themselves. But, the subjects any society either consciously or unconsciously avoids are quite often highly relevant to survival and adjustment, much as they are in individual psychopathology.

Repression is the Achilles Heel of modern societies, protecting them from questioning their basic assumptions and premises and allowing them labels and definitions which blind and often lead them toward self-destruction. Recent history includes so many examples, that repression should be an obvious and widely discussed fact of life. Human vulnerability to repression may be the precise reason no culture in world history has ever been continuous; sooner or later all have self-destructed. To casually assume our society will be any

different in this respect, from all those which have gone before us, is blind egoism.

As a practical matter, probably nothing will change, even
though labels and definitions will, as usual, be switched
around—much like the patient who couldn't afford an operation so he had his X-rays retouched. Advertising will continue programming us and our children to take our places on
the endless belt of empty-minded consumerism. After ten
generations or so of conditioning (only two or three centuries) genetically induced change could occur, according to
the sociobiologists (Wilson, 1977). It is not unreasonable to
believe that certain presently acknowledged human traits,
such as altruism, may disappear completely from humans.

JUST LOOK OUT THE WINDOW

In November 1978 I served as a script consultant on
AGENCY, a feature film under production in Montreal, star-
ring Robert Mitchum and Lee Majors. A typical violent,
bloody, sexed-up spy epic, the story concerned a large U.S.
ad agency purchased by some unspecified alien power. The
subversive strategy in the plot was to corrupt and destroy
American society through the use of subliminals embedded in
advertising.

The film's producers, nervous about their multimillion-dol-
lar investment, kept worrying about the credibility of the
plot's subliminal strategy. Apparently, they were concerned
that American audiences might laugh at the notion.

Their most frequent questions to me were (1) what
messages would you embed subliminally in ad media to
destroy North American society? and (2) what would be the
long-term effects, say, over a twenty-year period?

Each time I answered, they looked at me more and more
incredulously as though they thought I was putting them on,
or as though they considered me some kind of a nut. An
hour or so later, however, they would work the same two
questions again into our discussions.

My answers were simple.

U.S. society could be corrupted, disoriented, and very possibly destroyed by doing precisely what the mass media are
presently doing with subliminal embedding. I showed them
the Howard Johnson Clam Plate, the Johnny Walker Rocks,

the Parkay Softie, and several other similar examples. So much for subversive content.

As to long-term effects, I suggested they simply look out the window. The effects of massive subliminal indoctrination are already highly visible. Large numbers of U.S. children regularly freak out on every conceivable chemical they can swallow or pump into their veins. The U.S. family is a disaster area, with nearly half of all marriages ending in divorce. American men and women are alienated and distrustful of each other, their reproductive behaviors shunted through masturbatory fantasies of bizarre and unrestrained sexual indulgence. Our general population is anaesthetized toward reality by immersion in endless hours of mind-deadening media pap—a perverse, destructive manipulation into fantasies of instant gratification, endless sensual indulgences, and purposeless consumption just for the sake of consumption—and corporate profits.

One thing quite apparent from world history is the low survival rate for societies which repress their vulnerabilities* and imperfections by constantly repeating to themselves how perfect, beautiful, noble, inspired, and great they are. The Greek youth Narcissus never realized, even at the point where he was destroyed by his self-adoration, that the magnificent being he had fallen in love with was his own reflected image.

---

* Most curiously, in their September 10, 1979, issue Behavior Section, *Time* published a full two-column story on Dr. Becker's subliminal audio anti-theft device. The story was comprehensive and well written, detailing early experiments, Vance Packard's exposé of substimuli in his book *Hidden Persuaders*, Becker's successful weight-control clinic using subliminally embedded videotapes, the deep concern over mass manipulation expressed by a former executive director of the American Civil Liberties Union, and briefly discussed my research on the movie *The Exorcist*.

Perhaps *not* so strangely, neither I nor my books were mentioned. And, of course, *Time* carefully avoided any reference to the use of substimuli in advertising. The Becker story was written by the same staff writer who wrote the unpublished story on my work nearly two years earlier!

EPILOGUE ————————————

[*From Book V, Chapter V,* The Brothers
Karamazov *by Fedor Mikhailovich Dostoevski.*
The scene is a confrontation between Jesus
Christ and the Grand Inquisitor during the
Holy Inquisition.]

. . . and the Grand Inquisitor spoke to Jesus Christ:

"Didst Thou not say, in those days fifteen hundred years
ago, 'I will make you free'? Didst Thou not know man pre-
fers peace, even death, to freedom of choice in matters of
good and evil? Nothing is more seductive for man than his
freedom, but nothing is a greater cause of suffering.

"Yes, we've paid dearly for it. For fifteen centuries we
have been wrestling with Thy freedom. But now, it is ended
for good. Under us, people are more persuaded than ever
they have perfect freedom. They even brought us their
freedom, laying it humbly at our feet. Nothing has ever been
more destructive for man and his societies than freedom.

"Today, for the first time, it is possible to think of man's
happiness. Man was created a rebel, but we both know rebels
cannot be happy.

"We alone shall feed them, in Thy name, declaring falsely
that it is in Thy name. Never, never can they feed themselves
without us!

"No science will make them bread so long as they remain
free. In the end they must say to us, 'Make us your slaves,
but feed us.'

"There are three powers, three powers alone, able to con-
quer and hold captive forever the minds of these impotent

rebels and bring them happiness. Those forces are *miracle, mystery,* and *authority.*"

[*Miracle, mystery, and authority are the foundations for successful mass merchandizing—the wonderous products which work like magic, relentlessly proposed through high-credibility media.*]

BIBLIOGRAPHY ⸻

Arendt, Hannah. *The Life of the Mind, Vols. I and II.* New York: Harcourt Brace Jovanovich, Inc., 1977.

Becker, Hal. C. *Apparatus for Producing Visual Stimulation.* October 30, 1962, U.S. Patent #3,060,795; *Apparatus for Producing Visual and Auditory Simulation.* October 11, 1966, U.S. Patent #3,278,676.

Becker, Hal. C., and Judith F. Jewell. "Subliminal Communication and Videotape Feedback on the Treatment of Obesity." (lecture) Las Vegas, Nevada: American Bariatric Physicians Annual Symposium on Obesity, October 14–17, 1976.

Berenson, Bernhard. *The Florentine Painters of the Renaissance.* New York: Putnam's, 1896, pp. 30–31.

Berger, John. *Ways of Seeing.* London: Penguin, 1973.

Bevan W. "Contemporary Problems in Adaption Level Theory: A Symposium." *Psychol. Bull.,* 61 (3), 161–87, 1964a.

⸻. "Subliminal Stimulation: A Persuasive Problem for Psychology." *Psychol. Bull.,* 61 (2), 81–99, 1964b.

Bevan, W., and J. F. Pritchard. "Effect of 'Subliminal' Tones upon the Judgement of Loudness." *J. Exp. Psychol.,* 66, 23–29, 1963.

Black, R. W., and W. Bevan. "The Effect of Subliminal Shock upon the Judged Intensity of Weak Shock." *Amer. J. Psychol.,* 73, 262–67, 1960.

Boardman, W. K., and S. Goldstone. "Effects of Subliminal Anchors upon Judgements of Size." *Percept. Mot. Skills,* 14, 475–82, 1962.

Boring, Edwin G. *A History of Experimental Psychology,* 2nd ed. Englewood Cliffs, N.J.: Prentice-Hall, 1929.

Brown, Norman O. *Life Against Death.* Middletown, Conn: Wesleyan University Press, 1959.

Buechner, Thomas S. *Norman Rockwell: Artist and Illustrator.* New York: Harry N. Abrams, 1970, Plate 87.

Burnham, Sophy. *The Art Crowd.* New York: D. McKay, 1973.

Camus, Albert. *The Fall.* New York: Knopf, 1956.

Carpenter, Edmund, and Ken Heyman. *They Became What They Beheld.* New York: Outerbridge & Duenstfrey, 1970.

Cirino, Robert. *Don't Blame the People.* N.Y.: Random House, 1971.

Cirlot, J. E. *A Dictionary of Symbols.* New York: Philosophical Library, 1972.

Commoner, Barry. *The Poverty of Power.* New York: Knopf, 1976.

Dichter, Ernest. *Handbook of Consumer Motivations.* N.Y.: McGraw-Hill, 1964.

"Did Rembrandt Paint It Blue." *Holland Herald,* 9, No. 3, 10–15, Amsterdam, Netherlands, April 1974.

Diehl, Gaston. *Picasso.* New York: Crown Publishers, 1960.

Dixon, N. F. *Subliminal Perception: The Name of a Controversy.* London: McGraw-Hill, 1971.

————. "The Effect of Subliminal Stimulation upon Autonomic and Verbal Behavior." *J. Abnorm, Soc. Psychol.,* 57 (1), 29–36, 1958.

Ehrenzweig, Anton. *The Hidden Order of Art.* London: Paladin, 1970.

Ellenberger, Henri F. *The Discovery of the Unconscious.* New York: Basic Books, 1970.

Ellul, Jacques, translated by Konrad Kellen and Jean Lerner. *Propaganda: The Formation of Men's Attitudes.* New York: Alfred A. Knopf, 1973.

Escher, M. C. *The Graphic Work of M. C. Escher.* New York: Ballantine, 1972.

Foulkes, D., and A. Rechtschaffen. "Presleep Determinants of Dream Content: Effects of Two Films." *Percept. Mot. Skills,* 19, 983–1005, 1964.

Fraenger, W. "Die Versuchung des heiligen Antonius, Madrid." *Hessiche Blätter für Volkskunde,* 49–50, 1958, pp. 20ff.

Fuhrer, M. J., and C. W. Erikson. "The Unconscious Perception of the Meaning of Verbal Stimuli." *J. Abnorm. Soc. Psychol.,* 61, 432–39, 1960.

Gadlin, W., and H. Fiss. "Odor as a Facilitator of the Effects of Subliminal Stimulation." *J. Person. Soc. Psychol.* 7 (1), 95–100, 1967.

Galbraith, John Kenneth. *The New Industrial State.* Boston: Houghton Mifflin, 1967.

Gardner, Helen. *Art Through the Ages.* New York: Harcourt Brace Jovanovich, Inc., 1948.

Goldstone, G., J. Goldfarb, J. Strong and J. Russell. "Replication: The Effect of Subliminal Shock upon the Judged Intensity of Weak Shock." *Percept. Mot. Skills,* 14, 222, 1962.

Gordon, C. M. and D. P. Spence, *The Facilitating Effects of Food Set and Food Deprivation on Responses to a Subliminal Food Stimulus.* J. Person, 34, 406–15, 1966.

Gordon, G. "Semantic Determination by Subliminal Verbal Stimuli: A Quantitative Approach." Ph.D. Thesis, University of London, 1967.

Halpern, Steven. *Tuning the Human Instrument.* Palo Alto, Calif.: Spectrum, 1978.

Hart, Larry. "The Effect of Noxious Subliminal Stimuli on the Modification of Attitudes Toward Alcoholism." *British Journal of Addiction,* 68, 87–90, 1973.

Herbrick, Russell T. *An Historical-Descriptive Analysis of Selected Threshold Cues in Advertising.* M.A. Thesis, University of Akron, 1976.

Hilgard, Ernest R. *The Experience of Hypnosis.* New York: Harcourt Brace Jovanovich, Inc., 1965.

Howard and Hulbert. *Advertising and the Public Interest: A Staff Report to the Federal Trade Commission,* 30 (1973).

Janson, H. W. *The Image Made by Chance in Renaissance Thought.* New York: De Artibus Opuscula, XL, Essays in Honor of Erwin Panofsky, 1961, pp. 254–66.

Jobes, Gertrude. *Dictionary of Mythology, Folklore and Symbols.* New York: Scarecrow Press, 1962.

Jones, Stephen A. *Subliminal Advertising in American Broadcast Media.* New Haven: Yale Legislative Services, 1978.

Jung, C. G. *Collected Works,* XX Vols. Princeton, N.J.: Princeton University Press, 1967.

Key, Wilson Bryan. *Attitudinal Resistance to Technological Change in an Economically Underdeveloped Social System.* Doctoral Dissertation, Denver University, August

1971, sponsored by the Economic Development Administration, Puerto Rico. Available from Univ. Microfilms, 300 N. Zeeb Road, Ann Arbor, Mich. 48106.

————. *Media Sexploitation.* New York: Signet, Paperback Edition, 1976.

————. *Subliminal Seduction.* New York: Signet, Paperback Edition, 1974.

Klein, G. S., and R. R. Holt. "Problems and Issues in Studies of Subliminal Activation." In J. G. Peatman and E. L. Hartley (Eds.), *Festscrift for Gardner Murphy.* New York: Harper & Row Pub., 1960, pp. 75–93.

Kozyris. "Advertising Intrusion: Assault on the Senses. Trespass on the Mind: A Remedy Through Separation." *Ohio L. J.* 236 (1975).

Kroger, William S., and William D. Fezler. *Hypnosis and Behavior Modification Imagery Conditioning.* Philadelphia: Lippincott, 1976.

Laing, R. D. *The Politics of the Family.* Toronto: CBC Learning Systems, 1969.

Laing, R. D., and D. G. Cooper. *Reason and Violence.* London: Tavistock, 1971.

Laing, R. D., and A. Esterson. *Sanity, Madness, and the Family.* London: Penguin, 1964.

Ledford, Bruce R. *The Effects of Thematic Content of Rheostatically Controlled Visual Subliminals upon the Receiving Level of the Affective Domain of Learners.* Commerce, Texas: Office of Organized Research, Grant 1501–9718, East Texas State University, August 1978.

Leeman, Fred. *Hidden Images.* New York: Harry N. Abrams, 1976.

Lidz, Theodore. *The Person.* New York: Basic Books, 1968.

Lorenz, Konrad. *Civilized Man's Eight Deadly Sins.* London: Methuen, 1974.

Marcuse, Herbert. *Five Lectures.* Boston: Beacon, 1970.

————. *One Dimensional Man.* Boston: Beacon, 1964.

McLuhan, Marshall. *Understanding Media.* New York: Signet, 1964.

McLuhan, Marshall, with Wilfred Watson. *From Cliché to Archetype.* New York: Viking, 1970.

Meadows, Dennis L., Donella H. Meadows, Jorgen Randers, and William W. Behrens. *The Limits to Growth.* New York: Universe Books, 1972.

Miller, Henry. *The Time of the Assassins.* New York: Pocket Books, 1975.

Murphy, Gardner, and Joseph Kovach. *Historical Introduction to Modern Psychology,* 6th ed. New York: Harcourt Brace Jovanovich, Inc., 1972.

Offner, R. *Corpus of Florentine Painting,* IV 2:1. New York, 1962, Plate III.

Panofsky, Erwin. *Early Netherlandish Painting.* Cambridge, Mass.: Harvard University Press, 1953.

Peirce, C. S., and J. Jastrow. "On Small Differences of Sensation." *Mem. Nat. Acad. Sci.,* 3, 73–83, 1884.

Penfield, W., and L. Roberts. *Speech and Brain Mechanisms.* Princeton, N.J.: Princeton University Press, 1959.

Pine, F. "Incidental Stimulation: A Study of Preconscious Transformations." *J. Abnorm. Soc. Psychol.,* 60, 68–75, 1960.

———. "Incidental Versus Focal Presentation of Drive-Related Stimuli." *J. Abnorm. Soc. Psychol.,* 62, 482–90, 1961.

———. "The Bearing of Psychoanalytic Theory on Selected Issues in Research on Marginal Stimuli." *J. Nerv. Ment. Dis.,* 138 (3), 205–22, 1964.

Poetzl, O. (1917) "The Relationship Between Experimentally Induced Dream Images and Indirect Vision," Monograph No. 7, *Psychol. Issues,* 2, 4–120, 1960.

Popescu, Marin Metei. *Michelangelo the Painter.* London: Abbey Library, 1975.

Reed. "The Psychological Impact of TV Advertising and the Need for FTC Regulation," 13, *Am. Bus. L. J.* 171 (1975).

———. "Psychological Advertising: A New Area of FTC Regulation," 1972, *Wisc. L. Rev.* 1967.

Reuterswärd, Patrik. *The Face in the Rock.* New York: Macmillan, 1970. Article in *Art News Annual,* XXXVI, 99–110.

Rubinoff, Lionel. *The Pornography of Power.* New York: Ballantine, 1969.

Schramm, Wilbur. *Men, Messages, and Media.* New York: Harper & Row, 1973.

Schultz, Duane P. *A History of Modern Psychology.* New York: Academic Press, 1969.

Shevrin, H., and L. Luborsky. "The Measurement of Preconscious Perception in Dreams and Images: An Investigation of the Poetzl Phenomena." *J. Abnorm. Soc. Psychol.*, 56 (3), 285–94, 1958.

Sidis, B. *The Psychology of Suggestion.* NY: Prentice-Hall, 1898.

Silverman, Lloyd H. "Ethical Considerations and Guidelines in the Use of Subliminal Psychodynamic Activation." Unpublished paper utilized for clinical orientation, available from author.

——. "The Unconscious Symbiotic Fantasy as an Ubiquitous Therapeutic Agent." Lecture at American Psychoanalytic Association, Baltimore, May 8, 1976.

——. "The Reports of My Death are Greatly Exaggerated," *American Psychologist,* 31, No. 9 (September 1976), 621–37.

Silverman, Lloyd H. Abbot Bronstein, and Eric Mendelsohn. "The Further Use of the Subliminal Psychodynamic Activation Method for the Experimental Study of the Clinical Theory of Psychoanalysis: On the Specificity of the Relationship Between Symptoms and Unconscious Conflicts." *Psychotherapy: Theory, Research, and Practice,* 13, No. 1 (Spring 1976), 2–15.

Silverman, Lloyd H., Peritz Levinson, Eric Mendelsohn, Roseann Ungaro, and Abbot Bronstein. "A Clinical Application of Subliminal Psychodynamic Activation." *Journal of Nervous and Mental Disease,* 161, No. 6, 379–392, 1975.

Smith, G. J. W., D. P. Spence, and G. S. Klein. "Subliminal Effects of Verbal Stimuli." *J. Abnorm. Soc. Psychol.,* 59 (2), 167–76, 1959.

Spence, D. P., and C. M. Gordon "Activation and Measurement of an Early Oral Fantasy: An Exploratory Study." *J. Amer. Psychoanal.,* 15 (1), 99–129, 1967.

Spence, D. P., and B. Ehrenberg. "Effects of Oral Deprivation on Response to Subliminal and Superliminal Verbal Food Stimuli." *J. Abnorm. Soc. Psychol.,* 69, 10–18, 1964.

Spratt, John S. "Your Behavior and Cancer." *Missouri Medicine,* January 1974, pp. 22A, 22D, 23, and 24.

——. "The Subversion of Health Education by Advertising in Mass Media." Editorial published by the Cancer Center, University of Louisville, Health Science Center, 1978.

Tarangul, Marin. *Bosch.* London: Murray Sales and Service, 1974, Plates 47–48.

Thass-Thienemann, Theodore. *The Subconscious Language.* New York: Washington Square, 1967.

———. *Symbolic Behavior.* New York: Washington Square, 1968.

Tryer, Peter, Peter Lewis, and Joan Zee. "Effects of Subliminal and Supraliminal Stress on Symptoms of Anxiety." *Journal of Nervous and Mental Disease,* Vol. 166, No. 2.

Turnbull, Colin M. *The Mountain People.* New York: Simon & Schuster, 1972.

Wallace, Robert. *The World of Rembrandt.* New York: Time-Life, 1968.

Wertenbaker, Lael. *The World of Picasso, 1881.* New York: Time-Life, 1967.

Wilson, Edward O. *Sociobiology: The New Synthesis.* Cambridge, Mass.: Harvard University Press, 1977.

Worthington, A. G., and N. F. Dixon. "Changes in Guessing Habits as a Function of Subliminal Stimulation." *Acta Psychol.,* 22, 338–47, 1964.

INDEX